PARIS

PARIS

THE MEMOIR

PARIS
HILTON

DEYST.

An Imprint of WILLIAM MORROW

A hardcover edition of this book was published in 2023
by Dey Street, an imprint of William Morrow.

FIRST DEY STREET PAPERBACK EDITION PUBLISHED 2024.

DESIGNED BY RENATA DE OLIVEIRA

Library of Congress Cataloging-in-Publication Data has been applied for.

ISBN 978-0-06-322461-2

24 25 26 27 28 LBC 5 4 3 2 1

For the family I was born into,
the family I made,
and the family I found along the way.
I love you all.

PARIS

PROLOGUE

Dr. Edward Hallowell, author of *Driven to Distraction*, says the ADHD brain is like a Ferrari with bicycle brakes: powerful but difficult to control. My ADHD makes me lose my phone, but it also makes me who I am, so if I'm going to love my life, I have to love my ADHD.

And I do love my life.

It's June 2022, and I'm having one of my best weeks ever. My friend Christina Aguilera, my neighbor, invited me to be one of her top-secret special guests at LA Pride, and as my crew moved my DJ equipment out the door, I was so nervous and excited I left the house without my shoes and showed up at a backstage trailer in a tank shirt, velour track pants, and socks, which was even more embarrassing when I accidentally went into the wrong dressing room.

Some backup dancers were in there getting dressed and screamed for joy when they saw me.

So, selfies. Obviously.

I always try to do it myself—like hold the person's camera so it's angled down, which is important if you're tall, because it's so unflattering when the angle is up your nostrils or the person's hands are shaking because they're maybe nervous and a bit shy, which I totally relate to, so I did that with "Loves it! Loves it! Sliving!" and all the things, and then off I went in my socks, doing this thing my husband, Carter, calls the "unicorn trot": not fully running, more graceful than galloping, and less like skipping than dancing. I have a hard time going slow.

So then I'm there at Pride with Christina and about thirty thousand other people, all decked out in rainbows and sparkles, dancing, laughing, hugging, having the best time during my set, which came right after Kim Petras, who sang at our wedding last year—this beautiful ballad version of "Stars Are Blind" and then "Can't Help Falling in Love" as Carter and I walked down the aisle—which is why that song brought tears to my eyes last week at Britney Spears's wedding when our gorgeous angel princess bride emerged, after all those nightmare years, and floated down the aisle in Versace (because *Versace*, please) with that iconic Elvis Presley song, which has been sung at millions of weddings in Vegas, where my grandfather, Barron Hilton, started the whole Vegas residency trend by having Elvis at the Las Vegas Hilton International back in 1969, paving the way for Britney and so many other groundbreaking performers to flourish in that format, a perfect example of how one person's creative vision sparks a cascade of genius that goes on and on into the future.

Another perfect example: my great-grandfather, Conrad Hilton. Wait. Where was I?

Pride!

This crowd. Oh, my god. Energy. Love. Light. Unbreakable spirit.

I'm behind the board. It's like piloting a spaceship full of the coolest people in the galaxy. My set is structured around iconic music like "Toxic" alongside a sick BeatBreaker remix of "Genie in a Bottle" by Xtina, Queen of the Night, plus a lot of other dope originals and remixes, which I should put up on the podcast or YouTube, because this set is so much fun. (Note to self: Make playlist for this book.) I was so hyper-focused on my set (note to self: add Ultra Naté to playlist), it didn't even hit me until I was halfway through that I had left my phone on the counter in that trailer where I took the selfies with the half-dressed backup dancers.

Fuck.

I'm trying not to say *fuck* all the time. I don't want to wear it out, because it's such a good word for so many occasions. Noun. Verb. Job description. Fill in the blank. *Fuck* saves the day. So *fuuuuuuuuuuck!* Because I feel naked without my phone, and I'm super paranoid about someone getting hold of it and blasting the contents all over the internet, which has happened more than once, so thank God for Cade—best friend, guardian angel—who went and located the stray phone after I killed my set, and then we all went to the after-party Christina and I hosted at the Soho House downtown.

Now I'm home with my loves: Diamond Baby, Slivington, Crypto, Ether, and Harajuku Bitch, the OG chihuahua.

Shout out to Harajuku Bitch!

She's twenty-two years old. Multiply that by seven dog years; she's literally 154! She sleeps twenty-three hours a day and looks like Gizmo from *Gremlins*, but she's still here living her best life. I know one night I'll come home to find she's fallen asleep forever. I'm so scared of that night, and I hate that random intrusive thought. Intrusive thoughts are my nemesis, cutting through my joy even when I've been part of an epic event with people who lift me higher than high and my husband is up in bed waiting patiently for me to take my bath and do my skin-care routine, which he knows I never shortcut.

From the time my sister and I were little girls, our mom instilled in us the value of skin care; I always feel her with me in the soothing ritual. Skin care, if you're doing it right, means claiming a moment of tenderness in an abrasive world. You remove the mask—your brave face, your funny face, your enforcer face, your hard candy coating—and see yourself, cleansed and replenished, and it's like, "Okay. I'm good." You feel everything so keenly when you've just washed your face. Like a newborn feels that first sting of fresh air.

Kim Kardashian and I were making frittata and French toast coated with Frosted Flakes for breakfast one morning, and she said, "I don't know anyone who parties as hard as you do and looks as good as you do."

Skin care. Seriously. If you take nothing else from my story, receive this: *Skin care is sacred.* Most women who did coke back in the 1990s looked beat by the mid-aughts. That was a strong deterrent for me. I won't say I never tried it, but I wasn't about to sacrifice my complexion for it. Same with cigarettes. You may as well hit yourself in the face with a shovel.

These days, my only bad habit is spray-tanning. My sister Nicky can't stand it, but I'm kind of addicted. Otherwise, Carter and I are big on wellness and skin care. We always say, "Forever's not long enough." Taking care of ourselves is something we do for each other out of love. We want our good life to last.

After I put the frittata in the oven and set a cute little penguin timer, Kim said, "Now is the twelve minutes when we clean. *Clean as you go* is the rule."

My only rule is skin care. Sunscreen is my eleventh commandment.

You may be wondering: *What does all this have to do with ADHD?*

Nothing. Also everything. And anything. All at once.

ADHD is exhausting and exhilarating, and it's how God made me, so it must be right.

Carter doesn't fully grasp what it means to be ADHD, but he's the first and only man in my life who made an effort to understand. Early in our relationship, he spent a lot of time and energy researching ADHD, which is the most authentically loving thing any man has ever done for me. Most people sigh, drum their fingers, and let me know how insanely frustrating it is to be sucked into the endless spin cycle of my life. Carter rolls with it. Where most people see a dumpster fire, Carter sees Burning Man. He gets frustrated, for sure, but he's not trying to deprogram me.

Carter is a venture capitalist. M13, the company he founded with his brother, Courtney, is known for engaging with unicorns—start-ups valued at more than a billion dollars—like Rothy's, Ring, and Daily Harvest. Carter is a unicorn whisperer. He's sentimental and forward thinking, and he likes to be the boss, but he has a light touch. If we're in an 11:11 Media board meeting, talking about a contract, and I go off on a tangent about a better tool for impromptu IG videos and how that tool could be styled, manufactured, and marketed in a really fun, accessible way and I could promote them via cross-promotional content, and what if the nob was like a little otter or sloth or kangaroo—

Carter leans to whisper in my ear. "Babe."

Not in a mean way. Just to bring me back to center.

A while back I was featured in *The Disruptors*, a documentary about extraordinary people with ADHD, including will.i.am, Jillian Michaels, Justin Timberlake, the founders of JetBlue and Ikea, Steve

Madden, Simone Biles, Adam Levine, Terry Bradshaw, astronaut Scott Kelly, Channing Tatum—the list goes on and on. *The Disruptors* also features Dr. Hallowell and other psychologists and neurologists who've advanced the science of ADHD. The message of the film really flies in the face of the misconceptions and stigma.

The structure and function of the ADHD brain are a throwback to a time when you had to be a badass to survive, find food, and procreate. (Visual cue: Raquel Welch as the iconic cavewoman queen in *One Million Years B.C.*) The frontal lobe—home of impulse control, concentration, and inhibition—is smaller, because the primitive badass had to react on instinct, without fear. Neural pathways don't connect or mature at the same rate, because it was more important for the primitive badass queen to be better at picking berries and killing saber-toothed tigers than she was at reading novels. Dopamine and noradrenaline, powerful chemicals that regulate sleep and facilitate communication between brain cells, were on a slow drip, because she had to wake up at the snap of a twig.

I, like 5 percent of children and 2.5 percent of adults, am a primitive badass in a world of contemporary thinkers, a world that wants obedience and conformity. Even if we wanted to be the orderly people our loved ones want us to be, we don't have it in us. We must embrace who we are or die trying to be someone else.

The benefits of ADHD include creativity, intuition, resilience, and the ability to brainstorm. I'm good at damage control because I'm constantly losing things, showing up late, and pissing people off. I'm good at multitasking because I'm not hardwired to concentrate on one thing for a big block of time. Because my attention span is limited, I don't see time as linear; the ADHD brain processes past, present, and future as a Spirograph of interconnected events, which gives me a certain Spidey sense about fashion trends and technology.

It's easy to follow my bliss because my bliss is whatever interests me at any given moment. My brain chemistry craves sensory input. Sounds, images, puzzles, art, motion, experiences—everything that triggers adrenaline or endorphins—that's all as necessary as oxygen for the ADHD brain.

I don't just love fun. I *need* fun. Fun is my jet fuel.

The primary disadvantage of ADHD is that people around you are often inconvenienced, weirded out, or hurt by your behavior, so you're constantly getting judged and punished, which makes you feel like shit. Suicidal ideation is higher in people with ADHD. Self-loathing and self-medication are endemic. If the rest of the world says you're obnoxious or stupid or just not braining right, loving yourself is an act of rebellion, which is beautiful but exhausting, especially when you're a little kid. With that needy little kid always inside you, your life becomes an epic quest for love—or whatever feels like love in the moment.

I was never medicated as a kid—never tested for ADHD, as far as I know. Even if you have the most wonderful, loving parents in the world (and I do), diagnosis doesn't always happen early, especially for girls who are good at hiding the symptoms. Treatment of ADHD has traditionally focused on squashing undesirable behavior. In the 1980s, people had just started talking about being hyper or being on "the spectrum."

No one ever said, "Relax, little girl. There are many different kinds of intelligence."

Instead, people told me I was dumb, bratty, careless, ungrateful, or not applying myself. And none of that was true. I had to be creative and work hard to fit in, but I'm naturally creative and hard-working, so I was in it every day, grinding away, trying to fit in, until I grew strong enough to say, "*Fuck fitting in*," which is what I intend to teach my children from the beginning, no matter what their neurodevelopmental profile happens to be.

As an adult, I've been medication-fluid. When I was in my early twenties, a doctor explained what was "wrong" with me and put me on Adderall. That was a love/hate relationship that went on for about twenty years—me and Adderall—until Carter and I met with Dr. Hallowell.

Dr. Hallowell said, "I've been trying to explain to people since 1981 that this condition, if you use it properly, is an asset composed of qualities you can't buy and can't teach. It's stigma that holds us back. Stigma plus ignorance. A lethal combination."

I felt that lightning bolt you feel when someone speaks a hard truth you've always known but never heard anyone say out loud.

"Our kryptonite is boredom," said Dr. Hallowell. "If stimulation doesn't occur, we create it. We self-medicate with adrenaline."

ADHD can be a wellspring of creative energy, but creative energy's evil twin is a troublemaking compulsion. Want some adrenaline? Do everything the hard way. Get into train-wreck relationships. There are a million ways to screw yourself over for the sake of adrenaline. My imagination is infinite, but it takes me to dark places as easily as it takes me toward the light. Dr. Hallowell calls it the Demon, that snake that slithers into everything telling you that if it's bad you deserve it and if it's good it won't last. Of course, the Demon is a liar, but try telling that to my brain when it's craving a big bucket of deep-fried anxiety.

"Your greatest asset is your worst enemy," said Dr. Hallowell.

And my brain said, *Fuck*.

"Tell me, Paris, how is your self-esteem?"

"I'm good at pretending," I said.

He said, "That's common among people who live with ADHD."

Not "people who suffer from ADHD." Not "people afflicted with ADHD."

People who live with ADHD.

Some of us have discovered that ADHD is our superpower. I wish the *A* stood for *ass-kicking*. I wish the *D*s stood for *dope* and *drive*. I wish the *H* suggested *hell yes*.

I'm not bragging or complaining about it, just telling you: This is my brain. It has a lot to do with how this whole book thing is going to play out, because I love run-on sentences—and dashes. And sentence fragments. I'm probably going to jump around a lot while I tell the story.

The Spirograph of time. It's all connected.

I've avoided talking about some of these issues for decades. I'm an issue-avoiding machine. I learned from the best: my parents. Nicky says Mom and Dad are "the king and queen of sweeping things under the rug."

There is a hierarchy, and these are the rules in my family:

- If you don't talk about a thing, it's not a problem.
- If you hide how deeply something hurt you, it didn't happen.
- If you pretend not to notice how deeply you hurt someone else, you don't have to feel bad about it.

Of course, that's bullshit, and what makes it even crazier: *It's not good business.* I come from a family of brilliant businesspeople. How can we be so bad at emotional economics? Relationships, professional and personal, are transactional. Give and take. For better or worse. You invest, hoping for a good return. But there's always risk.

I love my mom, and I know she loves me. Still, we've put each other through hell and can't squeeze out more than a few words on certain topics. It's going to be hard for her to read this book. I won't be surprised if she puts it on a shelf for a while. Or forever. And that's okay.

I'm trying to take ownership of some intense personal things I've never been able to talk about. Things I've said and done. Things that have been said and done to me. I have a hard time trusting and don't easily share my private thoughts. I'm super protective of my family and my brand—the businesswoman who grew out of a party girl and the party girl who still lives inside the businesswoman—so it scares me to think about what a lot of people will say.

But it's time.

There are so many young women who need to hear this story. I don't want them to learn from my mistakes; I want them to stop hating themselves for mistakes of their own. I want them to laugh and see that they do have a voice and their own brand of intelligence and, girl, *fuck fitting in*.

PART 1

*Never regret anything,
because at one time it was exactly
what you wanted.*

MARILYN MONROE

1

People told me it was stupid to go skydiving the morning after my twenty-first-birthday party in Las Vegas, but back then, I didn't care, and now I know they were wrong. If you want to go skydiving the morning after a Level 9 rager, go for it. Your twenty-first birthday is prime real estate for stupid, and a lot of stupid things you do in your twenties lay the foundation for wisdom later on. As you wise up, you realize that all the stupid things you *didn't* do—those are the regrets. My twenties were like, *damn*, girl. Leave no stupid behind. Love the wrong men. Hate the wrong women. Wear the Von Dutch.

I have no regrets.

Okay, I have a few regrets.

Skydiving is not one of them.

When I decided to do it, I was thinking it would be a perfect cherry on top of a star-studded, multicity, balls-out birthday celebration that was lit AF—possibly the greatest twenty-first-birthday cel-ebration since Marie Antoinette—and I can say this with authority because partying is an area of expertise for me, a marketable skill developed over a lifetime of dedicated practice.

A BRIEF HISTORY OF MY PARTYING LEGACY

(Details to be developed at greater length later in this book.)

The parties I went to when I was tiny were mostly family gather-ings at Brooklawn, the home of my dad's parents, Barron and Mari-lyn Hilton, whom I called Papa and Nanu. You may have seen this house on my docuseries *Paris in Love*; it's the Georgian-style man-sion where I got married in 2021. Designed by legendary architect Paul R. Williams—who also created homes for Frank Sinatra, Lu-cille Ball, Barbara Stanwyck, and other Hollywood immortals—the house was built for Jay Paley, one of the founders of CBS, in 1935.

At that time, Papa was eight, living in a hotel with his big brother Nicky, baby brother Eric, and my great-grandfather, Conrad Hilton. My great-grandmother had left them (according to family mythol-ogy) because she didn't like the hardworking hotel life and gave up on Conrad ever having real money. (Mentally inserting "Bye, Feli-cia" gif.)

Conrad was later briefly married to the Hungarian socialite Zsa Zsa Gabor, who was broke but beautiful and happy to go out danc-ing every night. Zsa Zsa had a sparkling personality and developed an early version of the business model we now call influencing, get-ting paid to wear clothes, appear at parties, and talk up beauty prod-ucts so the brand names would appear in the Hollywood press. The marriage ended bitterly, and Conrad decided it was better to raise the boys himself. He brought them up with old-school Christian val-ues, making them work as bellhops and teaching them that work and family are jealous gods who will always be at war, fighting for a man's time and complete devotion. Papa married Nanu after World War II, and they had eight kids. Dad is number six. When he was little, they moved into the Jay Paley house and renamed it Brooklawn.

This all sounds like ancient history, but to understand my story, you need to know the Hilton of it all. People who knew Conrad Hilton tell me I'm just like him, and I take that mostly as a compliment. Mostly. He died two years before I was born, and despite what most people think, he left most of his fortune to charity. Papa worked. My parents worked. I'm a working beast. In 2022, I signed a massive deal to be the face of Hilton Hotels in ad campaigns and cross-promotions on my social media, and I love working with them, but I think that's the biggest money I'll ever get for being a Hilton.

But I am a Hilton, and that's huge. Here's me, acknowledging how blessed and lucky I am, okay? My family has been called "American royalty." I'm not downplaying the extraordinary privilege or the access it gave me. Experiences. Travel. Opportunities. I'm grateful for all of it.

The Barron Hilton family is huge, and we flock together, loving each other and minding each other's business, even though we don't see each other as much since Nanu died. When we were little, Nicky and I adventured around Brooklawn with our million cousins, climbing fences and playing kickball on the lush green lawn. Parties at Brooklawn were like full-on carnival events, with pony rides, petting zoos, bouncy castles, tennis tournaments, and Marco Polo death matches in the gigantic pool, which featured an elaborate mosaic—imported Italian tile depicting the signs of the zodiac. I'm an Aquarius, so I thought I should be the one that looked kind of like a mermaid, but that turned out to be Virgo. Aquarius was a beefy-looking dude with a jug of water on his shoulder. I probably cried when I found that out. Actually, I probably cried for three seconds and then decided I was the mermaid, no matter what the stars or some old Italian tile people said.

My parents, Rick and Kathy Hilton, spent the 1970s partying with Andy Warhol and the hippest possible crowds from Studio City to Studio 54. My dad is in real estate and finance, the cofounder of Hilton & Hyland, a massive firm specializing in high-level corporate and residential real estate. My parents did a lot of entertaining related to his business, and when Mom has a party, she plans it down to the last rose petal, all the little things that make her guests feel like they're part of something special. Everything is perfect, including the hostess. My mom styles herself and her surroundings with impeccable taste. She walks into a party and works that room like a royal—savvy, kind, and beautiful. People love her, because she genuinely cares about people, listens to them, and lets them feel savvy, kind, and beautiful, too.

True sophistication is the ability to fit in anywhere because you have a broad understanding of and respect for all kinds of people. Mom is sophisticated like that. She's funny and smart and stylish, but savvy is her real superpower. I had no clue how much silly energy she had bottled up inside her until she signed on to do *The Real Housewives of Beverly Hills* in 2021. It was like somebody popped a cork on a bottle of pink champagne.

When Nicky and I were little, before the boys came along, Mom schooled us on party manners. Which fork to use. How to place our feet when we stood for red carpet photos. We understood that our family name carried weight and drew attention. We had a certain place in society, which came with certain expectations. As little girls, Nicky and I attended super chic social functions, fundraising events, holiday galas, and fancy receptions at the Waldorf or the Met, where my parents mixed with lawyers, agents, politicos, and all kinds of extraordinary people who did big things.

One of my earliest memories is sitting on Andy Warhol's lap, drawing pictures at an after-party at the Waldorf-Astoria. He loved me and always told my mom, "This kid is going to be a huge star."

I love that my parents included us in all that. You might think fancy business and social events would be boring for a little kid, but I lived for those parties. I learned to appreciate the architecture of a good ball gown. I was exposed to great music: jazz combos, string quartets, and private performances by famous artists. I sat like a butterfly on a fence, eavesdropping on adult conversations about corporate maneuvers, real estate deals, fortunes being made and lost, ill-advised love affairs, and messy divorces. It was all about love and money, two things that fascinated me because everyone seemed to be under the spell of one or the other.

The first time I experienced going to a club environment, I was twelve. Nicky and I were friends with Pia Zadora's daughter Kady, and Pia was friends with our mom, so we got to go with Pia to a New Kids on the Block concert in LA. Because Pia was a celebrity, we got to go backstage—and we were, like, dying.

"We're going to Bar One for the after-party," the boys told Pia. "You should come."

Nicky and Kady and I were like, "We have to go! Please! *Pleeeeeeeease!*" We were all totally obsessed with New Kids. Pia was cool, so we went over to Bar One, and the bouncers let her right in because celebrity.

The atmosphere inside Bar One blew my tiny mind. I had an immediate visceral response like *yaaassssss* because—*LIGHTS MUSIC LAUGHTER FASHION MUSIC JOY LIGHTS WHITE TEETH DIAMONDS MUSIC*—a blast of the flashy sensory input my ADHD brain constantly craved. I didn't know I was feeling an actual shift in my body chemistry, but I knew I was feeling something real, and I loved it. Every part of me came alive—body, brain, skin, spirit—and it felt awesome.

Unfortunately, just as I was soaking all this in, we bumped into my mom's sister. Aunt Kyle was like, "WTF!" She dragged Pia aside for a brief, hissy conversation and then took us home, but I knew I had to go back.

In my early teens, I took advantage of every sneak-out opportunity I could create. I became one of those *Desperately Seeking Susan* club kids who ruled the nighttime world in the early nineties. The vogue dancers and drag queens took me under their wings and watched out for me, which is how I learned the key elements of partying like a rock star:

1. Stay hydrated.
2. Stay pretty (tipsy can be cute, but drunk is gross).
3. Wear boots—like good, sturdy platform boots—and comfortable clothes so you can dance all night and easily climb in and/or out of windows and over fences as needed.

I didn't drink or do drugs back then. When I was a kid, fun was the only party drug I needed. I wasn't there to get wasted; I was there to dance. Alcohol and drugs are for escaping reality, and I wanted all the reality I could get. The escape drinking didn't happen until later.

One night after the Pia Zadora club adventure, I tried to smuggle Nicky, our cousin Farrah, and our friend Khloé Kardashian into Bar One. Khloé and Farrah were little middle school girls, so I did Khloé up with full makeup, a long red wig, and a floppy black hat.

I told her, "If anyone asks, your name is Betsey Johnson."

I put Farrah on top of somebody's shoulders with a big trench coat. We put so much effort into our disguises, we were shocked when we didn't get past the velvet rope.

"I guess you need to be with someone famous," I said.

I didn't like how it felt to be rejected in front of everyone. I wasn't going to let it happen again. When I was sixteen, I hooked up fake IDs for Nicky and me. We weren't fooling anyone, but we were getting a little bit famous, so we had no trouble getting in Bar One (now Bootsy Bellows), Roxbury (now Pink Taco), and other hot spots.

My partying opportunities between the ages of sixteen and eighteen were limited, because I was locked up in a series of culty wilderness boot camps and "emotional-growth boarding schools." When I escaped for a few blessed weeks of freedom, I played it safe with small beach parties and living room gatherings where kids were just chilling and talking, until I made everyone get up and dance. Especially kids who were too shy or felt self-conscious about their bodies. They're the ones who need dancing most. This is still the rule at every gig I DJ in my virtual world or in real life: When you party with Paris, you dance.

At eighteen, I signed with a modeling agency, and what do you think people want to do after a runway show? Party with models. It's easy to think *no duh*, but move past the easy assumption that men are pigs and models are dumb. That's not fair or true or useful. Most men are basically decent, I think, and successful models travel all over the world. Traveling the world is the best education there is. Most models are in their teens and twenties, and sometimes that lack of maturity shows, but they're growing. Give them a minute.

Networking—knowing how to work a party—is a critical aspect of growing a business. In my twenties, I was so good at both partying and business, people started paying me to come to their parties. I didn't invent getting paid to party, but I *re*invented it. I'm proud to be called the OG influencer. Girls need to understand the value they bring to the party. It's a lot more than standing around looking pretty. Mannequins can do that. An accomplished party girl is a facilitator, a negotiator, a diplomat—she's the sparkler *and* the match.

Know your worth, girls. You're not lucky to be at the party; the party is lucky to have you. Apply as needed to relationships, jobs, and family.

Like my wedding in 2021, my twenty-first-birthday celebration in 2002 spanned multiple days and time zones. I'd already been partying in clubs for years, but I was sick of bullshitting bouncers, passing off fake IDs—as if they didn't know. It made pretenders of us all, and that seems like such a waste of energy. I was excited to be twenty-one and leave all that behind. This was my first time to go out all nice and legal, so I went big, planning parties all over the world and getting sponsors to pay for it all. My coming-of-age birthday bash was a dancing, drinking, hobnobbing multiverse that left people paralyzed with exhaustion.

Obviously, I coordinated an amazing wardrobe. This was a multiple-look event with a whole lineup of design-forward dresses, platform heels, accessories, and diamond tiaras. This was the genesis of my iconic silver chain-mail dress by Julien Macdonald—a dress Kendall Jenner cloned for her own twenty-first-birthday party in 2016. That's how timeless this garment is. I wore mine again (hell yes, I kept it!) on my last night in Marbella, Spain, when I was DJing there in 2017.

Julien made me the chain-mail dress to wear at my London party at the end of London Fashion Week, where I walked in his show. I was the bride, and the bride's dress was amazing, but the first time I laid eyes on that iconic chain-mail birthday dress, I was so blown away.

"This dress is *everything*," I said. "This dress is going to end up in a museum someday."

The weight and construction are exquisitely engineered, incorporating thousands of Swarovski crystals. It moves like a liquid Slinky. The neckline is cut clear down to Argentina, so double-sided tape is needed to prevent nip slip. That usually works pretty well until you work up a sweat on the dance floor, but dancing in that dress is better than a milk bath.

I fell on my face when I was running to hug somebody, so I thought I should get out of those six-inch heels. I think that's when I changed into a floaty blue mermaid dress. Backless but well built. At GO Lounge in LA, I wore a sheer pink mini studded with a trillion hand-sewn diamante beads. But nothing made me feel the way I felt dancing my ass off that night in the Stork Lounge in London in that silver Julien Macdonald dress.

I want every girl to feel that way on her twenty-first birthday: free, happy, beautiful, and loved.

Invincible.

Heatherette made me a turquoise mermaid dress covered in Swarovski crystals to wear at Studio 54 in New York. Le Cirque put out this extreme gourmet buffet and made me a gorgeous twenty-one-tier birthday cake. After that, there was a party in Paris, France, because *Paris*, and then Tokyo, where I sponsored a massive party for thousands of fans, because I could never leave my Little Hiltons behind. Then I went back to LA and did a rolling bash that moved from LAX to my house on Kings Road with friends and family I'd known and loved all my life.

My house on Kings Road was piled high with presents. Friends and fans all over the world sent roses, rings, bracelets, stuffed animals. So many sweet, thoughtful gifts. I was so touched by the loving words written in cards, letters, and emails. I wrote thank-you notes until my arm was ready to fall off.

Curating a party crowd is a skill. Andy Warhol was the undisputed mastermind of party curation. Prince inherited the title from him and took it to the next level with the secret sauce—music. That's what stays with me from all those parties. The music and the people. My sister and my cousins. Lots of childhood friends, like Nicole Richie. The hot matriarchs: Mom, Kris Jenner, Faye Resnick, Aunt Kyle, and Aunt Kim. Random legends like P. Diddy and the restaurateur Sirio Maccioni. All the family and friends who've been a constant in my life, but also a lot of cool people who came and went because some friendships just have their seasons, and that's okay.

This fascinating assortment of people danced to my handpicked playlist. Every. Body. Danced. This was before my professional DJ days, but I always had an instinct for the ebb and flow. Club music of the early aughts was made for raging:

Chemical Brothers, "Star Guitar"

Depeche Mode, "Freelove"

DJ Disciple, "Caught Up" featuring Mia Cox

Funky Green Dogs, "You Got Me (Burnin' Up)"

I also had to have my soul song: Ultra Naté, "Free."

At the Bellagio in Las Vegas, DJ AM played, so I knew the music would be on point. I didn't want that night to be over. For most of my adult life, if I slept without my dogs—and a lot of times even when I had them with me—nightmares chewed through my brain and tore up my stomach, so I was terrified to fall asleep. I put it off as long as I could, partying on—dancing, drinking champagne, dancing, dancing, drinking, laughing, dancing—until it was morning and my body was like, *Bitch, stop. It is overrrrrrrrr* . . .

And the next thing I knew, my phone was vibrating in my armpit.

Someone was pounding on my hotel room door.

"Paris? Paris, wake up. We have to get to the airstrip."

I opened my eyes. The room reeled like a disco ball.

"What? Why . . . are we . . . where are we going?"

And then I remembered that I had told everyone I was going skydiving.

No! Ugh.

This was going to suck, but I didn't want to embarrass myself by backing out. I pulled on a tracksuit. Even after I chugged a bottle of water, my mouth felt like a sandbox. The water made me feel kind of ill, like I was about to throw up, but there was nothing else in my stomach. Maybe a little cake. I'd been so busy dancing, I never really made it over to the buffet. Usually champagne is good hangover insurance, but I also had some shots or martinis or whatever people drink at their twenty-first-birthday party. My right eyeball was in supernova. My hair follicles were screaming.

On the way to a tiny airstrip outside Las Vegas, I kept telling myself: *Don't be lame, don't be lame, don't be lame.* I knew that if I vomited or cried or backed out, some of the people I was hanging out with would not keep that to themselves. Someone would be taking pictures and selling them. Some of these people were trusted friends, but others I didn't know that well or trust at all, and the hangover had sapped my energy to differentiate, so I defaulted to my *trust no one* mode and tried to pretend I was super excited.

"I'm really tired," I said. "I'm just gonna . . . yeah."

I covered my head with my jacket and trembled like a little wet dog.

We got to the private airstrip in the wide, dry nothing somewhere outside the city. I was so dehydrated and wrung out, I couldn't even comprehend all this information the guy was giving me. Something about "blah blah tandem instructor—blah blah jumping at thirteen thousand feet—blah blah freefalling for the first mile on the way down." And I'm sitting there like *What the fuck have I gotten myself into?* And then they strapped the whole apparatus on me, and shit got real. I was 100 percent sober, and I was scared.

Going up in this tiny, rattlecrap airplane, everyone else was laughing and talking—yelling because the engine was so loud. The happy yappy voices felt like scissors in my ears. I just sat there. Quiet. I always get quiet when I'm scared. Like a little rabbit going purely on instinct, huddled in a silent ball, ready to take evasive maneuvers. It's humbling to be reminded that no matter how big your life is, you are still a speck of dust that can be swept off the earth in half a second.

The goggles were tight on my face. That would leave a mark, I was positive. *Ugh.* I was sitting on the lap of this guy, a stranger, whose body was literally strapped to my body—our bodies spooned together—so that was weird, and my life was in the hands of this man, and the whole thing was so stupidly terrifying, I wanted to hurl.

Then they opened the door. A blast of freezing cold air roared in.

Now, above this door is the same sign you see above every door of every airplane. Red letters. All caps.

THIS DOOR MUST REMAIN CLOSED

There's a reason! When that door opens, the world ends. Your head gets sucked inside out. Your heart shrivels like a forgotten mushroom.

THIS DOOR MUST REMAIN CLOSED

But now this door is open.

I'm on this bench behind some other people, and every time someone jumps, everyone else scoots forward. Someone jumps. We all scoot forward.

Jump. Scoot.

Jump. Scoot.

My spoon-mate keeps pushing me closer to that door, yelling, *"Doing great, Paris. This is gonna be awesome, Paris. Almost there, Paris. Doing great."*

And then we're at the door. I feel the edge under my feet. The wind is so fast and loud, it whips away the sound of my screaming, like pulling a loose thread.

"On three!" says the guy, but if he ever said "three," I didn't hear it. It was like, "One," and then—

Nothing.

Everything.

Air.

Light.

Unbearable brightness.

A blessed rush of adrenaline.

I expected to feel like I was falling. Like the ground was flying up at my face. It's not like that. You start out at thirteen thousand feet—literally miles above the earth—so even though you're falling at 120 miles per hour, the space around you is so vast, the distance so great, your perspective is that of a slow-moving cloud.

There was nothing to hang on to. Nothing to let go.

I opened my arms and felt unpolluted joy.

Freedom.

Ecstasy.

Everything you want but will never get from drugs or money or even love.

All the constant cravings of my adrenaline-junkie brain.

Conrad Hilton was a religious man. He wrote a lot about God. Feared God. Wanted to know God. Craved God. He should have gone skydiving.

The tandem instructor released the chute, and I was caught up in a slow, quiet ride, suspended above the desert like a diamond on a delicate silver chain. I stopped thinking, stopped trying, stopped wondering.

The sky was crystal-blue perfection. The distant mountains

were wrinkled yellow and ocher, iced with midwinter snow. The wide-open desert gave up a thousand shades of gray, sliced with highways, dotted with boxy little structures.

The insignificance of anyone who'd ever loved or hurt me.

The insignificance of myself.

There was no audience to play for.

Only profound peace.

A state of grace.

We descended, riding the wind, borne on soaring updrafts.

Gratitude.

Elation.

Triumph.

I'm here.

I survived.

I'm not afraid.

I love my life.

Marilyn Monroe said, "Fear is stupid. So is regret." In general, I've found this to be true. Many times, throughout my life, the most terrifying moments have led to the most fulfilling. Free-falling over the Nevada desert is just one example. I want to tell you about a few others, even though I know not everyone is going to like what I have to say.

We all have that jump door inside us, and for a long time, I marked mine with red letters. All caps.

THIS DOOR MUST REMAIN CLOSED

Brace yourselves, bitches. We're about to pry it open.

2

I was born in New York City on February 17, 1981, three days after Valentine's Day: Aquarius sun, Leo moon, Sagittarius rising. Six months later, MTV made its official debut with the Buggles' "Video Killed the Radio Star."

It all adds up.

In the context of a technological renaissance, the story of my life makes perfect sense.

Everyone says I was a sweet kid. My parents have hundreds of hours of home videos to back that up. My dad was always an early adopter when it came to tech, and as soon as those bulky old-school camcorders became available, he got one and embraced the idea that everything should be recorded, for entertainment in the present and archival value in the future. He taped everything about my life, starting the day of my birth. I loved the feeling of his focused eye on me. In those moments, his attention was distilled to that little round lens, and there I was at the center of it.

Dad always called me "Star"—in the sense of "movie star," yes, but there was also a *how I wonder what you are* vibe.

When I was two, Cyndi Lauper dropped her first single—"Girls Just Want to Have Fun"—and my little sister Nicholai Olivia was born. Aunt Kyle says I was over the moon, crazy in love with Nicky from the second she came home. I have no memories of a life before her. She was my best friend and partner in crime when we were little girls. Mom dressed us in twin outfits. We played dress-up in Mom's closet, styling each other with scarves and jewelry and sashaying up and down a pretend runway.

I've been dragging Nicky into adventures and misadventures ever since. I counted on Nicky to back me up if I was doing something out of bounds, like hiding a ferret in a cage under my bed or climbing out my upstairs bedroom window and scrambling down the trellis when I was grounded. She's been trying to pump the brakes on me since she was old enough to understand the word *consequences*. When she was in junior high, she turned into a little tattle-tale, but I believe in my heart that she truly thought she was looking out for me.

From the time I was a toddler, my brain skipped and flickered with the chemical imbalance of ADHD. Sometimes it was too much. I had to get up and dance in the glow of my Disney princess nightlight. "Time out" or anything that required sitting still was torture for me. I'm sure I was a handful, but it was never in my nature to lie or be mean. Nicky and I went to etiquette classes, so I knew how to apologize like a good girl, and I got a lot of practice. To be a "good girl" you had to be quiet.

Obey.

Sit still.

I was incapable of these things, so I had to be adorable instead. I had to be cute, precocious, and coy. I had to act silly and put on a baby-girl voice, which came naturally when I was nervous, because tension in your neck and shoulders actually tightens up your vocal apparatus and makes your voice go high and glottal. (I learned that during vocal training for *Repo! The Genetic Opera*.) I sang and danced and put on shows in Nanu's living room with Nicky and our pets, but I wasn't into the idea of performing in public. Fundamentally, I've always been shy—an extroverted introvert, overcompensating with performative social-butterfly behavior.

When Nicky and I were preschoolers, our family relocated to Bel Air and moved into a house that my parents bought from Jaclyn Smith from *Charlie's Angels*. Jaclyn had built an elaborate playhouse for her little girl—like Barbie's Dream House come to life—which Nicky and I turned into a pet hotel. I always saved up my money so I could shop for animals at a dank-smelling pet store where they sold tropical fish, snakes, and other fantastic beasts. I wanted to love and comfort any little creature who came my way.

Nicky and I played elaborate games of dress-up and pretend, while Aunt Kyle snapped pictures and filmed us with her video camera. Mom has allowed only a sliver of that footage into public view. On one old home movie, there's a telling moment when my eight-year-old face is all crooked smile and smeared lipstick, my bangs are right out of "Forever Your Girl"—teased ragged with the appropriate hat—and I'm wearing Boy George blue eyeshadow and layers of bunchy, jewel-toned clothes typical of the late 1980s.

"Hey," says Aunt Kyle. "Aren't you that famous movie star?"

"Yes!"

"What's your name?"

"Paula Abdul." I run off, chasing a little black-and-white rabbit.

"Are you gorgeous?" asks Kyle.

"No." I hold up the bunny. "He is."

"Make a mad face," she says. "Make a happy face. Make a plain face with no emotion."

I do each of those on cue, into the game, but only briefly. The bunny was a lot more interesting to me.

My dad noticed and nurtured my love for animals. He took me to pet stores to see the puppies and to the exotic cat show to see the Bengal cats. We spent a wonderful day at the San Diego Zoo, where Dad booked a backstage VIP experience so I could see all the animals up close and help the zookeepers with chores. My grandparents had a ranch, where I got to ride horses. Dad took me fishing and dirt biking and showed me how to handle the newborn chicks in the chicken coop. That's when I felt closest to him. He and Mom were amazingly cool about my personal petting zoo of ferrets, rabbits, gerbils, cats, dogs, birds, snakes, guinea pigs, chinchillas, even a little monkey, and a baby goat that I kept next to the tennis court at Papa and Nanu's.

I had a whole community of rats named after all the people from *90210*: Luke, Tori, Jason, Shannen, Brian, Ian, Jennie, Tiffani, and Gabrielle. Yeah, I know what you're thinking—like *rats?*—but domesticated rats are actually very clean, sweet natured, and intelligent. I had a huge rat named Max who had enormous balls. One day when I was out in the yard cuddling Max, a ferret ran over to me, and poor Max screamed this bizarrely loud scream with his little rat mouth wide open, and then he bit me. I dropped him, and he ran off, waddling up the driveway as fast as he could with his weirdly large balls bouncing away. I started crying, not because I was hurt but because I thought I'd lost him.

"Max! Max!" I sat down on the driveway, sobbing.

Max looked over his shoulder at me and came waddling back. I scooped him up in my arms and kissed him and told him I wasn't mad. He seemed deeply embarrassed about the whole incident.

Rats are so sweet. I should get another rat.

(Note to Carter: Birthday rat.)

Sometimes Nicky and I got to visit Dad's office in Century City. (Later he and his partner, Jeff Hyland, moved to Canon Drive in Beverly Hills.) The energy of ringing phones and clattering fax machines made it feel like great things were happening, and Dad's secretary, Wendy White, kept it all humming without a hint of chaos.

You know how Batman has that brilliant old guy with the charming accent who looks out for him and makes sure the Batcave is in good working order? For as long as I can remember, that person in my father's life has been Wendy White, an extremely proper South African lady who tolerates no nonsense from anyone. She likes to remind people of that.

Wait. Maybe she just likes to remind me.

"I'm very strict, Paris. I don't take any crap."

Anyway, because she's saying it with her exotic South African accent, it really hits home. Wendy was always happy to see Nicky and me. She'd set us up with paper, pens, markers, and scissors so we could create collages or Christmas cards. I loved doing any kind of art, especially forms that challenged the flat concept of "coloring." I had a huge cache of supplies with which I created 3-D family photo displays and BeDazzled picture frames. Nothing was safe from my BeDazzler, a gadget you could buy off an infomercial and use to clamp rhinestones and fake gems onto virtually anything that didn't move. Now you can get them online. (Shout out to whoever invented the BeDazzler!)

I loved creating collages, sitting on the floor in Dad's office, surrounded by magazines, scissors, and glue. The endless depth and variety of the ad campaigns in *Vogue* and *Vanity Fair* gave me the same kind of buzz I got from good music. I could live in those layered images for hours. That's how my mind works best—free-associating bits and pieces. We usually made a huge mess that mushroomed out of control until Wendy got stern and made us clean it up.

Later on, as Nicky and I grew up, Wendy swooped in to facilitate whatever needed facilitating. She wrangled unhappy landlords, manifested plumbers and landscapers as needed, ordered unwanted houseguests to leave, and provided clarity whenever one of us was overwhelmed by the task of adulting. She's pragmatic, but she believes in love.

The day Carter and I were married, Wendy said, "Remember, life is a journey with all its ups and downs. Stay true to each other."

Again, with the accent. I will love Wendy forever, even if she someday gets the memo about retirement meaning you don't work anymore.

In 1989, I was eight years old and Nicky was six. The Berlin Wall came down, *The Simpsons* debuted on Fox, and my adorable little brother Barron Nicholas Hilton II was born. We loved him intensely. He was almost as good as a puppy. (Joking! Love you, Barron!) Mom was a 1990s power mommy, running the household and a business of her own, making sure everyone was well fed and properly groomed. She had a boutique on Sunset Plaza where she sold gifts, accessories, and antiques that reflected her impeccable taste. It was called the Staircase, which I love, because it was her way up.

Bethenny Frankel, a friend of Aunt Kyle's, was our nanny at the time. I think they were both around nineteen or twenty. Mom was running the store, so it was Bethenny's responsibility to collect Nicky and me from Lycée, the bilingual school where we studied in French and English. Nicky liked to go to Rampage—a Hot Topic/ Forever 21–sort of store in the mall—but I always begged Bethenny to take us to the pet store in Westwood to visit the tropical fish, mice, and parakeets. Sometimes we'd meet up with Kyle and go ice-skating or get candy from the Mobile Mart.

My mom and her sisters worked as models and actresses from early childhood through their teen years. Grandma booked photo shoots and small parts for them on a ton of different television shows. Mom was the prettiest brand of pretty by 1960s standards: half Irish, half Italian, hazel eyes, blond hair, porcelain-doll complexion. Mom was a Gerber baby and did early commercials for Barbie dolls. She had small parts in *Bewitched*, *Nanny and the Professor*, *Family Affair*, and *The Rockford Files*. When she was eighteen, she played a backup singer for Leather Tuscadero (played by Suzi Quatro) on *Happy Days* in an episode called "Fonzie: Rock Entrepreneur Part I." She and another girl did the choreography in their ballet flats, stepping back and forth, singing "oooooo" and "da da da" as Richie (Ron Howard) wailed on an alto sax and Fonzie (Henry Winkler) looked on hungrily from a booth at Arnold's Diner.

Mom went to Montclair College Preparatory School in LA, where she was besties with Michael Jackson, one of the many hard-working industry kids in her class. Meanwhile, Aunt Kim and Aunt Kyle were both in Disney's *Escape to Witch Mountain*, and Kyle had a recurring role on *Little House on the Prairie*. All three sisters worked consistently through their teens. I always thought it was a positive experience, but there must have been something not great about it, because Mom felt strongly that Nicky and I should not get into modeling or performing. We did a few mother-daughter fashion shows for charity, but nothing professional. Just for fun. My dream was to become a veterinarian when I grew up, and my parents encouraged that.

Nicky and I weren't allowed to wear makeup or revealing clothes. Our mom was strict about that, which was fine with me. I wanted to be comfy. Shorts, tees, tracksuits. Always ready for action. Our mom valued modesty and grace. We didn't talk about things she considered private or gross or unseemly. I still have trouble with that myself.

When Carter suggested swimming with sperm whales as a honeymoon activity, I was like, "No. I can't be associated with the word 'sperm.'"

"Okay," he said amiably. "Humpback whales then."

"Honey. 'Hump'?"

He laughed. He thought I was joking. He doesn't get why I'm so hypersensitive. I don't fully get it myself, but it is what it is.

As a preteen, I was athletic, clever, and completely without fear, which is probably the most terrifying kind of kid to parent, but my mom and dad were a strong parenting team. Sometimes I could bat my eyes and baby-talk Dad into things Mom had already said no to, but most of the time, they were a united front. They were strict, but I felt safe and loved in my immediate and extended family.

Nicky and I went to Buckley, a tony private school in Sherman Oaks, filled with the children of Hollywood executives and industry people. When I was in fifth grade, we were all crazy for these Reebok Pump sneakers that inflated when you pushed a little basketball on the side. I needed those shoes, but when Mom took me to Pixie Town to get them, they had only one pair left.

Mom tried to tell me, "These won't work. They're two and a half sizes too big."

I did not care. They were so cool. I piled on a few extra socks, pumped them as much as they would pump, and wore them to school the next day, thinking I was killing it. Right away, some girl was like, "Oh, my god, Paris! You look like Ronald McDonald." And then everybody piled on laughing at me as I ran for the bathroom, wanting to die. I pulled myself together and threw the shoes into someone's locker on my way to the pay phone to call my mom.

"I hate you! Why did you buy me these shoes? Everyone is so mean."

Mom calmed me down and brought me a pair of shoes that fit, but I had a hard time coming back from that. Once you're on that end of the bully dynamic, school can get pretty torturous. My grades started to slide.

When I was in sixth grade, everyone was in love with Edward Furlong, the kid in *Terminator 2*. He was all over *Tiger Beat* and *People* and started a whole hair trend. Buckley was K–12, so when the tenth-grade boys with their Furlong side bangs invited me to sneak off campus and go to McDonald's at lunchtime, I was like, "Sure!" And obviously, I couldn't walk around town in a dorky knee-length skirt, so I rolled it up and styled it short and got in trouble for that. I wasn't doing anything with these boys. I just liked the attention.

(I ended up dating Eddie Furlong when I was eighteen. He was an animal-rights advocate, so we had that in common. A few years later, I heard he was arrested for freeing the lobsters from a grocery-store lobster tank, which sounds so epic. *Run, little lobsters, run!* I wish he'd thought of it when we were together.)

At the end of the school year, the principal told my parents I was not welcome to come back for seventh grade, which sucked, because it meant leaving my middle school bestie, Nicole Richie.

Nicole was in my class at Buckley, and her family lived close by, thank God, so we still had each other. Together, we aspired to be the kind of cool girls Bethenny and Kyle were. We were eager to bring that energy to the early boy-girl parties and simultaneously experienced our first kisses (with different boys) during the same game of Spin the Bottle.

I transferred to a K–8 Catholic school in Los Angeles. John Paul II was pope at the time, and only half the nuns were wearing the old-school *Sound of Music* habits, but they were all as mean as ever. I'd start a math test feeling like *I got this*, but after a few minutes I couldn't keep still. The numbers jumped around every time someone coughed.

There was a bird outside the window.

My sleeves felt uneven.

Sister Godzilla had a mole on her chin.

"Paris, sit still."

It was like that mole was yelling at me, which made me giggle, and then Sister was walking toward me, saying she was going to call Mom, and Mom was getting so tired of being called. And getting notes. And meeting with the principal. My grades hadn't hit rock bottom yet, but my parents knew I could do better.

"You're one of the smartest kids I know," Dad kept telling me. "You just need to apply yourself. Have some self-discipline."

Cheerleading was a lifesaver. I wore myself out learning the drill team choreography, the perfect balance of physical and mental workout. After sitting in school for several hours, it was such a relief to jump around, flailing and yelling, getting positive attention for the first time all day. I was feeling myself in the cheerleading arena. One of the cool girls.

I kept an ornately BeDazzled diary in which I recorded all the middle school cheerleader drama and page upon page of ideas for inventions, thoughts about life, poems, dreams, doodles, tirades against anyone who hurt my feelings, odes to whatever boy I was crushing on, and lavishly illustrated stream-of-consciousness stories about wild horses, unicorns, and animal kingdoms.

At some point, I heard Nicky say "That's hot" and it resonated with me. I wrote it in my diary and doodled flowers and fireworks around it. It's such a great statement, isn't it? Positive. Unpretentious. The word *hot* is evocative; there's energy in it—hot pink, hot shit, Red Hot Chili Peppers. And if you say it to the next person you meet, I guarantee you'll see them smile. I mean, don't be creepy about it, but who doesn't love a little positive affirmation? If you see something you appreciate, shout it out. Toss a spark of positivity into the world.

It's like "I see you"—but hotter.

Suddenly there seemed to be a lot of things in my world that deserved this little accolade, and I recorded them faithfully in my diary.

Mom got me markers with glitter in them. That's hot.
We learned how to diagram sentences. That's hot.
Nicole is sleeping over the whole weekend. That's hot.

It caught on. Pretty soon all the kids in my class were saying, "That's hot." Like I made "fetch" happen! (*Mean Girls* reference. That's hot.)

My dad traveled a lot for business, and my parents don't sleep apart. To this day, if he goes, she goes. So, we traveled a lot as a family, or Mom would travel with Dad while Aunt Kyle looked after us, which was great because Kyle always encouraged Nicky and me to invite friends over. There were a lot of sleepovers with Nicole—my middle school bestie. We thought we were edgy as hell because we knew all the words to Sir Mix-a-Lot's "Baby Got Back."

Mom, Kim, and Kyle presented a fabulous model for sisterhood dynamics. Mom tells me now that their mother was super strict when she was a kid, but Grandma apparently chilled out somewhat after she divorced my mom's dad and married her second husband. Kim came along five years later, and Kyle was born five years after that. Grandma divorced that guy and got married and divorced twice more after that, so those girls went through a lot when they were growing up, but they came out of it with beauty, business sense, impeccable style, and a natural joie de vivre I've always admired. They supported, defended, and loved each other unconditionally, but they could depend on each other to tell the unvarnished truth. If one of them had broccoli in her teeth, the other two would tell her. Their lively conversations were always full of laughter and confidences. Mom loves cracking people up.

One night I passed by my mom's room, and I heard Mom talking in an exaggerated little puppet voice. Kim and Kyle were laughing so hard they were practically crying. I don't remember the exact lines, but I heard something like "*Nicole says I should just go up to him and tell him I think he's hot. Kim says I should tell one of his friends that I like him and see what happens . . .*"

It took a minute to sink in. She was reading from my BeDazzled diary.

I was so angry I couldn't move. I stood behind the door, frozen, fuming, humiliated. There was nothing mean-spirited in my aunts' laughter; they just thought it was super cute. And I'm sure it *was* super cute. I'm sure Mom just wanted to share this super cute thing with her sisters. After she dug through my sock drawer. And read my diary. In a Lamb Chop–puppet voice.

In the realm of bad things that happen to kids, this is not a big deal. I get that. I'm just mentioning it because the moment stayed with me for a long time. Like when a glass slips from your hand and breaks in the sink. In the big picture, it's not a big deal, but in that moment, you know the fragile nature of things, and it makes you feel weirdly fragile yourself.

I don't know what happened to my diary. I wish I still had it. I suppose, if I saw it, I would laugh, too. But I would also recognize that it was a thing of beauty. Sometimes we forget what it means to be a creative spirit in that precious moment before you become self-conscious, forced to admit that, yeah, you really do care what other people think of you. Especially people you love and look up to.

In 1994, I was thirteen, and my baby brother Conrad Hughes Hilton was born. I started paying more attention to music and fashion. I worshipped Madonna and Janet Jackson. I didn't understand half the lyrics in Salt-N-Pepa's "Shoop," but I could lip-sync along with that and most of Da Brat's "Funkdafied" and Snoop Dogg's "Gin and Juice."

On New Year's Eve, my family and Nicole's family and a bunch of other people we knew went to Vegas. My parents love Vegas, so this get-together was a big tradition for all of us. Usually, the grown-ups went out to dance in the New Year while the kids played board games and watched movies in the hotel suites with nannies. But that year, Nicole and I begged for our own room. We lobbied hard, pointing out how insulting it was to be babysat at our advanced age.

"We're teenagers! We're old enough to babysit each other."

We finally convinced our parents that, if they let us stay in our own hotel room, we'd watch *Dick Clark's New Year's Rockin' Eve* and put ourselves to bed right after midnight.

Obviously, that didn't happen.

By nine o'clock, we were bored and talking on the phone to two Buckley boys who were a little older than us. Happy coincidence! They were in Vegas with their families, too. The boys came over to our hotel room and suggested we all take a walk. Nicole and I had been forbidden to leave that room, but we wanted to be cool, so we said we could only walk around the hotel for a little while, but then it seemed like we should avoid any chance of running into our parents, so, clearly, the practical choice was to walk down the Strip with the boys.

That was a lot of fun. We weren't trying to drink or smoke or anything like that; we just wanted to be out there where the action was. Music poured out of every door. Happy, beautiful people celebrated in flashy clothes and party hats. At midnight the street was full of light, cheering crowds, and honking car horns. We made out with the boys—nothing beyond first base—and then they went off to do their own thing.

Nicole and I continued walking on our own. Walked and walked, taking it all in, window-shopping, laughing, and chatting. People poured out of the casinos and hotel bars—so many people—heading for after-parties. It was super crowded and a little scary. Nicole and I kept going, arms linked so we wouldn't get separated.

Finally, I said, "We should get a cab and go back to the hotel."

Nicole agreed, but everyone else on the street had the same idea. This was long before the days of Uber and Lyft. You hailed a cab on a street corner or stood in a queue outside a hotel, but there were so many people it was impossible to even see a cab, much less get in one. Eventually, we went up to a police officer who looked busy but friendly.

"Excuse me," I said. "Is there anywhere we can get a cab? There's like a million people waiting in line."

The cop shined his light on me and said, "How old are you?"

"Twenty-one." We didn't miss a beat.

He folded his arms. "Show me your ID."

"I don't have it on me," I said. "I lost it."

"What's your name?"

"Jennifer Pearlstein," I said. "This is my friend Leslie."

"How old are you, Jennifer?"

"I told you! Twenty-one!"

"No, you're not."

"Eighteen?"

"You are not eighteen," he said, "and it's illegal for you be out on the Strip after nine. There's a curfew. You want to get arrested? I should arrest you right now."

Nicole and I insisted we were *so* eighteen and just in town on business, but the cop wasn't having it. He ordered us into the back of the cop car, and we sat there like, *Holy crap! What do we do? What do we do?* while he stood on the corner, talking into his shoulder radio.

We waited for a long time. It seemed like two hours, so it was probably about fifteen minutes in real time. Nicole and I whispered back and forth, getting our story straight, planning a strategy. Then the cop opened the car door and Nicole blurted out, "Her name is Paris Hilton! We're staying at the Las Vegas Hilton! Her mom is Kathy Hilton!"

"*Nicole.*" I elbowed her. "Oh, my god."

"We're so sorry, officer. We didn't mean to do anything wrong," Nicole said. She gave him my mom's phone number, and a little while later, my dad showed up to collect us. All the way back to the hotel, he yelled at us, as one would expect.

"What were you thinking? Do you have any idea what could have happened? You are grounded, Star. Grounded!"

I was like, "Grounded from what? I'm already in Las Vegas."

"Grounded from Nicole," said Dad. "Obviously, the two of you are a bad influence on each other. You are no longer allowed to hang out."

Nicole's parents were just as mad as mine, so it was like double trouble. They put us in separate rooms and told us we weren't allowed to speak to each other. When we got back to LA, our moms confiscated the phones in our rooms, but Nicole's house was across the golf course from mine, and we discovered that if we stood on our balconies and screamed, it echoed over the green, and we could hear each other.

Love will find a way. There was no keeping us apart.

Nicole Richie and I were ride or die from our terrible twos, and we'll stay that way until world ends. When we were teenagers, riffing off each other, doing silly voices, everyone around us was dying. We were dying. I'm dying now just thinking about it! I don't know what it was; we just seemed to resonate like a tuning fork. We were having so much fun, a kind of Lucy and Ethel comedy magic happened, and that was the magic of *The Simple Life*.

Nicole is so genuinely kind and sweet, she catches people off guard with her raunchy one-liners, and the reaction she gets from people is comedy gold. Comedy has to be fearless, and Nicole doesn't hesitate.

One of our favorite activities was making prank calls, which we learned from the prank-calling GOAT: my mom. Mom can disguise her voice and make you think a delivery person is on the way over with a hundred Hawaiian pizzas or that she's locked in the trunk of her car or literally anything. Once she and Nicky took me to lunch at a little vineyard and made me think I was at a surprise wedding in which I was the bride.

Inspired by Mom's epic prank-calling example, Nicole and I spent hours up in my room answering want ads in the *Los Angeles Times* or dialing boys from our class and pretending to be the appointment secretary for a professional sports scout. These calls usually went down pretty much like the ones Nicole and I did with random numbers we found on a bulletin board in a laundromat when we were shooting *The Simple Life*.

RANDO: Hello?

ME: *(putting on a low, raspy voice)* Yes, I'm calling regarding the room for rent.

RANDO: It's big. You'll like the furniture. It's bad.

ME: I don't like bad furniture, dear. Wait. Bad means good? I don't know teenager lingo. I'm a lonely old man.

RANDO: Bad means good.

ME: It says no smoking. I love my cigs.

RANDO: No smoking.

ME: Okay. Am I allowed to go naked in the pool? I live in Caliente right now, which is a nudist colony. You don't have a problem with nudity, do you?

(Click)

3

I turned fourteen in February 1995. I loved *Toy Story* and *Jumanji* and hopping up and down with one arm in the air, singing at the top of my lungs to Montell Jordan's "This Is How We Do It." I was in eighth grade at the Catholic school. We wore uniforms—boxy basics—but Nicky and I found ways to shorten the skirts and style them in our favor with Hello Kitty accessories, clever shirt-tucking techniques, and blown-out hair. I couldn't wait to get home and kick that plaid skirt and starchy blouse into a corner. I tore around in surfer shorts with baggy tees and sneakers. I slept in boxers and baseball shirts I swiped from Dad's clean laundry.

I was a tomboy, but I certainly didn't think of myself as a child. I had a beeper and my very own phone line, which connected to my very own answering machine. I recorded the answering machine message over and over, trying to make my voice raspy and alluring like the phone sex lines that advertised on late night TV.

Hey, it's Paris. I'm not here right now, but I really want to talk to you . . .

I lay on my bed in the evening, gossiping with my friends about very grown-up things like whether Rachel and Ross on *Friends* would ever get together and what was happening on after-school reruns of *Beverly Hills, 90210*.

Shannen Doherty was the bad girl icon of the mid-nineties. You couldn't check out at the grocery store or buy candy at the newsstand without seeing her all over the tabloids. She posed almost nude for *Playboy*. She partied with guys, feuded with girls, and then— *unforgivable!*—she left the show. The same audience that made her the breakout star of the show turned on her, and we all went with that flow: "What a slut. What a bitch." All the generic comments that apply to the girl everyone loves after she becomes the girl they love to hate.

Mom had her hands full with the boys, so my messes and my pets and my bouncing around were increasingly getting on her nerves. We'd always been close, but now we were feeling some of the friction burn that happens naturally between moms and teenage daughters. Mom was super conservative; I was super *not*. I blasted Onyx's *Bacdafucup* on repeat and wore rude message tees from Gadzooks. I mouthed off and failed to write thank-you notes, and whenever I wanted to avoid the gauntlet of parental permissions, I climbed out my bedroom window and maneuvered down to the ground like Super Mario. The nuns complained about my school-day fidgeting, shit-disturbing, and lack of attention.

I was frequently grounded, and my solution to that was to sneak out. One time, Nicole and I hatched a plan to go to a school dance we were supposed to be grounded from because of our generally unruly behavior. We went to a store called Judy's in the Beverly Center and bought twin outfits: velvet shorts with crop tops and fishnets. (Not in good taste, but not horribly inappropriate. You see sexier getups on *Dance Moms*.) Then, we went to her dad's house on the pretense of working on a school project or something, put on the outfits, and pulled baggy pants and jackets over them. Off we went to the dance with both sets of parents thinking we were at the other person's house.

We got a huge thrill out of stuff like that.

The planning! The intrigue!

We never did anything terrible; we just loved feeling free and trying to outsmart anyone who we thought was trying to keep us down. We almost always got caught and grounded again, which seemed terribly unfair to us at the time. We were just exploring. *What is it like to feel sexy? What does sexy even mean?* Totally valid questions for teenage girls to be investigating.

But it's problematic when girls go into that exploratory phase feeling secretive and ill informed. If the message you send is "We don't talk about such things," then—guess what!—your kids move toward adulthood with the idea that being an adult means keeping secrets. The nuns didn't teach us anything about reproductive health in biology class. We certainly didn't cover *Lolita* in English class. Mom didn't talk about things that fell into nebulous categories like "private" and "dirty." I learned the basics from feminine-hygiene ads in *Seventeen*. My understanding of sexuality was a fog machine of Madonna videos, Calvin Klein commercials, and a vaguely naughty impulse that made me feel the same sting of guilt I felt when I swiped a tube of lip gloss from Mom's purse.

So, with middle school graduation just around the corner, in my mind, I was pretty much in high school. Which pretty much means grown up, right? When the yearbook came out, all the eighth grad-

ers were pictured in our caps and gowns, and my picture was cap-
tioned: "Finest Girl."

That's another great word, isn't it? Like "You're doing fine.
You're okay." Or "Nothing wrong with this little girl. She's fine!" Or
maybe *fine* like delicate, like a dragonfly wing.

But obviously, this is *fine* like *hot*. Like *sexy*. I was the *sexiest* of
the eighth-grade girls! Because sexy eighth grader—that's a thing,
right?

Like a Halloween costume?

I was fine with being "Finest Girl." I leaned into that.

Meanwhile, all the girls in my class were crushing on this hand-
some young teacher. Always saying how ridiculously hot he was.
Very Abercrombie. Tousled hair. Penetrating eyes. Everyone loved
him, including the nuns.

But he chose *me*. The Finest Girl.

"I've got a crush on you," he said, flashing a flirty smile.

He made me feel noticed in an important, grown-up way. He
flattered and teased me and said that all the other girls were talking
about me behind my back because they were jealous. Jealous of my
hotness. Because their boyfriends probably wanted to break up with
them the second I walked into the room. He asked for my private
phone number and cautioned me not to tell anyone.

"It's our secret," he said, and I kept that secret like candy under my pillow. I never felt like I was being manipulated. I felt like I
was being worshipped. I was Marilyn Monroe waiting to happen.
He couldn't help the way he felt because I had cast my spell on him.

Why wouldn't I love this narrative? It was all about me, me, gorgeous little me. The focus was on my intoxicating beauty instead of
his inappropriate behavior.

Mr. Abercrombie called me almost every night, and we talked
for hours about how amazingly mature, beautiful, and intelligent I

was, how sensual, misunderstood, and special. He reminded me that Princess Diana was thirteen years younger than Prince Charles. And Priscilla Presley was my age when Elvis fell in love with her. I deserved a rock star. I deserved a prince. Because I was a princess. I deserved to be cherished and loved in a way eighth-grade boys know nothing about.

Mr. Abercrombie made me believe that I was rare and precious, and you know what? I *was*. Every eighth-grade girl is rare and precious. Every eighth-grade girl is a treasure, like a priceless work of art, so you'd like to think that every eighth-grade teacher will be like a security guard in an art gallery. He's not there to enjoy the beauty; he's there to protect it. He's there to enforce the rules, and Rule Number One is: *DO. NOT. TOUCH.* Keep your fingers, lips, and man bits off the masterpieces. It should be obvious that the Girl with a Pearl Earring deserves a chance to smile her wistful smile without some creepy guy feeling her up. Because damage to that precious work of art can be hidden, but it can never be undone.

My teacher asked me almost every night, "Are your parents home?"

One night when they were out, I said, "No, it's just the nanny."

"Come outside," he said. "I'm waiting for you."

I threw on sneakers, climbed out my bedroom window, and slid down the drainpipe. Night air filled my lungs, along with the smell of mown grass and gardenias. I saw a late-model SUV idling at the top of the driveway. I climbed into the passenger seat. Teacher pulled me into his arms and kissed me.

The intensity of it stunned and delighted me. My brain lit up, flush with adrenaline, curiosity, and a host of feelings I couldn't even name. This terrifying blissful kissing went on for what seemed like a long time and seemed to be evolving into something more. I don't know where he would have taken it if my parents hadn't pulled into the driveway.

Headlights spilled across the windshield, and the spell was broken.

I glimpsed my dad's stunned face. Teacher jammed his key in the ignition and peeled out. I clutched the edge of the seat as we fishtailed down the driveway. He sped like a maniac through the posh streets of Bel Air and Westwood, reeling around corners, freaking out the whole time.

I giggled. Nervous. Heart pounding. Ears ringing. Oh, my god! I wasn't wearing a seat belt! This was like Bonnie and Clyde!

"*Fuck! Fuck! Fuck!*" Mr. Abercrombie sounded like he was crying. "My life is over. What am I doing? *Why did you make me do this?*"

Eventually, he circled back and dropped me off in front of my house. He didn't even kiss me good night like I imagined somebody would if you were on a date. It didn't happen like a rom-com; he just dumped me out of the car and sped away. I sprinted across the yard, scrambled up the drainpipe, climbed in the bedroom window, and dove under the covers. My parents burst into my room, beyond furious, both of them screaming at me. There were too many words to sort out. A solid wall of outrage.

I blinked my big eyes and said in a dreamy baby voice, "What? What are you talking about? I've been sleeping."

I didn't know what else to do. I'm sure they didn't believe me for a second, but whatever—I just wanted them to go, and obviously, they just wanted to be gone, so they went out of my room, and no one ever mentioned the awkward incident again.

The school year was almost over, but that last month or so was fraught with drama at school and home. I never told a soul, but somehow, people seemed to know. Maybe I imagined it, but things felt different. He was still Mr. Abercrombie, but I was no longer the Finest Girl. I was the Shannen Doherty of the Catholic school. Everyone loved to hate me. Nothing I did was right. I didn't know how to feel or what to do, and I was trying to process it all in the lonely, confusing space of secrecy.

During the school dance after the graduation ceremony, I went over to McDonald's, and when I came back, the chaperones wouldn't let me in.

The nuns were like, "You're done, bitch. GTFO."

I mean, they probably didn't use those exact words, but they were clear. I had to call my mom to come and get me, knowing she'd be livid and embarrassed.

That was the end of my happy life in Barbie's Bel Air Dream House.

Mom and Dad sent me to live at my grandmother's house in Palm Springs—just for the summer, I thought, but it turned out to be for much longer.

I don't know if there were any repercussions to the teacher or if there was any attempt to prevent him from choosing another little girl. My parents never volunteered any information, and I never asked, but I assume the fear of bad publicity would have prevented them from making a scene or pressing charges. I understand how they could have reasoned that this was in my best interest.

For twenty-five years, I framed this episode in my mind as "my first kiss," because, even though it wasn't my first kiss, it made all the kisses that came before it seem like the kisses I gave my ferrets. I never allowed myself to talk or even think about what it really was or why I climbed out the window to kiss that stupid pedophile. It took decades for me to actually speak the word *pedophile*.

Casting him in the role of child molester meant casting myself in the role of victim, and I just couldn't go there. I couldn't accept that all his praises—all those affirmations an eighth-grade girl desperately needs to hear—came from a place of malevolence, and I was stupid and vain enough to buy it. It was like dreaming about a lover's gentle touch but then waking up to realize it was actually a roach crawling on you. I couldn't reconcile the fact that I had enjoyed something that was, in reality, utterly vile. I feel physically ill now, seeing it in that perspective.

I wanted to be a spider, not a fly, and as it played out, I was the one who was disgraced and sent away, so I must be the one at fault, right? As surely as plastic bags make the wind blow, the shame was on *me* for ruining this poor man's life.

And the shame is still on me.

Even now, knowing in my grown-up mind that no child is ever to blame for inappropriate adult behavior, my face is literally burning as I sit here telling you this terrible secret. I'm not sure I'll ever be able to fully shake it off. But it's a key part of my story, the catalyst for much of what followed.

I cried when I read Marilyn Monroe's memoir *My Story*, and I was inspired by the fact that she found the courage to talk about being molested by her aunt's neighbor when she was in grade school. The man groomed her with charming banter and lured her into his room with smooth kindness. He locked the door and felt her up, telling her she was so beautiful he couldn't help himself. Then he unlocked the door and told her to never tell anyone. He tried to give her a nickel for ice cream, but little Norma Jeane threw the nickel in his face and ran to tell her aunt, who scolded her for lying about this neighbor, who was an upstanding gentleman. A few days later, her aunt took her to a religious revival meeting, where the man who'd molested Marilyn loudly prayed for her sins to be forgiven.

"I cried in bed that night and wanted to die," Marilyn says in *My Story*. "I thought, 'If there's nobody ever on my side that I can talk to, I'll start screaming.' But I didn't scream."

It's infuriating to me now to think about how readily Marilyn and I both accepted that narrative about our physical appearance being the excuse for someone else's criminal behavior. But how could we not?

We were given a choice:

A: "You are a stupid child who was deceived, used, and thrown away like garbage."
B: "You are an irresistible siren whose beauty and allure have the power to change someone's mind, sway their soul, and alter their behavior."

Given the choice between victim and influencer, Marilyn and I embraced our siren selves.

4

The microclimate of Palm Springs makes for prime resort real estate. The surrounding area is a blazing hot frying pan full of scorpions and cactus plants, but Palm Springs is positioned to benefit from shadows cast by the San Jacinto Mountains. The weather stays nice most of the time. High-society people started going there in the early 1900s because the warm desert air was good for dainty Victorian women's problems like consumption and hysteria, which was their catch-all term for PMS, menopause, or whatever condition gave a woman the crazy idea she was allowed to express an opinion.

According to legend, Marilyn Monroe was "discovered" by a William Morris talent scout (in the sense that Columbus "discovered" America) as she lounged by the pool at Charles Farrell's Racquet Club in Palm Springs in 1949. Conrad Hilton came along in the early 1960s and built a luxury hotel there with a ninety-nine-year lease.

By the time I arrived in Palm Springs in summer 1995, the Racquet Club was between owners and overgrown with weeds. Half the stores in the Palm Springs Mall, including the anchor stores, I. Magnin and Saks, were closed. Downtown Palm Springs was still a playground for the Hollywood elite, but the neighborhood where I lived with my mom's mom was mostly full of little old ladies with blue hair.

My grandmother was not one of them.

My grandmother's hair was coppery red, the color of a brand-new penny, and she didn't step outside without applying fire-engine-red lipstick. She was glamorous. Always decked out in diamonds. She enjoyed her jewelry—the more the better—and she made it all look beautiful. Gram Cracker was a force of nature who shifted the energy of every room she walked into. She was a character. Loved being social. Loved being gorgeous. Instead of trying to fit the typical mold, she relished being herself.

In a word, Gram Cracker was *sliving*.

Sliving is a word I invented a few years ago at a Halloween party. I started to say "slaying" but took a sharp left toward "living your best life," and "sliving" came out. We all died laughing, but I was thinking, *That's a great word. Ima trademark that shit like yesterday.* I may have been slightly tipsy. But it is a great word! It's a movement and a lifestyle. And my grandmother was sliving personified.

Looking back, I'm so glad I had that time with her. She showed me what style is, what strength is, and how the two fit together. It seemed to me like she ruled that town. Everyone loved her style and spirit. Even as a kid, I recognized that. She didn't have the resources I saw on the Hilton side of my family; she made things happen with audacity and strength of will.

"Work hard and be independent," she told me. "Don't let a man tell you your life. You're a star—the most gorgeous thing on the planet. Men will bow down to you, but you have to know what you want and go for it."

One day I came home upset because a boy was being mean to me in class. Gram Cracker knew his parents, so she called him on the phone and straight up cursed him out, like, "Listen, you ugly little pimple face, don't fuck with my granddaughter. If you so much as speak to her again, I'll come over there and destroy you."

Language aside, she set a powerful example: Stick up for the ones you love—and love yourself enough to stick up for *you*.

I loved my summer with Grandma, but when summer ended, Mom came and enrolled me in ninth grade at Palm Valley School, a private college prep school in Rancho Mirage, an easy half hour commute from Grandma's house. I didn't see this as punishment for what happened with my teacher. Lots of kids go away to prep school. It's not a big deal. Also, I guess, since they had to be away a lot, they felt I was safer with Grandma than I was with a nanny. I was smarter than most of the nannies. I was not smarter than Gram Cracker. Nobody ever was or will be.

I was devastated to learn that my family had moved back to New York City without me. My grandma's house was definitely the nicest of all the places I would be imprisoned, but I was stuck living next to a golf course in the desert while my family took up residence in the Waldorf-Astoria. This was a bitter pill to swallow. I was a fourteen-year-old kid. I wanted to be with my family. I needed my mom. I missed the clean smell of Chanel No. 5 on her wrists. I missed trying on clothes in her overflowing walk-in closet. I longed for those amazing afternoons at the zoo with my dad. My little brother Barron was growing taller so fast, I hardly recognized him. My little brother Conrad was a toddler; I hardly had a chance to know him or play with him or love on him the way Nicky and I had loved on Barron when he was a baby.

I was not a bad girl.

I could be mouthy sometimes, uncooperative and stubborn. In other words: *I was fourteen*. If your fourteen-year-old kid walks around like a perfect little angel all the time, they should probably be tested for Lyme disease. I'd never had a drink of alcohol or tried any kind of drugs. Never smoked a cigarette. I didn't swear or lie (much), and even though I had the kind of arguments teenage girls routinely have with their moms, I loved my parents, and I knew they loved me. It just hurt me so deeply to think about my family having breakfast and hanging out in front of the TV—all the little things that were happening without me. I cried a lot, wanting my mom, wanting my siblings, just wanting to go home.

I didn't know what my family wanted. Not me, apparently.

So, I did what people do when they don't have the family they need: I made one. That's a good skill to learn, because pretty much everyone, at some point in life, goes through a phase when they're estranged from the family they're born into. For many people, it's more than a phase; it's a lifestyle. So many of my LGBTQ friends and fans exist in that space, and without oversharing my own stuff, I've always tried to make them feel seen and loved. I get it.

Thank God for Gram Cracker.

She and I got along like peas in a pod. I never expected her to play the role of demure old lady; she never cast me as the Catholic school girl. We were just ourselves, Gram Cracker and me. She told me at least a thousand times, "Before you were born, a psychic told me, 'This baby girl will someday be one of the most photographed and famous women in the world.' Brigitte Bardot, Audrey Hepburn, Marilyn Monroe, Grace Kelly—you'll be bigger than all of them."

I'd never been allowed to wear makeup, go on real dates, or hang out at the mall before. Grandma wasn't uptight about any of that. She schooled me on all the sensitive topics Mom declined to talk about: boys, bras, mascara, and other matters that were all totally appropriate and necessary for a girl of fourteen. She took me to the salon and let me get my honey-brown hair bleached blond and cut in layers like Farrah Fawcett. She schooled me on current makeup trends: matte foundation, exaggerated lip liner, plucked-to-perfection eyebrows, and subtle glitter finish. She was the master of the Nefertiti eye—an icy blue or lavender lid with silvery white up to the brow bone—but I preferred the early grunge trend that favored a smokey eye.

Grandma let me go to the mall on weekends and made sure I had money for the food court. She let me date and go to parties. I was allowed to have male and female friends over to watch TV in my room, so I didn't have to sneak out. I was free to do a lot more than my parents had ever allowed, but my grandmother set boundaries, and she wasn't kidding.

Ninth grade was the last year that I really got anything out of school. I never cut classes. I did my homework and thought about college. I was dating my first real boyfriend, Randy Spelling, who lived with his parents, Aaron and Candy Spelling, and his sister, Tori, in a legendary 56,500-square-foot mansion called the Manor. Randy's house had a movie theater, a bowling alley, and a lot of other things that made it fun to be his girlfriend. He was a couple years older than me and had a driver's license, so he came to visit me in Palm Springs, and once he rented a cool bungalow with a pool and hot tub. We made big plans for the weekend. Not sex plans. Just fun. I was a virgin and very clear about the fact that I would be saving myself for my husband.

Raised with a Catholic view of virginity, I looked up to my mom and wanted to marry someone just like my dad. They were loyal and kind to each other. Cherished each other. I wanted to be cherished like that, and it was ingrained in me that to be the right kind of wife, you had to be a virgin when you got married. She drilled it into my head that guys only want what they can't have, so giving it up meant being unwanted the next day. She said blow jobs were beneath me. "That's for girls who are desperate. You don't have to get on your knees. You're Paris Hilton."

Mom always told Nicky and me, "Never sell yourself short or give yourself away to someone who doesn't appreciate your value. See yourselves as the Chanel purse. You're the Hermès original, not the thrift-store knock-off."

So, even though I was crazy about Randy, I was like, *Be the Birkin.* And Randy was cool with that. We could still have a fun weekend, right?

It wasn't just going to be the two of us; it was a whole group of kids. Very *Beverly Hills, 90210* kind of thing. I packed some cute clothes in a little suitcase and told Gram Cracker I would be spending the weekend with my friend Crystal, and she was fine with that because she was good friends with Crystal's mom. It didn't occur to me that because they were such good friends, my grandma would call her to check on me. I don't know how she got the address of the rented bungalow, but I think it proves my point about her Palm Springs network. She booked it over there and pounded on the door while we were all out back chilling in the jacuzzi. I went inside and looked out through the peephole.

There was Gram Cracker, yelling, "Paris, I know you're in there!"

I grabbed my suitcase, bolted out the back door, and scrambled over the fence. This bungalow was on the edge of a golf course, so I ran barefoot across the green, dodging sand traps and sprinklers, all the way back to my grandma's house. She came home a little while later, and she was righteously pissed. I tried to run every story I could think of—*I swear I was at Crystal's! We were in the guesthouse so her mom blah blah blah*—yeah. Forget it. There was no lying to Gram Cracker. She looked at me with her laser-beam eyes and saw right into my soul. She didn't ground me, but she lectured me about integrity and consequences and made me feel horrible for trying to deceive her.

Compared to what high school students are up to today, this was pretty tame, but Mom and Dad had done their best to keep Nicky and me sealed in a Tupperware container of love and privilege, sheltered from the world from the day we were born. Mom grew up working and married young; she never really had a chance to experience "normal" teen years—if there is any such thing—so I think that period in my life scared her. The Hilton name was important to them. And to me. I was proud to be a Hilton. But I wanted to be Paris, too.

High school made me feel like I was queen of my own destiny, looking good and feeling confident, hanging out with friends at Micky D's.

Sometimes I went over to LA on the weekend to spend the night with Papa and Nanu and hang out with friends, and we usually ended up at Century City Mall, which was *way* better than the mall in Palm Springs. Whenever we were there, my friends and I ran into these two older guys, in their late twenties. They were so cute and nice and grown up in their mall clothes, and we felt very grown up about their wanting to be friends, hang out, get our beeper numbers, and call us up to shoot the breeze.

One weekend, I was at the mall with a not-super-close friend—let's call her Iffy—and we ran into these two hot guys, and they invited us to hang out at one guy's apartment that was not far. The invitation didn't feel weird or out of bounds, because these guys weren't strangers; they were nice guys we'd known for a while. They were older, but we weren't little girls; we were in high school, after all. This was midmorning on a Saturday, and Iffy's parents were expecting us to be home for dinner.

So Iffy and I went over, and we were playing music and dancing, just hanging out. One of the guys kept trying to get me to drink this wild berry wine cooler, but thinking ahead, I had brought a bottle of Sprite with me.

I kept saying, "I'm good with my Sprite."

But he kept coming over to me with this wild berry wine cooler, wild berry wine cooler, wild berry wine cooler. He kept saying, "Don't be a baby. It doesn't even taste like alcohol. It's hardly anything. Like Kool-Aid. Look, you have to drink it now, it's already open. We can't waste it. Just take one drink."

I took a sip. It was syrupy sweet, tinged with blue.

After that, I don't remember much. Broken pieces. Fragments. Echoes. White noise. Black silence. I became aware of a crushing weight on me. Suffocating me. Cracking my ribs. I felt a jolt of panic and tried to get up, but the impulse was lost, as if something had severed my spinal cord. When I tried to scream, there was no air in my lungs. All that came out was a small, raspy *"stop . . . what's happening . . . stop . . ."* until this guy clamped his hand over my mouth—like, aggressively—like, *hard*. He clamped down on my face and whispered: "It's a dream. It's a dream. You're dreaming."

That creepy whisper in my ear—like a mosquito.

And then . . . nothing.

I woke up alone in a room I didn't recognize. Late-afternoon sun beat through the streaky windows. My eyes felt like two stones in my skull. My lips felt swollen and tasted like blood. My body ached, unstable, like I'd been torn in half and glued back together inside my clothes. I didn't know if my friend had abandoned me or was dead in the other bedroom. I needed to throw up.

I went into the bathroom, vomited, and washed my face with cold water. Before I opened the bedroom door, I pressed my ear against it. The apartment was silent. I carefully opened the door and stepped into the hallway. The guy was standing in the middle of the living room between me and the front door.

My throat closed. I couldn't breathe. The way he was standing there—it seemed like he wasn't going to let me leave. It seemed like he wanted me to be afraid. But then he smiled and said, "Hi."

I said, "Where's Iffy?"

He said, "They left earlier. I think they went for lunch. And then you fell asleep. Right? You remember falling asleep?"

I said, "I was . . . yeah. I—I must've fallen asleep."

He said, "Did you, like, have any weird dreams? Do you remember anything?"

I focused on the front door and said what I thought he wanted me to say: "I don't remember anything. I was just asleep. That's all."

He kept shuffling back and forth on his feet in a weird, awkward way, asking me if I remembered anything, asking me if I had any bad dreams. I just acted like I didn't know what he was talking about, saying I really had to get back because people were waiting for me, and finally, he stepped aside just enough for me to squeeze past him and get out the door. I tried to run, but my legs were liquid cement. All I could do was stagger down the stairs, terrified to look over my shoulder.

I don't remember where I went or how I got back to Grandma's house in Palm Springs. My memories of that day and the days that followed are jumbled and strange, like they've been chopped up and processed in a blender.

I never told my grandmother. She kept asking me, "Why are you so moody these days? We're gonna change your name to Miss Moody." And I kept pretending to laugh.

Spring 1996 was Celine Dion singing "Because You Loved Me."

Summer 1996 was Bone Thugs-N-Harmony singing "Tha Crossroads."

Randy was becoming less cool about not having sex. I was fifteen. He was almost nineteen. We'd been dating for a year. All his friends were like, "Yo, he's gonna cheat on you if you don't hook up with him." All his friends and some of mine had already done it. (Or so they said.) I knew something was wrong with me. I wanted to be kissed and held, but if he touched my boobs or anything else, my whole body turned to stone.

I drank champagne before we did it. That helped.

Going forward, it made a much better "How I Lost My Virginity" story.

Once upon a time. With a cute boy who loved me.

I didn't let myself think about that day at the mall guy's apartment. I certainly didn't tell Randy about it. I never told Nicky. I never told Mom. I didn't even tell Carter until recently. It happened so long ago, and so much has happened since, what would be the point? To be honest, I've hardly thought about it since it happened. Thinking about it made me feel ruined and embarrassed and sick to my stomach, so I shoved it into the deepest, darkest corner of my mind. I refused to see the long shadow it cast.

But something strange has happened to me in the past few years. A shift in perspective, maybe. Or a shift in the way I process those memories I'd rather dismiss as a bad dream. You know how you see a spiderweb lit up with dew? You see all the connections: cause and effect. You see life spinning outward and death caught in the sticky strands. There's beauty in the design that brings that galaxy together, and I see myself—I see Star—at the center of it all.

I'm not saying the world revolves around me; I'm saying *my* world revolves around me, just as your world revolves around you.

And we can't see far enough to know how many worlds intersect with our own. But they do.

Things like what happened to me don't happen in a vacuum. Somewhere, I'm certain, there are many other women trying to forget the bad dream of that apartment. Maybe if one of them had told someone, it wouldn't have happened to me. And maybe if I had told someone, it wouldn't have happened to somebody else. That's why I'm telling you now.

Because shame is dangerous. Poisonous.

And not just for those who carry it.

Do you ever wonder why two out of three sexual assaults go unreported? Or do you have the luxury of not caring? A lot of people who hear the story of a fifteen-year-old girl being sexually assaulted or exploited automatically think: *Stupid girl*. Our culture is so good at spinning it that way, we even say it to ourselves. For decades, every time that creepy mosquito voice whispered through my nightmares, I woke up thinking, *Stupid stupid stupid girl!*

Even the most woke, feminist, cool, enlightened people you know—oh, don't even try to lie about it—you know that's where you go. Who's more generous, evolved, and progressive than Pink? Nobody! She's effing awesome. Brilliant! And she seems like a great mom, which makes me like and respect her even more. But when everyone was buzzing about a sex tape of a certain teenage girl from a soon-to-be-hit TV show—a girl who said emphatically over and over that she did not want the tape out there—the takeaway was "Stupid Girl." The whole video is a not-at-all-subtle send-up of "porno paparazzi girls" in general and, specifically, me, in a parody of my infamous sex tape.

That tape, made when I was not legally old enough to be served a rum and coke in a bar, was released and monetized against my will, but when that thing hit the internet, the full weight of public outrage, scorn, and disgust came down on me instead of on the massive crowd of people who bought and sold it, sparking a steady drip of fake Paris Hilton sex tapes, and blazing a trail for a whole cottage industry that would ruin the lives of other vulnerable teenage girls in the future.

Pink sang about *"outcasts and girls with ambition"* and said, *"That's what I wanna see."* But she chose not to see it in me.

To be clear: I'm not mad at Pink.

There's no Pink–Paris "feud." That's not a thing. I have the attention span of a gnat, which means I suck at holding grudges. Anyway, anger doesn't help; honesty does. So, I'm being honest right now.

Doing advocacy work in the troubled-teen space has taught me the toxic nature of silence and shame, and looking back, I see myself trying so hard to reestablish ownership of my body, to reclaim what was natural and good in me, and that made a lot of people so uncomfortable, they didn't look beyond it or wonder, "What's really going on with this kid?"

At a tennis tournament last year, I met a very sweet acquaintance of Carter's who said he knew me from Palm Valley High. I searched through decades of names and faces piled up in my jumbled memories of that time.

"Oh, hi!" I said, trying to look like I had a clue who he was. I seriously didn't remember him at all. But he mentioned an incident that did ring a bell.

One Friday night, there was a ninth-grade sleepover movie night where you were supposed to show up at the gym in pajamas with a favorite stuffed animal and stay until morning. Most of the girls arrived in sweats, flannel pajama pants, and baggy T-shirts, with Care Bears and plush dogs. I showed up in a little silk romper from Victoria's Secret, looking like I was headed for a party at the Playboy Mansion. It wasn't like crazy sexy lingerie or anything, but it was hot pink and pretty short. And I had a live ferret. The chaperone called my grandma and told her I couldn't stay.

When I told Carter about it, we laughed until we cried.

"Maybe it was the ferret," he said. "That could be a health code violation. And a liability issue."

Because that's how my husband's beautiful, nerdy, sexy, compulsive fixer brain works. He really wanted to make it about the ferret.

"Sure." I patted him on the knee. "I bet that was it."

I don't know how much Mom and Dad talked with Grandma about my life in Palm Springs, but they must have been comfortable with it, because I stayed there for about a year. My parents visited on a regular basis, took me on a couple of family vacations, and eventually decided to bring me home.

I was thrilled to be going home to my family but heartbroken at the thought of leaving my grandma. During that year that I lived with her in Palm Springs, both our lives had been turned inside out, but we got through it together. That's what made it bearable.

I don't know if she already knew she had breast cancer. If she did, I'm not sure she told my mom, and I know Mom didn't tell Nicky and me until it was obvious that Gram Cracker's fierce red hair was falling out. I was a grown woman living on my own by that time, but I was scared. Those are scary words, *breast cancer*, and I was crushed by the thought of saying goodbye to Gram Cracker. She was unbreakable. Or maybe I just saw her that way because I couldn't stand the idea of losing her.

She powered through it for a while, and I let myself believe everything would be fine. But it wasn't. The treatment was hard on her. The last time I saw her, I cried and clung to her. I said, "I don't want to leave you here. I'm scared I'll never see you again."

"Get over it," said Gram Cracker. "I'm not going anywhere."

"Promise! Promise you're not dying."

"Well, I'm not dying *today*—unless you drown me in all these tears."

She handed me a Kleenex and helped me fix my makeup. Before I left for the airport, she took my face between her hands and kissed my forehead.

"I'll always be with you," she said. "Every time you see a hummingbird, that'll be me."

Kathleen Mary Dugan Avanzino Richards Cartain Fenton was born in Nebraska in 1928. She was the single mom and manager of three extraordinary daughters. She was outrageously loving and relentlessly herself. In the series *American Woman*, produced by Aunt Kyle, Alicia Silverstone played a character based on my grandmother, and there's a great scene where she challenges a guy who's messing with her daughter: "You know, Jerry, I see you. You're just a dark, rainy storm cloud hovering over a beautiful tree, and you try to scare everyone with your thunder and your lightning, but you know what? My daughter can take anything you rain down on her. Because she's that tree. She's a goddamned redwood."

The show is fiction, but that moment is true to her character—true to her fierce belief in her daughters and granddaughters.

Gram Cracker died in 2002, when *The Simple Life* was still in development. She never got to see the psychic's vision come true, but she didn't need to. It was her own vision that made all the difference; she had faith in me right down to the last beat of her heart. Whenever I see a hummingbird, I feel her arms around me, and when I did my first NFT drop—trying to bring fierce, talented women artists into this powerful new space—I collaborated with Blake Kathryn on "Hummingbird in My Metaverse," which featured planets in flux and a hummingbird in flight.

Shout out to Gram Cracker.

Wherever she is now, I know she's watching over me.

5

Papa told me that for more than a decade, his father kept a picture of the Waldorf-Astoria Hotel under the glass on his desk. On this yellowing photograph, Connie had written "The Greatest of Them All." The story of how Conrad Hilton studied, pursued, purchased, and restored the Waldorf is like *Moby-Dick* with a soaring limestone monument to art deco instead of a great white whale. You can read about it in Conrad Hilton's memoir *Be My Guest*.

Short version: He saw it. He wanted it. He kept grinding until he made it happen.

The Waldorf is forty-seven stories high and occupies an entire midtown block bordered by Park and Lexington Avenues between Forty-ninth and Fiftieth Streets. If you come in by the Park Avenue entrance, you're welcomed by *The Spirit of Achievement*, a gracefully aggressive art deco sculpture by Nina Sæmundsson. Every time I swing a business deal, get an idea, or score a victory that makes me feel like a boss bitch, I think of her outward-and-upward wings. I love the way she stands on tiptoes, her body long and strong, her face composed and focused.

The hotel is a stunning work of art and architecture, home to countless treasures. The 1893 World's Fair Clock has gone to the New-York Historical Society now, but it used to stand in the Waldorf's Peacock Alley, where Mom taught me and Nicky all the etiquette of high tea the way they do it at Kensington Palace. Everywhere I looked, there was a priceless painting or Ming vase. Tucked in a corner on the mezzanine level was Cole Porter's piano.

The list of world leaders, royalty, Hollywood stars, and industry magnates who've resided at the Waldorf is longer than the building is tall. Marilyn Monroe lived in suite 2728, the same suite where a diamond smuggler was found murdered forty years later. John F. and Jackie Kennedy spent their honeymoon there. My family lived in 30H. Michael Jackson lived in 30A with his kids. Barbra Streisand and Frank Sinatra were also in the building. You couldn't pass through the lobby or get on the elevator without bumping into a foreign dignitary, movie star, or Rolling Stone.

The Waldorf is a hub for high-society and upmarket business functions, so there's always fascinating people milling around, interesting conversations going on, and big parties happening.

Also, there's a salad named after it, and the salad is weirdly yummy, even though it combines mayonnaise and whipped cream with a handful of other things that seem like they shouldn't go together but do. It's like ADHD in salad form.

Here's my recipe for a classic Waldorf salad:

A couple of tart green apples. I don't know how many. How
would I know how big the apples are in your produce
aisle? You do you.

Celery. Go big, because fiber.

Walnuts or pecans. Or both. Fear not the extra. Toast them
a little if you aren't easily distracted.

Red grapes. However many you don't eat while making the
salad.

Sugar. Probably just a little.

Salt. Let's say a pinch. Because pinch is fun to say.

Mayonnaise. It sounds gross, I know! Blop some in there.
You'll thank me later.

Whipped cream. Or Cool Whip. I'm not a purist. I
suppose you could substitute Greek yogurt and make the
dressing on the side, but why not just embrace it?

Sprinkle with edible glitter or pink sea salt and serve.

Voilà! Waldorf salad.

You're welcome.

Back to the Waldorf.

My family had moved into a sick apartment at the Waldorf while
I was in Palm Springs with Gram Cracker, and I was hella jealous.
How could I not be? You have to understand, this was not like a
hotel room or even a hotel suite. This was a twenty-five-hundred-
square-foot condo with Italian marble, art deco architectural details,
stunning light fixtures, and city views from every location, including
the bathtub.

It was a little awkward at first, trying to fit in with the rhythm of
the household, which was a lot different from the laid-back California household we had before. Everyone was doing their own thing,

and I didn't really have a "thing" right away. Mom had created a beautiful room for me with white linens, a fluffy pink rug, and all the dolls and stuffed animals I loved when I was little. The only problem with it was that I wasn't little anymore. A lot had happened. I was fifteen now. In high school. I had my own ideas about what I wanted my life and personal space to look like, but I kept this mostly to myself. I didn't want to seem ungrateful, because I was *so* grateful!

SO. DAMN. GRATEFUL.

Grateful to be home.

Grateful to be loved.

Grateful for the family sounds around me.

My adorable siblings—I loved them so much. I loved watching cartoons with my little brothers, who bounced all over and climbed on me. I loved running around the hotel with my little sister, who swiped my clothes and tried to boss me around. I loved my parents, who were always busy with interesting things and still made time to scold me about school and etiquette and blah blah blah. I'm not being ironic here. I was happy to be back in the arms of my perfectly imperfect family. I wouldn't have changed a thing about any of them. I was like, "Yaaaassss! Thank you, God!"

Believe me, I was fully aware how blessed and fortunate I was.

The whole block was alive with activity and excitement 24/7. Sometimes Nicky and I got dressed up and invited ourselves to parties. Or we'd sneak into an empty ballroom after a big event, running around in our PJs and bare feet, picking over the fancy dessert carts and checking out the leftover gift bags. It was Candyland for two teenage girls who were increasingly obsessed with fashion, music, and art.

That summer, we vacationed in the Hamptons, and that felt like another homecoming for me. I was in a familiar place with the people I loved. Guys kept hitting on me and telling me I should be a model, which is a thing guys say, so who cares, but back in New York, the people saying that Nicky and I should model were legit people in that world. Agents. Designers. Photographers. We realized we could make some money of our own.

"Absolutely not," said Mom. "Not until you're eighteen."

Nicky always keeps a cool head in conversations like this, so I let her do most of the talking.

"You and Dad were just telling us in the Hamptons that we should get a job," she said.

"We meant babysitting," said Mom. "Working at an ice cream shop. Something like that."

"Mom," said Nicky, "you were modeling when you were a little baby."

"That was a different time, and it wasn't my choice."

"Are you saying you didn't want to do it?" I asked.

"I'm saying no one asked me. I wanted to sing," said Mom. "I worked hard at that. I had a recording contract. But then I got pregnant, and I had you to take care of, and that's the life I chose." She said it as if she had simply turned the page from one chapter to the next. I couldn't read the look on her face.

If you ask my mom how she gets through difficult conversations, she says, "I go like this." She brings her hand down across her face like a curtain, and when her hands are folded in her lap again, she's wearing the perfect smile of a Stepford wife. So perfect. So pretty. It's a skill I eventually learned. My Stepford smile. It gets a lot of play.

We didn't exactly have Mom and Dad's permission, but we started booking jobs. We figured we could pop out, do the job, and pop back home without Mom and Dad ever knowing. Most of the time, that worked, but every once in a while, someone would call our mom and say, "Oh, yeah, I just saw Paris and Nicky shooting over at [whatever place]," and then we had to face her when we got home. She didn't like it, but we chipped away at her resolve.

Three Possible Reasons Mom Didn't Want Us to Work as Models

1. She knew more than we did about the modeling/acting world and didn't want us to learn things the hard way.
2. It was painful for her to see us working because it raised a lot of "what ifs" in her mind. Just like seeing Nicky with her beautiful kids raises "what ifs" in my mind.
3. She secretly did want us to do it, but she wanted us to own it. Conrad Hilton taught Papa and Papa taught Dad that it's dangerous when rich kids don't have enough "dragons to slay."

Maybe it was some combination of all three. Bottom line: She said no to every runway show and photo shoot I got offered.

In the fall, Mom and Dad took Nicky and me to interview at Sacred Heart, a prestigious Manhattan school for girls. A nun escorted us around, showing us the whole place, telling us all about Saint Madeleine Sophie Barat, the founder of the Society of the Sacred Heart.

"We teach by her example," said the nun. "Saint Madeleine Sophie Barat said, 'Be humble, be simple, bring joy to others.' Our girls learn about living a meaningful life."

I didn't want to go there. I don't know what it was about that place—the uniforms that reminded me of my old school, the classrooms full of rigid rows—but I knew immediately that it was going to be so fucking hard. I knew myself. My ADHD was still undiagnosed, so I had no language for my challenges and quirks, but I felt certain that I would be hated by the irritable nuns and prissy girls and end up hating myself.

After the tour, Nicky and I had to be interviewed by the nun in charge of admissions. I fidgeted and bounced my foot while she and Nicky had a great conversation about blah blah blah, and then the nun asked me, "What did you like best about the school, Paris?"

I tried to sound breezy. "Nothing."

"Well, what did you like best about your school in Palm Springs?"

"Art. Field hockey." I squirmed in the uncomfortable chair. "Look, I don't want to go to this school, so I'm not trying to impress you."

"I see," she said.

"This place sucks. I'd rather kill myself."

I felt my mom's eyes drilling into me like lasers. The nun organized the papers on her desk.

"I'm afraid you're not Sacred Heart material, Paris." She beamed in Nicky's direction and said, "*You* are."

In the fall, Nicky went to Sacred Heart, and I went to Professional Children's School, where I could opt into a curriculum that focused on the fashion industry. Macaulay Culkin and Christina Ricci and a lot of other young actors, ballerinas, and models went there. Macaulay's apartment was right next door to the school, so we had parties there after school.

I thought this would be the coolest school in the world, and it was, but I found it unbearable to be in one place—even a cool place—for hours at a time. Pouring adolescent hormones into an ADHD brain is like dumping gasoline on a fire. Many teenage girls with ADHD struggle with mood swings, weight gain, anxiety, panic attacks, and a lot of unfamiliar, frightening physical and emotional turbulence that lead to their being isolated, judged, bullied, and punished, which makes it all a thousand times worse.

I felt like there was a snake pit inside me. It was impossible to keep my mouth shut and my hands still, even though I was inwardly commanding myself—*mouth shut, hands still*—and digging my nails into my forearms. Sometimes it was too much. I just had to take off and walk around New York. I jogged along the path and played with random dogs in the park. I trotted down Fifth Avenue, and the windows went by like a slide show, something colorful and wonderful in every store.

My parents went away for a couple of weeks so Dad could take care of some overseas business. Barron was seven, and Conrad was a toddler, so the nanny had their hands full and I had plenty of space to do whatever I wanted. Even more freedom than I had in Palm Springs. And New York was a million times more fun.

I waited for Nicky to get home from school and said, "Let's go out."

She was ambivalent. "I'll go Friday," she said, "but not on a school night."

"Come on. Why not?"

"Because I'm not a moron. I want to get good grades."

Nicky was thirteen and kinda bossy. She frequently forgot who was the big sister around here. Whatever.

I went down to the Waldorf lobby, grabbed a copy of *Time Out New York*, and flipped to the back, where they listed everything going on in the city at night. Every kind of music you can imagine—jazz, pop, karaoke, classical—and all sorts of quintessential New York happenings—gallery openings, drag competitions, performance art, and fashion shows. Best of all, they listed all the clubs, DJs, and underground raves.

Time Out New York became my daily homework assignment. I got good at scoping out the best parties and music and DJs. I slept most of the day, spent a couple of hours playing with Barron and Conrad or talking on the phone in Nicky's room while she did her homework. After everyone went to bed, I headed out with just enough cash in my pocket to grab something to eat on the street. Party people didn't show up at the clubs until midnight, and you couldn't really know where the raves were happening until bar time, so midnight was the sweet spot. Plenty of time to pop into a few clubs and overview the situation before bar time.

Like the song says: *You don't have to go home, but you can't stay here.*

A group of us would jam ourselves into a cab or hop on the subway and go to a warehouse or an abandoned shopping center or a defunct department store to dance and go wild until morning. The music pulsed so loud that there was no way to make conversation, but that was okay. We didn't need words. It was all about the feeling: freedom, abandon, adrenaline. I wanted it to go on forever, but eventually, sweaty and exhausted, I found my way back to the Waldorf, slipped past the doorman, and leaned against the cool, clean elevator wall until the doors opened. I went in as quietly as I could, took a shower, and fell into bed as everyone else got up to get ready for school.

It was easy to lose track inside the brick walls and blacked-out windows. When raves went late, and later, and so late it was early again, I figured it was better not to go home at all. I crashed at a friend's house, slept all day, and went back out the next night.

One morning I got off the elevator and found my parents waiting with a hybrid look of rage and relief on their faces. Mom was devastated, wrecked with tears. Seeing how hard it was on Mom made Dad even more furious.

"Where have you been? Do you know what we've been going through? Do you know what we've been imagining?"

I was so tired. I just wanted the confrontation to end, so rather than try to explain, I apologized and promised it would never happen again. And I wanted to mean it. I hated how this hurt them, but

I felt like they should trust me to take care of myself and be cool with it. Obviously, that was totally selfish and idiotic. Why would any parent be okay with that? I certainly won't be okay with it as a mom.

But I tried to sell it to them: "Calm down. I'll be fine."

"There are predators," Mom said. "Predators are out there waiting for girls like you."

"No one's going to mess with me," I said. "Not with the paparazzi always hanging around taking pictures."

"*What?*"

To be clear, we're not talking about the storm of paparazzi that followed me around later in my career. This was a few groggy die-hards who camped out on the street every night, waiting for someone famous to come out of certain clubs that were known to be popular with certain celebrities. I wasn't famous, but I had a famous name. Sometimes it was the best they could do. A picture of "Paris the Heiress" was worth a little something, so they'd call out to me, "Hey! Hey, are you the Hilton girl?"

"Hey, boys!"

"Where are you headed, Paris?"

"Oh, you know."

"Is that your boyfriend?"

"No, we're just hanging out."

I always gave a cute pose and tried to be polite. If I had been walking alone in a dark street or getting into a cab at 3:00 a.m. without anyone seeing the license plate, I'd have been scared. I felt safer knowing the paps—always guys back then—would be out there waiting for me, trying to make me look over my shoulder and laugh, showing predators that I was seen and accounted for.

For some crazy reason, Mom and Dad did not find this comforting.

Obviously, first and foremost, they were concerned for my safety;

in addition to random stranger danger, they were legitimately scared that kidnappers might see this girl from the rich family and take me for ransom. But they were also worried about what people would say if their underage daughter was seen hanging out in nightclubs and raving till dawn.

Now that I'm in the driver's seat of a billion-dollar brand, I understand how distraught my parents were at the idea of my picture showing up on Page Six, the *New York Post*'s gossip section. My father had invested heart and soul to build this luxury real estate business in the context of a family where the bar for success was set incredibly high, and my mom was beside him every step of the way. They didn't want me running around upper Manhattan embarrassing them. When you're building a brand, embarrassment comes with a price tag.

I didn't see why anyone should care what I did. I was just a teenager living my life. I wasn't done up to be sexy. I wore baggy pants and tank shirts with sneakers. My hair was cut short in a cute little bob, just long enough for Cindy Lou Who pigtails, and I kept my makeup natural because I danced like I was running a marathon four nights a week.

When you're sneaking in and out like I was, you need skills like a ninja, so I wasn't interested in getting trashed. I just wanted to be part of the scene and dance with the rest of the ravers. I walked around sipping Sprite from a champagne flute, holding an unlit cigarette between my fingers. I loved the over-the-top fashion and makeup, the creativity that went into those looks, and the way everyone accepted everyone else on the dance floor. There was no one who didn't belong. The pulsing music and laser lights were in sync with the unique rhythms in my brain. I know it sounds counterintuitive, but the chaos was comforting.

Meanwhile, my parents were getting calls and emails from the school, so they were unhappy. The whole school situation caused friction between us and made Mom cry, and this made me feel terrible. I kept promising to do better—and I really wanted to—but I kept failing tests and ditching classes. Eventually Professional Children's School kicked me out.

I enrolled in tenth grade at Dwight, a private school that was kind of a last stop for stoners and other rich kids who'd been rejected everywhere else. I still see jokes about it online. "DWIGHT: Dumb White Idiots Getting High Together." Weed wasn't my thing at all back then, so I felt like I didn't fit in at Dwight any more than I did at Sacred Heart. They put me in a class with only two other kids who had a lot of issues. It was scary and weird. Plus, I was bored as balls. The endless school day felt like being waterboarded with a vanilla milkshake. Getting kicked out of that school was a relief.

I begged my parents to be chill. "Why can't I just work? Just let me get an agent and start modeling full time."

Agents were interested in me. I was good on the runway—long legged and tall like Dad and Papa—and the designers I modeled for were thrilled whenever I showed up on Page Six, unlike my parents, who acted like it was the end of the world. Being at school made me feel like shit about myself. Being backstage at a runway show—everyone rushing back and forth in a fog of hairspray and frenetic energy—I felt tall and confident. Modeling gave me an opportunity to shine, while every school day felt like another setup for failure.

Mom and Dad were pissed at first, but then they got weirdly quiet. They sent me to a therapist, who was kind of a joke to me, but it seemed to make them feel better. I understood the gravity of the situation, but I thought I was handling it. Getting work. Learning the business. Cultivating connections.

It made me feel like *I* was going somewhere.

Like I could really be successful at this.

In February 1997 I turned sixteen. I wanted my party in LA so Gram Cracker and Papa and Nanu and all my LA cousins and friends could be there. Mom worked with Brent Bolthouse and Jen Rosero to throw an incredible sweet-sixteen party at Pop, a club on Highland where kids under eighteen could go on Thursdays and Saturdays. That was one of my first-ever nights out in Hollywood and definitely the sweetest sweet-sixteen I've ever been to.

My mom threw an epic, epic party.

Everyone was dressed to kill. Brent brought in DJ AM. Nicky and I and all our friends felt so grown up. *We're at this club! With this amazing DJ! And we look so hot!* It was thrilling.

"You were bright eyed and bushy tailed," Brent tells me now in a big-brotherly way, but I didn't feel like a kid anymore. Before I stepped out on any runway, I looked in the mirror, and there was a woman looking back at me. It was helpful that Wonderbra was having a moment—maybe because the trend was for women to be skinny, which made them naturally flat chested. Wonderbra was born in the 1960s during the reign of the bullet bra, and it was ready for a comeback. I embraced that dynamic and made it work for me, and later on, like 2015ish, I designed my own dream push-up bras under the Paris Hilton brand.

I have to be careful wearing push-up bras these days, because it always sparks rumors that I'm pregnant, and the most annoying thing that could possibly happen when you want to have a baby is constant Twitter and tabloid rumors that make people go, "Paris looks pregnant. Pregnant, Paris? Still not pregnant? How 'bout now? You look kinda pregnant. Why aren't you pregnant?" Ugh. Stop talking. It's beyond.

Wait. What were we talking about? Reverse engineer for a sec.

Wonderbra.

Bolthouse.

Sweet sixteen.

Yaasssss! I felt so ready to go out and conquer the world. I was excited about driving. You can get wherever you need to go in New York in cabs or on the subway, but I figured I'd end up in LA most of the time if I pursued modeling, acting, and music, which seemed to be the direction I was heading. Veterinary school was not going to do it for me, but I loved the idea of using my platform to do activism on behalf of animals the way Tippi Hedren and Brigitte Bardot did.

Since I wasn't in school, I could sleep in and be fully rested when I went out at night to explore the city. There was always something interesting going on, beautiful clothes to look at, fascinating people to watch, dancing to be done. The challenge of sneaking out was like a game, and I was good at it. When 30H was dark and silent, I'd tiptoe down the hall in my tracksuit and sneakers. I dragged my friends out with me, if they were willing to go, and I made a lot of new friends who were night owls like me.

Mom and Dad were killing it—running multifaceted business endeavors and managing massive teams—which should have made it easy for me to come and go as I pleased, but Mom's a smart cookie. If she found a business card or cocktail napkin with a phone number on it, she changed the 1 to a 7 or the 3 to an 8. I'd call these people and they'd be like, "What the hell?"

Nicky was a relentless tattletale. Except when she wanted to come out with me. But that was only on weekends. She was a homebody most school nights. Not me.

When the school year ended, we went to the Hamptons, where everyone was calmer and happier, in beach mode, until we heard that Princess Diana had been killed in a mad car chase fleeing the paparazzi. Nicky and I were devastated. We adored Princess Diana. Now she was in Heaven with Marilyn, forever young, forever perfect. We didn't stop to wonder why everyone wants women to stay young if dying is the only way to do it. And I didn't connect her death with the paps who waited for me outside the clubs at night. To me, they were just a well-meaning gaggle of basic sweetie pies. So flattering and funny.

We were on the other side of the looking glass back then, consuming all those tabloid photographs that made Diana an icon.

"They killed her," Mom said flatly. "They hunted her down like a pack of coyotes. Do you see now? Do you understand what I've been trying to tell you?"

I did, but if I wanted to succeed as a model, I needed to be seen. I had to be out there getting photographed.

We went back to New York, and—as my parents feared—pictures of me did start showing up in the tabloids. Dad was silently irate. Mom cried daily. They raged that I was breaking their hearts, becoming a bad influence on my siblings, throwing my life away, acting like a spoiled, out-of-control brat. It was the same dialogue over and over.

> THEM: "What are people thinking right now—that we let
> our children run around town all night? What are we
> supposed to do? Move to the moon?"
> ME: "Oh my god, leave me alone! I'm so sick of this
> conversation."

It was brutal.

Mom literally locked me in my room at night, but I was pretty savvy and managed to escape a few nights a week. Sometimes I could bribe Barron with promises that if he would sneak the key from Mom's room, I would let him come with me. Whispering through the locked door, I primed him with stories of the wonderland that is New York at night, telling him how we would dance and eat candy and have as much McDonald's as we wanted. With total trust in me, he'd go get that key.

"Okay, now, you go to bed and go to sleep," I told him. "I'll come and get you when it's time to go out."

What—*No, that didn't happen!* I was lying. Please. He was a second grader. Even I had my standards.

Sometimes party nights went on for days, and I came home to find Mom sitting on my bed crying. Gram Cracker came and stayed for a week, and I was hoping she'd be on my side, but she wasn't. She slept on a cot outside my bedroom door so I couldn't open it without her knowing.

I knew I was scaring the living shit out of my parents.

I knew it was cruel. And dangerous.

I loved my family, and I hated myself for hurting them.

Truly, I don't understand some of the choices I made, and I'm absolutely not encouraging any fifteen-year-old to drop out of school and party thirty-six hours a day.

ADHD—diagnosed or undiagnosed—doesn't authorize you to churn your family inside out or endanger yourself. I'm not offering my ADHD as an excuse. But I wonder. What if the therapist I saw back then—the guy I shrugged off as a joke—had diagnosed and treated my ADHD? What if anyone at any school I attended had tried to facilitate instead of fix me? I wonder how things might have been different if my parents had said, "We don't love the modeling thing, but we'll support you if you agree to a few ground rules." I wish they'd said that. Maybe they did say that, and I don't remember. Trauma often robs a person of the surrounding memories—which is inconvenient, but merciful.

I'm making a real effort to understand what this situation was like for my parents. Because I will never understand what they chose to do about it.

"To save your baby—you'd do it, too," Mom says on the rare occasion she's willing to talk about it. She says it with absolute certainty, even now, knowing how it all went so wrong. "You would do the same."

Not in a million fucking years, I think, but I don't say that out loud. I don't have it in me to argue with her, because I can't bear the thought of anything that will separate me from my family ever again. Instead, I put my arms around her neck and say the one true thing I can say: "I love you, Mom."

In autumn 1997, *South Park* debuted on Comedy Central.

The first Harry Potter book was published.

Madeleine Albright became the first female secretary of state.

Bell bottoms and platform shoes came out of the closet, paired with cropped tanks and anything that had a Union Jack to play up the Cool Britannia movement sparked by the Spice Girls.

"I knew there was a takedown in the works," Nicky told me later, "but I didn't know the details."

My last night at home was unremarkable. I had dinner with my family. Mom cooked. We ate. We talked and laughed. No one acted angry or odd or nervous. I decided to stay in that night. I don't know if that decision helped or hindered the "takedown" plan.

I chatted on the phone with friends and went to bed. I was sound asleep at about four thirty in the morning when my bedroom door crashed open, and someone tore the covers off me. A thick hand grabbed my ankle and dragged me off the mattress. I was instantly awake—hyperawake—in a state of panic, shrieking, struggling. My mind instantly went to the obvious.

I'm about to be raped. I'm about to be murdered.

Here the memory shatters—a broken mirror in my mind.

Two men.

Hands on me.

Coffee breath.

Body odor.

One of them clamped a sweaty palm over my mouth, wrenching my head back, shutting off the air I needed to scream. The other held up a pair of handcuffs that reflected the light from the hallway. The way he dangled them in his stained fingers—he seemed to be enjoying it.

He said, "Do you want to go the easy way or the hard way?"

I chose the hard way.

Clawing, kicking, screaming, I tried to break free. One man had my upper body, the other had my legs. My thrashing only made them grip harder as they carried me out into the hallway.

This is a nightmare. This is a nightmare.

I kept trying to wake myself up, the way I do now. The way I did for decades when the scene replayed in my head night after night.

I see this girl in a flimsy Hello Kitty nightshirt. She twists in writhing terror, screaming, *"Mom! Dad! Help me!"*

And then I see my mom and dad.

Their bedroom door is cracked open just enough for them to peek around the edge, faces streaked with tears. They press against each other and watch as two strangers drag me out the door into the darkness.

PART 2

*Be ever watchful for the opportunity
to shelter little children . . .
as they must bear the burdens of our mistakes.*
CONRAD HILTON

6

Once upon a time in Palm Springs, a furniture salesman named Mel Wasserman was on his way to a local diner and saw some teenagers on a street corner, protesting whatever people were protesting in 1964. According to legend, Mel invited them to his house for spaghetti dinner and offered them a place to stay for the night. They could even stay longer, he said, but they had to live by his agreement, which included a strict code of appearances and behavior and participation in group "therapy sessions."

Wasserman was a disciple of Charles E. Dederich, founder of Synanon, a violent cult that had been driven underground but never fully eradicated by the FBI. From 1958 until 1991, Dederich and his hench-bitches—aka "The Imperial Marines"—lured young people into the cult, promising to cure them of drug addiction and homosexuality. His methods included verbal abuse, physical violence, forced abortions and vasectomies, and psychological torture. "The Game" was like a verbal Fight Club. "The Trip" was a marathon weekend of sleep deprivation, brainwashing, and physical challenges. (Imagine being strapped to the bottom of a roller coaster for seventy-two hours.)

Wasserman saw the opportunity to monetize all this and took it to the next level. He moved to a compound in the San Bernardino Mountains and re-created the cult environment, now calling it an "emotional growth boarding school." Slick marketing targeted vulnerable parents who felt they'd lost control of their teenage children. He rebranded "The Game" as "Rap," and "The Trip" became a series of "Propheets." (That extra *e* makes it sound *suuuuuper* legit, doesn't it?)

Wasserman named his "school" CEDU—short for Charles E. Dederich University—but because of the lawsuits and bad press surrounding the cult, promotional materials claimed it meant "SEE yourself as you are and DO something about it."

The CEDU business model was so successful, Wasserman and his disciples—plus a few venture capitalists who saw the potential gold mine—opened sister schools in states where oversight laws were lame and authorities were willing to look the other way. They gained accreditation and developed lucrative partnerships with private insurers and state agencies so they could siphon money from Medicaid and the foster-care system.

In the 1990s, Maury Povich and Sally Jessy Raphael legitimized CEDU and made bank off "wild teen" episodes featuring kids—mostly pretty girls—sent off to boot camps and boarding schools for "tough love." Later, Dr. Phil got on board, including video of the violent transport of a teenage boy who was dragged out of bed by dudes three times his size, the same way I was.

According to the *Salt Lake Tribune*, the state of Alaska spent more than $31 million in Medicaid funds to send 511 kids to facilities in Utah between 1999 and 2005. An average of $60,665 per child. And that's kids funded by the taxpayers of just one state. The millions CEDU raked in from insurance claims and private payers will never be known.

Working-class parents mortgaged their homes and took second jobs to send their kids to CEDU. Wealthy parents came in with deep pockets, so CEDU aggressively courted them, especially celebrities. My parents were not alone. Michael Douglas, Clint Eastwood, Roseanne Barr, Barbara Walters, Montel Williams, Marie Osmond—the list goes on. CEDU and other facilities like it were a trending solution for the upper-class problem child. Programs expanded to take in kids as young as eight years old, staffed with loyal "graduates" who were too damaged to make it out in the real world.

TLDR: That random spaghetti dinner at Mel Wasserman's ballooned into a fifty-billion-dollar-per-year business we call the "troubled-teen industry."

That's how you entrepreneur: Recognize a problem—or create one—and offer your product as the solution.

I get it.

When Nicky and I were little, if she got a hundred dollars for her birthday, I used to set up a little store in my room and invite her to come shopping.

"This plush designer teddy bear is so full of love," I said. "It's like hugging a magic cloud. A *love* cloud. I should keep him because he makes me so happy. But I want *you* to be happy. So, I guess I could part with him for a hundred dollars."

She gladly handed over the hundred bucks, and within hours, I was down at the pet store, acquiring a hamster castle or a new best friend for my chinchilla.

Am I proud of this? Of course not. Much. The point is, it takes one to know one. I see Mel Wasserman for exactly what he was: an opportunist.

An evangelist with the soul of a furniture salesman.

He knew that people who couldn't afford fifty bucks for a new coffee table would do anything—pay anything—for the hope of healing their broken family. He offered therapists financial incentives to send kids his way. They handed parents a royal-blue brochure that showed a fabulous lodge, spectacular scenery, and happy students playing tennis and riding horses.

Actual copy from a CEDU brochure used in the mid-1990s:

Founded in 1967, CEDU High School is the nation's original emotional growth boarding school. Students build mastery through a rich curriculum of academics, performing and visual arts, outdoor education, recovery, and emotional growth. Students exhibiting behavioral and emotional difficulties create a successful future by learning to express themselves emotionally, artistically, and intellectually. CEDU High School's unique art infusion approach motivates students and engages them to explore thoughts and feelings. Arts are woven through college preparatory academics, adventure education, and the original CEDU Emotional Growth Curriculum. The result? Teens rediscover their dreams and families reunite.

Kudos to the copywriter. Evil genius.

Desperate parents latched on to the idea of this artsy, intellectual place where "tough love" would fix a broken child they loved but could not understand. A staff psychiatrist made regular visits to the CEDU campus to supply prescription drugs and report back to parents on their child's progress.

Most of those kids were like me: disobedient ravers from conservative families and ADHD kids who got kicked out of school. Some had experimented with weed or molly, but none of us were as street smart as we thought we were. A lot of kids were gay—or gay-*ish*—which upset their religious parents. Foster-system floaters came from bad situations that had nothing to do with them, but they had to be parked somewhere that looked okay on paper. Other kids lived in darker worlds: addiction, violent predatory behavior, and suicidal depression.

The decision to send me away is a rough topic for my parents. They haven't shown me any records, so I don't even know the exact dates when all this happened. I have some theories, but I don't know exactly how they found CEDU or who convinced them that this was their only option.

"This wasn't about a kid ditching school and talking back," says Mom. "We did it to save your life."

Dad says straight up, "You needed to go there. You were out of control."

End of conversation.

To me, that feels like blame—*You made us do it!*—but I love my parents, so I can't bear to take that coping mechanism away from them. We're all living with the brutal legacy of this the best way we know how, and they have expressed regret, in their way.

"I'm sorry you had such a hard time."

"I'm sorry you had to go through all that."

For a long time, I just wanted to hear them say, "I'm sorry we made a terrible mistake." But they're just not there yet. Maybe they never will be. And that's okay.

To be fair, I've never said, "I'm sorry I pushed you to the point of desperation."

So here we go.

Mom and Dad: I apologize. I am so sorry. Not knowing where your child is—that's a kind of psychological torture, too. I'm sorry I was insensitive to how cruel that really was. I'm sorry my choices put you in a place that must have seemed like a no-win situation. I love you, Mom and Dad. And I forgive you, even if you don't ask. Hopefully, we can all redirect our anger in a positive direction—like state and federal legislation that kicks the crap out of the troubled-teen-industry con artists and keeps them from destroying other families in the future.

Moving on.

TRIGGER WARNING: This next part is really hard. Take care of yourself, okay? In *Psychology Today* (a review of James Tipper's book *The Discarded Ones*, November 2012), Jann Gumbiner, PhD, compares the programs I survived to "Jim Jones's Guyana, Patty Hearst's kidnapping, or Zimbardo's Prison Experiment." A lot of people will find it upsetting. And they should. It should make you want to cry and throw this book across the room and yell, "This is wrong! This has to change!" I find it upsetting, too, but I don't cry about it that much anymore.

The terrible truth is, I became numb after a while. When you endure horror day after day, month after month, it becomes normalized. I built high stone walls around my heart—walls that no one could break through or climb over for more than twenty years. My MO was to not think about it, not talk about it. Don't feed the beast. Don't give it any oxygen. It'll go away. For a long time, I made that work, but every now and then, some random thing would trigger a flood of memory and anxiety and crush my soul all over again.

The spin-control sorceress inside me is moaning: "No! Not

this! Don't go there!" Like I said before, I'm not comfortable talking about private parts and bodily functions. I worry about how it might impact the brand I've worked so hard to create—a brand that's all about beauty, laughter, impeccable fashion, lovely fragrances, high-tech innovations, luxurious living, and the sophisticated art of not taking myself too seriously.

But people need to know what we're talking about when we use sterile terms like "congregate care facility" and "troubled-teen industry." I mean, think about that word—*industry*—in the context of children as raw material. I can't soft-pedal this just so you and I (and my parents) don't have to feel bad. That's how these people have been able to continue abusing children and tearing families apart for decades with zero regulation and oversight. I will not—I *cannot*—let them hide in the shadows any longer.

In 2021, I collaborated with Dayzee via Superplastic on an NFT drop built around a simple message: *THE TRUTH WILL SET YOU FREE*. These pieces speak to the way my story has been steered by the media, partly because I was afraid to tell it myself.

That's changed. *I've* changed.

When I realized that my story was a sledgehammer to that wall of silence and shame—that I had the power to free myself and maybe save someone else's life—everything I was scared of seemed trivial. I was finally ready to become the hero I needed when I was living in that hell.

None of the names used in these chapters are real, for obvious reasons, and I'm not pretending to remember every conversation word for word. For much of the time that I was locked up, I was being force-fed drugs intended to dull my wits and make me comply. I think they wanted to hide their actions by clouding our memories. I feel like Alice, trying to reassemble a broken looking glass. To the best of my ability, I'll tell you exactly what happened. Some details are burned clearly into my memory; others are foggy, but research and the testimony of fellow survivors back me up.

This is my truth.

Someone else may remember it differently, but this is my perception of this experience, as I experienced it. Please be patient with me. I'm sitting here with my eyes closed, my heart pounding, trying to remember a lot of shit I tried hard to forget.

7

The back of the black SUV was specially rigged so you couldn't open the doors or windows from the inside. The two men were like giant, 'roided-up meatheads, so they had no trouble shoving me in there, even though I was kicking and struggling with every shred of strength I had. As the Waldorf disappeared behind me, I scrunched into a ball, overcome with a weird, uncontrollable trembling. I was shaking so hard, it felt like my teeth would rattle out of my mouth. Looking back, I know I was in shock. I must have been crying, because they kept barking at me to shut up.

I assumed at first that my mother was right; someone had seen me in the tabloids, and they were kidnapping me for ransom, so I begged and pleaded with them, "Please, whatever you want—my parents will pay you."

They laughed. One of them said, "You brought this on yourself. Your parents had no choice. They're doing this for your own good."

My parents—wait—what now?

"You're gonna learn," one kidnapper said. "You're gonna get schooled."

what the fuck what the fuck what the fuck

(Typically the transport service is recommended by the therapist. They say it's easier for everyone. Well worth a few thousand dollars.)

On the way to the airport, they made me understand that my parents had hired them to transport me to a "special boarding school" in California. They provided proof; my mother had packed a little bag for me with socks, underwear, toiletries, some pictures of my family, and a basic wardrobe of casual school clothes. They told me the place they were taking me was secluded high in the mountains and that the counselors there would use "tough love" to fix what was wrong with me.

"There's nothing wrong with me," I said. "I'm not going there. I'm not getting on any fucking airplane with you."

The kidnapper showed me the handcuffs again. "Up to you. Do you wanna get on the plane nice and quiet or do you want to get carried on in handcuffs?"

"Fuck you!" I kicked the back of the seat, and they laughed.

"Do that again, and I'll have to restrain you," he said. "For your own safety, of course."

At the airport, they gave me a velour tracksuit and sneakers from the bag Mom had packed. I crawled into my soft, familiar clothes, grateful for that last thread of home. This was before 9/11, so walking into the airport and getting on an airplane was a very different thing. You just went in and went to the gate. Walking through the terminal,

I kept my eyes down, feeling like everyone was staring at me. I wasn't exactly famous back then, but in New York, I was often recognized—that Hilton girl, that socialite wild child from Page Six—so the last thing I wanted was to walk through JFK in handcuffs.

"I'll be good," I promised in my baby voice, willing myself to stay calm and be smart. Flanking me, gripping my arms, these two refrigerator-sized men steered me down the concourse, and I hurried along between them, looking for any possible opportunity to get away.

There were none. This was happening.

They were professionals, trained to cover all the bases. I had no choice but to go along with it until I could figure out a way to escape. Crammed into the middle seat between them, I tried to sound like I was excited to go to my new school. *Oh, what? It's in the mountains? How cool is that?* I smiled and pretended to sleep, thinking they could drag me to this boarding school, but they couldn't make me stay. I was confident. I had plenty of experience sneaking out of the house and slipping away from guys who got grabby on the dance floor. As soon as the sun went down, I'd be out of there.

My confidence fell to shit as we drove eighty miles from LAX to Running Springs, California. The road snaked upward into the San Bernardino Mountains. Cars got farther apart and more run down. Trees got taller and closer together. My ears throbbed with the rising altitude. My eyes burned with exhaustion. A cold, hard knot developed in my gut.

We came to an iron gate. It opened.

We drove in. It clanged shut.

The Walter Huston Lodge was built by the Academy Award-winning grandfather of Anjelica Huston back in the 1930s. He was an engineer first and an actor second. The grand, historic structure had a massive stone fireplace, vaulted ceilings, and thirteen guest rooms where his Hollywood colleagues stayed. It was a good place to get away from it all. Far from prying eyes.

Huston died in 1950, and the place sat empty, I think, until CEDU bought it in 1967. The school had been forced from its original home by neighbors who insisted that zoning, which did allow for a school, did not allow for CEDU, because this place—no matter how Wasserman tried to sell it—was not a school. Freaky stories and disturbing rumors went around. Weird stuff went on there. Sex orgies, drugs, chanting, screaming. So much screaming. They didn't want that in their neighborhood, so CEDU relocated to Huston's hidden mountain retreat.

A good place to get away from it all.

I was taken into the lodge. I remember a room with two staffers: sort of a messy-looking hippie guy and a gross woman with a pointed weasel face.

(No offense, weasels. Love you.)

Four or five other students, male and female, stood there watching. Weaselmug shut the door and said, "I need to search you for contraband. Take off your clothes."

I said, "No, that's not—I swear, I don't have anything. How would I have anything? I was at home. I was sleeping."

"Take off your jacket."

When I didn't take it off, she repeated the thing about "the easy way or the hard way," saying there was no use fighting what was going to happen because my parents had given them medical power of attorney and she could inject me with sedatives if she wanted to.

I unzipped the jacket and handed it to her.

The next little while is kind of like white noise in my head, but I can still hear her voice, flat and repetitive, like a broken shutter banging in the wind.

Take off your shoes.
Take off your socks.
Take off your shirt.
Take off your bra.
Take off your pants.
Take off your underwear.

She took each item and handed it to somebody who ran his hands over every seam and then stuffed it into a bag. I vaguely remember standing there naked in front of all those people, shaking uncontrollably, my knees clenched together, my arms hugged tight across my chest.

When she said *cavity search*, I thought it was a dental inspection. That's the only context in which I'd ever heard the word *cavity*.

Seeing that I didn't understand, Weaselmug said, "We have to make sure you don't have drugs or weapons hidden in there."

"In . . . where?"

I couldn't make sense of what she was saying. Because she could not be saying what she was saying. That could not happen. Everyone else stood there, and their faces were like—I don't know.

I don't know.

Just . . . bad.

Staring at me. Snickering. Shuffling their feet. These boys weren't much older than me.

The woman pulled on a latex glove and said, "Are you going to cooperate, or do we need to have these guys hold you down and pull your legs apart?"

I hated the whimpering rabbit sound that came out of me. It wasn't my clever baby voice; it was genuine panic.

"Let's go," she said. "Squat down and cough."

I squatted and tried to cough, but all I could do was sob and gasp for air.

"Are you going to cooperate, or—"

I hacked a hard cough.

She felt around between my legs and then made me stand up, bend forward, and hold my butt cheeks apart while she groped inside me with her gloved fingers. When it was over, she handed me some stained magenta sweats. They were gross, but whatever. I was desperate to cover myself. I put on the sweats without arguing and wiped my nose with the sleeve.

"We're gonna keep her in pinks," Weaselmug announced. "Transport says she's probably a runner."

She gave me socks. No shoes.

"Shoes are a privilege you'll have to earn."

I know she meant to humiliate me with those hideous magenta sweats, but pink has always been my power color. The way I walk has nothing to do with what I wear. You think a model loves every look that gets put on her? At sixteen, I'd worn some amazing clothes on the runway, but I'd worn my share of nightmare getups, too. I had already learned that the walk comes from within. You wear the clothes; the clothes don't wear you.

On the set of *Paris in Love* in 2021, I was shooting a funny little dream sequence in which I zipped down the street to a church on an electric scooter, dressed in a bridal mini with pink sliving gloves, angel wings, and platform heels that were high enough to make the producer nervous.

"Paris," she said, "how are you feeling about riding a scooter in those heels? Do you feel confident about that?"

"I'll do anything in heels," I said.

"I love that answer, but . . ."

"I was born in heels."

She wrote something on her clipboard and said, "I'm verbatim saying that. Just so you know."

I tweaked it to "I was born in Louboutins" and was about to post it on Instagram when I got a FaceTime call from Rebecca Mellinger, head of impact at 11:11 Media and now 11:11 Impact, the foundation I started so I could translate all my anger and sadness about the troubled-teen industry into meaningful action. Impact is a key part of my business model these days. It doesn't make money, but it's the thing that matters most. It helps people, and that makes it immensely satisfying.

Rebecca is a fierce administrative warrior who spearheads my legislative efforts, cultivates media, and organizes events. We were in the process of getting congressional support for a bill of rights that would force transparency and other safeguards in congregate-care facilities. I was jumping into the conversation as needed, even though I was in the middle of wedding preparations and an intense shooting schedule.

"Senator Merkley has a couple questions," Rebecca said. She passed the phone to Senator Jeff Merkley of Oregon, who was supporting this piece of legislation along with Representatives Ro Khanna (CA-17), Buddy Carter (GA-01), Rosa DeLauro (CT-03), Adam Schiff (CA-28), and Senator John Cornyn of Texas.

I held my phone at arm's length, just above my right temple. (Another fundamental right: your best photo angle.) I didn't feel like I had to explain the sparkly angel wings, because whatever you're wearing—that's *where* you are, not *who* you are. You rock it and do what you need to do.

"Senator Merkley," I said, "thank you so much for your support. We need to fine-tune the private referrals piece of this. As it's written, the focus is on children who come through the foster-care and juvenile-justice pipelines."

I straightened my shoulders, flexing my angel wings.

"I understand the need to advocate for kids in foster care," I said, "but I can tell you from personal experience: A lot of kids come into this system from loving homes. Wealthy homes. Their parents are deceived and screwed over. Transparency is their only hope. I won't leave those kids behind."

Rebecca wrapped the call, and I buzzed off to church on my scooter.

I can do anything in heels.

8

A girl with a bland expression and mousy hair took me to a room with four bunk beds. I don't remember her name, so I'll just call her Blanda.

"This is you," Blanda said cheerfully, indicating a top bunk with a yellowed pillow and blanket. "I'm over on that side. Sometimes there's four in here, but right now, it's just us. I'm your big sister!"

"No," I said. "You're not. I have a sister. It's not you."

I crawled up into the bunk and curled into a ball, wishing the ceiling would fall down on this bitch.

"Yeah," she said, "I read in your profile you have a little sister. Little brothers. I'm an only child. But now I have you, little sister!"

"Please stop talking."

"This is all for your own good. I read in your profile how you were, like, totally kicked out of every school in the world and, like, doing drugs and sleeping around."

"That's bullshit," I said. "That's not true."

"Now's not the time to run your anger, Paris. Wait for Rap tonight, and then take care of your feelings."

I covered my head with my arms, thinking, *What does that even mean?*

"I need to talk to my mom," I said. "I need to call my mom right now."

"Maybe in a couple weeks. That's a privilege you'll have to earn," said Blanda. She handed me a thick binder. "Here's everything about what to do and what not do, a glossary of terms you need to memorize, and all the stuff you'll need to work on in each of the Propheets."

"Whatever."

"You can't stay up there. I'm supposed to show you around and get you familiar with the rules."

"Don't bother," I said. "I'm not staying."

"Don't say that!" Blanda whispered, wide-eyed and urgent. "You'll get us both in trouble. If you try to run, they'll bring you back, and then you'll be sorry. If you don't work the program and stay in agreement, you'll end up going to Ascent. Or even Provo. Trust me, you do not want to get sent to Provo. We just want to help you, Paris. We just want you to know yourself and nurture the child within you, your little you. You'll be amazed how fast the next two years fly by."

"Two years?" I dropped down from the bunk so I could look into her face and see if she was fucking with me. "*Two years?*"

"You'll graduate when you turn eighteen, and by then, you won't even want to leave. A lot of the team leaders and counselors are graduates. They're required to work the program right alongside us."

"How long have you been here?" I asked.

"Two years plus a little. It went by like *that*." She snapped her fingers. "I wish it could be longer. I'm kind of dreading turning eighteen. C'mon. We've got a lot of information to cover. Starting with the basics: This is your drawer."

She pulled a wooden drawer open. There were underwear and socks in it, but they weren't mine.

"Before breakfast, they inspect drawers, beds, floor, everything in the room. If it's not within agreement, you get written up or put on bans. Bans is like, you can't talk to anyone, and no one can talk to you, or like, if you're on boy bans, you can't look at or talk to boys, and they can't look at or talk to you."

Walking around the mountainside in my socks, I tried to step over the slushy patches and autumn snowdrifts. I saw kids hauling rocks, digging holes, and stacking cinder blocks to make a retaining wall. There was a tennis court with no net, a horse barn with no horses, and a storeroom with cleaning products stacked on shelves. Blanda showed me the kitchen where kids were opening cans, the laundry room where someone else was folding towels. She showed me a cement shower room where there were several shower heads on the wall and drains in the floor, but no dividers or curtains. Two girls were on their hands and knees, scrubbing.

"Don't look at them," Blanda whispered. "They're on bans."

All the while, she chattered away, reeling off a long list of bizarre rules.

No swearing, singing, humming, or throat clearing.

No dancing, skipping, or spinning.

No touching, hugging, kissing, or holding hands.

No crossing your legs. No shuffling your feet.

No whistling.

No breathing too loud or smacking your lips while eating.

No talking about music, sports, television shows, movies, news events, your parents, your siblings, your friends, your clothes, your room, your school, or anything else about home.

No mention of Marilyn Manson.

No mention of candy, pizza, hot dogs, cheeseburgers, lasagna, McDonald's, Burger King, or Wendy's.

No talking about bikes, skateboards, or inline skates.

No looking out a window without permission. No opening a door without permission. No going to the bathroom without permission. No asking for permission to go to the bathroom, open a door, or look out a window.

No asking for food or water. No eating outside mealtime. No leaving food uneaten on your plate. No asking *why* or *why not*.

No eye rolling.

No sighing.

No snoring.

No slouching.

No shrugging.

No fidgeting, nail biting, skin picking, or scratching.

No whining. No crying. No yelling.

"Except during Rap," she added. "During Raps, you have to participate. Really get in there and use your big voice. If you don't participate, you'll get blown away. If you see someone who's not working the program or staying in agreement, you should totally call them out during Rap. And report them to a counselor. If you don't report, you're just as guilty as the rule breaker, you know? And you're, like, *harming* that person if you don't tell on them, because you're keeping them from doing their emotional work."

I was beginning to understand the need for a glossary. Bans, Raps, Propheets, in agreement/out of agreement, working the program, running your anger, taking care of your feelings—it was a lot.

And a lot of bullshit. The rulebook was a labyrinth of setups where it was impossible to avoid punishment. Like the whole thing was designed to make you suffer and fail.

That night, in the upper bunk in those gross pink sweats, I sobbed my guts out for hours. I finally drifted into a headachy half-sleep, but I kept jolting awake from a nightmare—a hand gripping my ankle, a grimy palm clamped over my mouth—and then I sobbed again until I drifted again, repeating the cycle over and over until Blanda poked me and said, "Paris. It's five thirty. We gotta clean the room."

We made the beds, straightened our drawers, and wiped down every surface including the floor. There was no mirror, but I caught a glimpse of my face in the window, and I looked beat.

"You're not allowed to look out the window!" Blanda hissed, and I wondered, if they really didn't want you to look out the window, why were there no curtains? Before I turned away, I tried to take in a breath of sunrise.

Someone came to inspect the room and let us go to breakfast, which was some kind of grayish hot cereal. Jobs were assigned. I vaguely recall a group with a couple of other girls and a few dudes carrying wood from a stack at the bottom of a hill to a stack halfway up the hill. Eventually, we were told to go to a table for lunch. Two slices of bread and a slice of bologna. After lunch we worked for a few more hours, and then Weaselmug yelled that it was shower time.

We went to the place where the showers were, and girls started to peel off their clothes. I just stood there. Lined up against the wall were half a dozen staff people—male and female—watching the teenage girls undress and shower. These men and women chatted and laughed and called out pervy remarks.

I stood in the doorway.

Like, frozen.

Like, *What. The. Actual. Fuck.*

The most disturbing thing was the blank stares of the naked girls as they washed themselves in the lukewarm spray. They were used to it. This was their life. They just accepted it.

Weaselmug rapped her knuckles on the back of my head and said, "What are you waiting for, an invitation?"

A middle-aged male guard said something like, "Need help with your panties?" and the rest of them laughed.

Staring at the floor, trying to face the wall, I undressed, showered as quickly as I could while the staff made cow noises and dog noises and limp jokes about carpet not matching drapes. I wrapped a scratchy towel around myself and stood there shivering until we were allowed to go to our rooms.

Whoever was working in the laundry had left clean socks and pink sweats on my bed.

"When do I get my own clothes back?" I asked Blanda.

"After they get labeled, I guess. But you won't need those," she said. "They'll give you whatever they want you to wear."

I'd slept only a few hours in the past three days, so I said I wanted to lie down and skip dinner.

"Dinner's not optional," Blanda said. "And after dinner, we go to Rap."

I don't remember what we ate for dinner, only that I forced myself to swallow every last bite because a girl across from me whispered, "If you don't eat it, they'll feed it to you."

It was early—maybe five or six—when we went to the "Rap" thing. I can't separate that night from any other because this bizarre thing happened several nights a week for literally three or four hours. I'll try to describe it, but I don't know if it's possible to fully understand it unless it's happening to you.

A bunch of people sat in a circle of chairs.

Loud music played over the house speakers.

I don't mean loud music played; I mean music played loudly.

It was always some insipid soft rock or easy-listening-type song—John Denver or Kenny Rogers or something—I don't remember ever hearing the voice of a woman. I'm trying to think of some specific ones, but I've blocked those songs out for the most part. Fellow survivors have mentioned the Randy VanWarmer song "Just When I Needed You Most," and I do recall that one getting a lot of play at CEDU and the CEDU sister schools where I was held later. You've probably heard it in an elevator. The chorus goes *"Youuuuuuuuuuuuuuuuu left me just when I needed you most."*

This one song played over and over and over on repeat while everyone sat down and the team leaders—Weaselmug, Hippie Mess, and the recent graduates who now worked here on some sort of fucked-up Stockholm Syndrome career path—went around and spooled off paper towels in little piles here and there and then set the rolls of paper towels strategically around the circle.

"What the hell . . ." I whispered.

The guy sitting next to me huffed a little half laugh and said, "Whatever you think you know—you don't."

Around the circle, kids shrank into themselves, looking like hamsters in a snake pit. Or they perched on the edges of their seats, eyes alive, eager for the game to begin.

"Blanda, would you like to start?" said Weaselmug.

Blanda stood in front of the boy next to me and said, "Jason, I saw you talking to Paris just now. Aren't you on girl bans because you winked at Deirdre last week? I mean, it's out of agreement is all I'm saying, and you know, I guess you're probably thinking you're going to fuck one or both of them, which is a total fantasy, because no self-respecting girl is going to fuck a fat, ugly slob like you. It'll never happen, but you're so oblivious, you don't even know what a shit human being you are. I know you're secretly gay. I saw in your file about your child molester uncle, and it's like, not even he wants you around now. What does that tell you?"

I waited to for this dude to tell her to shut up or go screw herself. He sat there, staring at the floor, saying nothing.

"Where is that selfish desire coming from, Jason?" asked Hippie Mess. "Was that I or Me looking at Paris and Deirdre with selfish thoughts—dirty thoughts—disgusting sexual fantasies? Was that I, the liar, or Me, the feeler?"

"I," the dude mumbled.

"Right! Look! Look what you're doing right now," said Weaselmug. "I is biting Me's lip!"

"Selfish asshole," said another girl. "On bans all the time. Too stupid to work the program. Too selfish and dumb and lazy to do the emotional work. It's no wonder his family was like, get the fuck out, you piece of crap. Because no one can stand you. Not even the people who are legally obligated."

Like a floodgate opening, people piled on, everyone talking at once, their voices tangled in that weird, loud music like *What a jerk-off! Why are you even alive, you piece of shit? Your family can't stand YOUUUUUUUUUU LEFT ME because you suck at everything you do. You pretend you're a writer—like you're going to write a book someday and rat everybody out YOUUUUUUUUU LEFT meanwhile, you're too stupid to spell your own name you worthless piece of shit why don't you YOUUUUUUUUUUU LEFT ME kill yourself and put everyone out of their misery? Oh wait—I forgot—you tried and you couldn't even do it right.*

This went on and on and on and on for what seemed like forever until his face crumpled and tears streamed from his eyes, and still they kept at it and kept at it and at it and at it and at it until he bent forward with his face in his hands, wailing like a wounded animal.

"Run your anger, Jason," said Hippie Mess. "Take care of your feelings."

The dude sobbed deep, wrenching sobs, choking on the words, "I can't—I can't—I'm a piece of shit and I try—and—and I tried not to look at her and I was thinking about wanting to—to see her—and like—wanting to jerk off because I'm a sick piece of shit! I'm weak and perverted and a dumb-shit asshole!"

Tears and slimy boogers dripped down on the floor in front of him. Weaselmug nudged a wad of paper towels over with her foot.

"I want to know why Paris hasn't said anything," said one of the girls. "She's just sitting there like a prissy little stuck-up rich bitch."

"Uh, you don't know me," I said, "and what happened to the no-swearing rule?"

Hippie Mess winked at me and said, "Talk dirty, live clean."

"You were right to put her in pinks," said Blanda. "She told me she's gonna run. She said the program is bullshit, all the girls here are fat, stupid pigs, and if she can't get out, she's going to burn this place down."

I gritted my teeth and said, "Fuck you, Blanda. I never said that."

"I heard you were slacking on chores," said Weaselmug.

"She was slacking! She was slacking!" Jason hiccupped. "She was mincing around like she was too good for everybody while I went up the fucking hill eight hundred times."

"I don't have any shoes, you moron."

As soon as I said it, I knew it was a mistake to defend myself. The entire circle zeroed in on me, a monster made of saucer eyes and black hole mouths.

She thinks she doesn't have to work. She was slacking today on the job. Lazy little bitch. Stupid spoiled whore. YOUUUUUUUUU LEFT ME think you can come in here and flash your tits around and not work your program JUST WHEN I NEEDED YOU MOST make all the guys slobber all over you and slack off on chores.

A roaring tide of raw verbal sewage came at me. Like when you see film of a flooding river. Dark water full of debris. It was worse than sticks and stones; this was like bricks and broken glass. It was relentless, and it lasted a long time, like *who do you think you are YOUUUUUUUUU got kicked out of like every school in the world stupid spoiled YOUUUUUUU LEFT ME JUST WHEN I NEEDED YOU fucking stupid lazy bitch you think you're all that your family hates YOUUUUUUUUUUU toxic fucking influence on your siblings and they don't give a crap about YOUUUUUUUUU stupid spoiled fucking stupid lazy spoiled bimbo YOUUUUUUUUUU LEFT ME JUST WHEN can't admit just admit it just admit it what a stupid spoiled liar slacking until you end up going to Provo and I hope they beat the shit out of you and* and on and on and on like that until I bent forward with my arms over my head, trying to protect myself from this storm of words and spit and cruelty. I couldn't breathe. Waves of nausea rolled through my stomach. My pulse hammered in my head. I felt like my soul was being sucked out the top of my skull. I heard someone screaming and realized it was me.

That's the objective of Rap: to force a person past the last jagged inch of what they can stand. You'd like to think you'll sit there and be tough or yell back or walk out or whatever, but there were beefy Imperial Marine throwbacks standing guard all around to make sure nobody went anywhere.

"That's it, Paris. Run your anger." Weaselmug shoved a wad of paper towels in my face, hugging her moist, flabby arm around my shoulders.

Blanda turned on a girl sitting across from me.

"Why are you sitting on your ass, Katy? Why aren't you helping Paris take care of her feelings? Your chickenshit lack of participation is harming everyone in this room!"

As suddenly as it had turned on me, the circle beast wheeled on that girl, bellowing and berating her until she gulped and sobbed and drowned in that riptide of cruelty and horse shit, and then they moved on to someone else, destroying one person after another.

Weaselmug praised the most aggressive attackers and ridiculed anyone who was hanging back or not being brutal enough. If you refused to participate, you were "out of agreement" and next up for annihilation. These kids knew each other well enough to target each other's soft spots. Whatever it was that cut the deepest—they found that vulnerable place, drilled down on it, and tore the person apart like a pack of hyenas.

This went on and on and on. For hours. I am not exaggerating.

For *hours* this went on.

And on and on and on.

Youuuuuuuuuuuuuuuuuuu left me.

It's a song about being abandoned. This was the message drilled into us during those endless sessions: *Whoever you were counting on—family, friends, anyone who ever said they cared about you—just forget them. They lied. They left you. Just when you needed them most. Anyone who says they love you—they don't. Because you are not worthy of love, and if you love yourself, you're just fucking delusional. You are helpless. You are worthless. You will never be loved. Your family has rejected you. We're your family now, and the only way to survive is to be like us.*

People rocked and wailed, spewing snot and drool, bawling self-hatred, their noses running, their eyes red and streaming. Some kids screamed until their faces were freckled with the little red dots you get when tiny blood vessels burst under the skin—the ones that come from violent vomiting. The only way to make it end was to confess. You had to spill some dark secret, share your terrible thoughts, or divulge some creepy thing about yourself.

People confessed to doing and thinking horrific things—raping a cousin, killing a dog, wanting to stab parents and strangle girlfriends—which was utterly terrifying to me, because I thought these confessions were all real. I was like, *Who are these people?* It didn't even cross my mind that some kids were just making shit up, saying whatever they had to say to make the abuse stop.

The ritual dragged on for hours until everyone in the circle was spent and sweating. It was late—after midnight—and we'd been up since stupid o'clock that morning. I told the hippie counselor, "I have to lie down. I'm going to pass out. I'm going to throw up. Please. I have to go to bed."

"Soon," he said with another weird little wink. "First we *smoosh*."

I was like, *what the fuck what the fuck what the fuck*. I couldn't imagine how this whole scene could get any more messed up, but—yeah.

It did.

Everyone gravitated to a conversation pit in front of the fireplace—"a horseshoe of cushy couches" is how it was described in the brochure—and these kids who'd been ripping each other's guts out five seconds earlier got down on the floor and snuggled up with their heads on each other's stomachs and their limbs entwined. Weaselmug sat with her legs wide apart. Blanda sat in front of her. Another girl sat between Blanda's legs, leaning back on her chest, like they were all on a bobsled. Weaselmug grinned and stroked Blanda's greasy hair.

Blanda said, "C'mon and smoosh, Paris!"

I was like, *Oh, hell no.* No, no, no, no, no . . .

Three girls cuddled up with Hippie Mess, cooing and giggling. Some dude who was in the room when I was strip-searched tried to drag me onto his lap. He opened his legs and tried to bobsled me, for

Christ's sake! I was like, "Get off me!" and tried to twist away, but Blanda grabbed my wrist and shook her head.

"Smooshing is not optional," she said. "It's part of the program."

"I guess I should have prepared you," Hippie Mess chuckled, pulling the girls closer. "Smooshing is all about feeling. *I* is thinking; *Me* is feeling. There's an ongoing battle between the two."

"*I* is bad," said Blanda. "You gotta stop thinking. *I* can't work the program. You gotta let *Me* do it." She looked up at Weaselmug for approval, and Weaselmug kissed the crown of her sweaty head.

People kept trying to lean on me or drag me into their laps. I worked my way into a corner, pulled my knees to my chest, and hugged my arms around my shins, trying to become small, like a walnut in a hard shell. When they finally let us go to bed, I climbed into the bunk and covered my head with the blanket. I tried to keep it together, but I was so deeply shaken—I won't lie—I cried and cried. Again, I was gripped with that deep trembling. Every muscle in my core ached with fatigue.

Blanda whispered in the cold darkness: "If you don't smoosh, you'll get the worst chores. Scrubbing toilets or cleaning up puke. You'll get blown away every time during Rap."

I said, "Please shut the fuck up."

I lay there looking out on the moonlit mountain. This place wasn't a lockdown, but it was surrounded by a tall fence. That didn't scare me. I'd scrambled over the tall fence at Brooklawn countless times to rescue a stray frisbee or just because it was fun. I'd scaled chain-link barriers around urban rave venues and wrought-iron gates at a friend's house.

I can hop a fence.

If you don't believe me, google "Paris Hilton climbs fence"; there's a surprising number of pics and videos, and I look surprisingly good in them.

Check out the *Daily Mail* from September 2007. I'm wearing an adorable French Connection sequined shift dress—geometric color blocking, white, gold, and silver with a joyful pop of yellow—silver pumps, and a Fendi Forever Mirror bag. Silver like the pumps, but it has a texture, so it's not too matchy-matchy.

This look was perfect for a Prime Time Emmy after-party, but I was there with a guy who was acting kind of beyond, like he had expectations or whatever, so I decided to ditch him and spend the night at the home of a friend who lived near the Hollywood Municipal Park, where the party was.

It was getting into the wee hours, as they say, and my friend wasn't answering the phone, so I asked one of the paps to hold my shoes, which he gladly did, because they'd followed me from the party and were excited to take pictures of me scaling the fence. I'm sure they anticipated a clear crotch shot, but—sorry, boys!—I know how to do it with my legs together. Like sidesaddle.

Fence hopping is a skill that comes in handier than you might think.

So, back at CEDU, I figured that was the easy part. The fence I could manage. But then what? We were in the middle of nowhere. It was pitch black and freezing cold at night. Without shoes, I wouldn't be able to run very fast or very far. I tried to think, tried to make a plan, but the freight-train roar of the Rap echoed inside my head.

"You'll get used to it," Blanda whispered.

No, I promised myself. *I won't.*

9

My memory of the following weeks is a blur of shock and exhaustion. I stumbled through each day in my pink sweats and gym socks, trying to avoid speaking or being spoken to, trying to swallow my humiliation and terror, trying to avoid eye contact with the boys who hissed and spit at me during Raps. If they looked at me, I was the one who got in trouble.

I counted down the fourteen days I had to get through before I could call my parents and wear shoes again.

"Two weeks," I reminded Hippie Mess, using my sweetest baby voice. "You said I could call my parents. I can't wait to tell them how beautiful it is here."

He smiled and said, "Cool. Blanda and I will be right beside you. To support you."

Oh.

This is a fun moment to share another bit of actual copy from the CEDU brochure:

> *CEDU has experienced a great deal of success with*
> *students who are manipulative, unmotivated, and*
> *lacking in direction. These adolescents often have strained*
> *family relations, poor communication skills, rebellious*
> *or withdrawn behavior patterns, and have possibly*
> *experimented with drugs or alcohol.*

My parents had been counseled by the psychiatrist who made weekly visits to the school that I would try to lie and manipulate them into letting me come home. He told them the only way to literally save my life was to be strong and refuse to listen to my begging and pleading.

When I sat down for my fifteen-minute phone call, Hippie Mess and Blanda sat right next to me, listening in. I had planned to blurt out everything as quickly as I could before they cut me off, but when I heard my mom's voice, my throat choked up, and I started crying.

"*Mom . . . Mom . . .*"

I needed those fucking shoes. I was afraid to say anything that would give the counselors an excuse to keep me in pinks, so I tried to send Mom a secret message. I used the baby voice, which she knew was fake AF. (Who do you think I learned it from?)

"Mom, I just . . . it's like . . . I'm really . . . really . . ." I couldn't do it. Words poured out of my face. "Mom, please! You have to get me out of here! This place is fucked up! You don't even know!"

"Paris, honey, I know it's hard. You just have to hang in there and work the program."

Work the program?

It was scary to hear CEDU-speak come out of my mother's mouth. I'd been operating on the assumption that my parents had no idea what was happening here. Now I didn't know what to think.

"Mom, they—this isn't like—like, in the shower—"

Gently but firmly, Hippie Mess took the phone from me and said, "That's all for today, Paris."

I tried to hold on to the receiver. "No! No, I get fifteen minutes!"

"Paris," he said, "you don't want to lose your call privileges, do you?"

"I won't say anything bad. I won't tell. I swear."

He hung up the phone, severing the connection—that small thread of love in my mother's voice. It would have been less painful if he'd cut off my finger.

"You want to make another call two weeks from now, don't you?"

"Yes."

"Okay then. Work the program."

Another week went by. And then another.

I was so fucking exhausted. I tried everything to sleep—counting, playing music in my head, imagining myself dancing under the strobe lights—but if the blanket touched my foot, I jerked wide awake with my heart leaping out of my chest because I was back in that moment of the thug grabbing my ankle.

I bolted out of bed in the morning and cleaned the room. If there was a hair on a pillowcase or a wrinkle in the blanket, the team leader would tear apart my bunk, dump my drawer, and tell me to start over. And then they'd tear apart Blanda's stuff just to make her hate me. Sometimes they didn't give a reason; they just tore up the room to mess with us and make us miss breakfast.

Working outside in stocking feet was unpleasant, but working inside was worse. Working inside meant scrubbing toilets and floors with creepy staff people hanging around smoking and leering and making menacing comments to girls who were down on hands and knees. Outside, there was cold, clean air, and carting rocks and logs up to the top of the hill gave me a better view of the surrounding area. It looked like miles and miles of nothing but trees, but every once in a while, I saw dust coming up from a gravel road or a wisp of smoke from a chimney, which gave me some idea of where the town might be.

I forced myself to eat the sort of food I wouldn't feed a dog, because I had to stay strong. I tipped my head up and drank shower spray to supplement the inadequate water we were given after hours of manual labor.

Stay hydrated. Stay pretty. Be ready to climb out a window.

During "school" hours, we were required to write "dirt lists" and "disclosures," owning up to all our "cop-outs"—sins, evil thoughts, bad things that we had done or that had been done to us. These confessions were used as ammunition during Rap. I refused to get in there and blow people away, so I was constantly on bans, but I never offered anything of substance on my dirt list, so they had only the limited information in my file to blow me away with.

These broken CEDU people practiced cruelty like a martial art: largely self-defense but lethal as needed. The person getting blown away would sit there with big, wounded, watery eyes, and, for the moment, it was tempting to pounce. You wanted to feel safe, and there's a brittle shell of power in being a bully. But that shell of safety is weak and unstable, and what goes around comes around, so the bullies were more terrified than anyone else. The kids who did the hurting were just as damaged as the kids they victimized.

The nightly smoosh was just—*ugh*. Beyond. There was literally no escape from it. Thinking about it makes me want to fall into a tub of sea salt and hand sanitizer. We all did what we had to do to survive, and it left deep scars. I don't know who those kids were or if they'll ever see this, but it wasn't their fault. Or mine. None of it.

The cinder block of shame we carried out of that place was never our burden to carry. It belongs to the people who made that place.

After about a month, I was told I was going to my first Propheet. Basically, each Propheet has some theme, like the "I & Me Propheet" or the "Journey of Self Propheet" or "Whatever-the-fuck-ever Propheet"—it made no difference to me. You had to sit through several hours of lectures by team leaders and counselors, who read from voluminous scripts written by the great god of furniture sales, Wasserman himself.

There were bizarre exercises including one where a kid had to lie on the floor, a "trainer" shoved a towel in their mouth, and the kid had to bite down and try to keep their head on the floor, while the "trainer" yanked on the towel, fighting to lift them up. (And yes, this is as violent as it sounds. There were stories about people losing teeth and a girl whose jaw was so messed up she needed surgery.)

After that, there was a marathon mega-Rap that started in the evening and lasted until morning. You had to stay awake and continuously engaged in this ritual until breakfast time the following day—and that was the first food or water you were given during this whole insane event.

This was a huge group thing that mostly took place outside with a lot of physical activities, so—*thank you, God!*—they gave me shoes. I made sure I was sitting close to the perimeter. Two or three hours into the lecture, when everyone was supposed to stand up and chant, I nipped over to the nearby enforcers and said, "Hi, boys!" in a sweet, flirty way the paparazzi always liked.

One of them said, "Hi."

The other one said, "Get back in your group, Hilton."

"I really, really need to visit the little girls' room," I said with a giggle. "Just a quick tinkle. *Pleeeeeease?*"

The first enforcer smiled and glanced toward the front of the group. Everybody was waving their hands in the air, so there was no way the speaker could see us. The enforcer nodded toward the restrooms and said, "Hurry."

I had scrubbed toilets in there many times, mentally measuring the window. It was small and high on the wall, but I'm tall, and I was super skinny from a month of hard work and inadequate nutrition. I got on top of the toilet, clawed my way over the sill, and dropped to the ground on the other side of the building. I darted across the yard, keeping to the shadows, climbed the fence, and ran like hell. Without looking back, I scrambled down a steep embankment, through thick underbrush, into the mossy forest.

People were always saying, "Don't go into the forest. There's dead kids in there. If you try to run away, they'll kill you and hide your body in the woods."

I didn't believe that, and if I had, it would have made no difference. All that mattered was getting away from there. I don't remember thinking anything other than *run run run*. I went in a generally downhill direction, just going on instinct. I saw a dirt road below me and ran parallel to that until I had to cross a little stream. I didn't want to get my shoes wet, so I crossed the road and angled down the mountain until I found a paved road.

Every time I heard a car coming, I jumped the guardrail and hid in a ditch or behind some bushes.

It was late afternoon. The sun disappeared behind the ridge. I was cold and scared, but I was on fire with adrenaline. I felt like I was in a movie. This was some James Bond shit! Sticking close to the road, hiding from approaching vehicles, I ran for what seemed like a long time. I don't know how far. Eventually, I saw a bright yard light through the trees and followed the glow to a small parking lot outside a roadside travel place—like a combination restaurant and gas station. By the side of the building, there was a pay phone.

Oh, God. *Thank you*.

Remember pay phones? Do pay phones even exist anymore? Thinking about how grateful and relieved I was to see that grimy outdoor phone bolted to a pole—it makes me want to buy one and install it in my foyer.

Using a trick all club kids know, I lifted the receiver and toggled the flippy thing underneath until an operator came on.

"Operator," she said. "Do you require assistance?"

"Yes! I need to make a collect call to—" *Fuck*. I didn't know who to call. My parents might not listen. Gram Cracker was too far away to do anything. "I need to call Kyle Richards."

I gave her my aunt's phone number.

The operator asked, "Who should I say is calling?"

"Star," I said.

Kyle answered and accepted the charges. "Paris, honey—"

"Kyle, you have to save me. Please. And don't tell Mom. Just come and get me, Kyle. *Please*. Please, hurry. This place is fucked up. The people are crazy abusive, and Mom doesn't—"

"What do you mean by abusive? Did one of the other kids hit you?"

"No, it's not—*please*. I'll tell you when you get here. You have to come right now. *Please*. I need you to get me out of here."

"Where are you?" she asked, and I told her the address listed on a card next to an ad for a taxi service.

"Okay, just wait there," said Kyle. "Don't go anywhere."

I went behind the building and scrunched down in the weeds. After a little while, a police car rolled into the parking lot.

"Have you seen a blond girl?" the cop asked someone coming out of the restaurant.

Shit. Shit. Think. Think. Think. Hide.

A door on the back of the run-down building was blocked

open, probably venting heat from the kitchen, and there was a narrow stairway just inside. As soon as the cop went away, I crept up the stairs and went behind some boxes of Christmas decorations and things where there was a kind of crawl space over the rafters. I scrunched into the shadows and waited, looking down on the restaurant below me, inhaling the smell of fried chicken and potatoes, letting the music move through me. I didn't know until that moment that it was possible to be physically hungry for both food and music, but I was.

Hours went by. Cops came and went. The enforcers from CEDU came and went. The bartender shrugged. "Nope. Haven't seen her."

Perched on a narrow board, I forced myself to stay awake so I wouldn't fall. That was the hardest part. I was so tired. Kyle was coming from LA. It would take a while, but she was coming, and we would drive fast, away from this shithole place to a town with a McDonald's. The waitress went back and forth, serving burgers and soup of the day. Oh, God, I was so hungry. Eventually, she chased the last of the late drinkers from the bar, set chairs up on the tables, and mopped the floor, chatting with the cook as he cleaned the kitchen.

They turned out the lights and left.

Fuck my life.

Now Kyle would have no way to get in. She was probably outside right now. I stretched my cramped legs and crept down the stairs. I pressed my ear to the door. Nothing. I opened it a crack and peeked out at the silent parking lot. Moths flittered around the lightbulb above the phone booth. I went to the pay phone and called Kyle again. She accepted the charges, and I was like, "Kyle, where are you? Did you call the police?"

"No," she said. "No, of course not."

A heavy hand clamped around my neck. I tried to hold on to the phone, but the enforcer lifted me off the ground and threw me into the SUV. They drove back to the school, which was actually only two or three miles away. I guess I was running in circles part of the time.

People were still at the Propheet thing, looking like a bunch of red-eyed zombies. Weaselmug looked like this was the happiest moment of her life. She hauled me up in front of everyone and said, "Well, look who it is!"

I didn't even see the back of her hand coming at me. Next thing I knew I was down on the ground. An enforcer hauled me up, and they just went crazy on me, hitting and choking me, and shrieking at everybody to *look what happens*. And everybody looked. Their eyes were as big as soccer balls. A lot of them were crying. No doubt, this was an intense thing to witness, and I suppose that was the whole point. That's why they didn't need barbed wire or steel bars or iron doors. There was something a lot stronger keeping people inside.

They had horror stories about dead kids in the woods.

They had everyone teed up to tell on everyone else.

They had the people who love you fooled.

Aunt Kyle was in her twenties when this happened. Not much older than me. We've never talked about it, but looking at it from her perspective at the time, how would she not call my mom? Her big sister. My parents did what you're supposed to do when your kid disappears; they called the police. I was angry when I was younger, but the more I learn about how hideously clever CEDU sales tactics were, the more compassion I feel for my family. At every step, they genuinely believed they were doing the right thing for me.

I mean, think about it: On the advice of a mental health professional, you send your struggling kid to this beautiful boarding school that costs a fortune. When the kid tries to run away, do you believe the kid who's been royally pissing you off? Or do you believe the psychiatrist who says the kid is a crazy, incorrigible liar?

I'm not the crazy one, you are!—say 100 percent of crazy people.

Local law enforcement often have financial arrangements with these places; they get a reward for returning runaways and ignoring allegations of abuse. And c'mon. Dead kids in the woods? That's like a B-movie plot.

Isn't it?

I mean, that can't be real.

Or do we just not want it to be real?

We don't want to believe that a monster named James Lee Crummel—a convicted child molester and serial killer who hanged himself in 2012 while on death row at San Quentin—was connected to a long string of horrific crimes, including the murders of two boys who disappeared from CEDU's Running Springs campus in 1993 and 1994. Department of Justice missing-person investigator Bill Gleason reported that Crummel regularly accompanied the visiting psychiatrist, Dr. Burnell Forgey, on his trips to CEDU. I don't know if Dr. Forgey is the same doctor who consulted with my parents, but he was there at the same time I was, hard-selling parents on the idea that their kids needed to "work the program" for two years.

According to a June 7, 2012, article in the *Orange County Register* ("Mom vs. Child Killer: Guess Who Won?" by Lori Basheda), Crummel was "not the first or the second, but the *third* convicted sex offender who, over the years, had lived with Forgey." Forgey was arrested the year after I left CEDU. He was charged with multiple sex crimes that went back years. From the *Los Angeles Times* ("Other Possible Molest Victims of Psychiatrist Are Being Sought," May 6, 1998, by Thao Hua and Scott Martelle): "According to court documents filed by the Orange County district attorney's office, Forgey is suspected of having oral sex with the teenager under his care while Crummel allegedly sodomized—"

Oh, Jesus.

I can't.

Just—*no.*

Just google it.

Fuck.

Fuck that place.

What the fucking *fuck?*

Why do these monsters get to be part of my story? I fucking *hate* this. I don't want to talk about this. I don't want to think about it. I can't think about it.

I have to think about—think—fucking *think*—

Something that makes me feel strong.

Platform boots.

My Burning Man boots. Or the sick platform boots I wore with my hot-pink bride's dress for the neon carnival part of my wedding. The boots were white, but my stylist spray-painted them to perfectly match my Alice & Olivia high-low gown, which incorporated yards of tulle with a brilliantly constructed bustier, and it was everything. Every. Thing.

Think.

Something that makes me feel safe.

My dogs.

My little fur angels:

- Dollar
- Prada
- Slivington
- Harajuku Bitch
- Marilyn Monroe
- Prince Hilton
- Princess Paris Jr.

- Tokyo Blue
- Peter Pan
- Diamond Baby
- Tinkerbell, the OG Hilton pup

Think. Goddammit.

Something that makes me feel happy.

My friends.

One time Demi Lovato and I were shopping, and the topic of Taco Bell came up, because we're both obsessed with Taco Bell. She told me she has Taco Bell pillows on the furniture in her screening room. I love Demi.

Another time, back in 2006, Britney Spears and I were at a party in a friend's bungalow at the Beverly Hills Hotel. We got bored and wanted to go back to my house, but these people didn't want us to leave, because—let's be real—I know how this sounds, but if you had Britney Spears and Paris Hilton at your party, would you want them to leave? They were like, "No! You can't go yet!" and I didn't want to be rude, so I pulled Brit into the bathroom and said, "Let's use my little trick." I opened the window and popped the screen out.

Brit was like, "I can't climb out the window." Because she was wearing a cute little cocktail dress.

I told her it would be fine and helped her climb out. We were dying. Laughing so hard. But we got out. We ran down an alley, and the second we came around the corner, we were swarmed by paparazzi. I pulled Brit back into the shadows so we could check each other. As friends do. I tweaked Brit's hair. We did lip gloss.

Finest Girls. Camera ready, bitches.

We went back out, trying to make our way to the car. The paparazzi did what they do, calling out to get us to look their way.

"Paris, look left! Left, Britney!"

"Britney! Paris! Over here!"

"Paris, is it true you and Lindsay got into an altercation last night?"

I didn't really respond. We were just trying to get to the car, right?

"Paris! Britney! One more, one more, one more!"

"Paris, Lindsay says you hit her!"

"What's the feud between you and Lindsay?"

Now they all got on board: *Did you hit her? Did you hit her? Did you hit her?*

It was raining a bit, and Britney was freezing cold and in a hurry to get in the car. I was wearing jeans, so I opened the door for her and stood there to block any immodest shot that might result from her getting into the passenger seat. I went around to the driver's side.

They kept asking—*Did you hit her? Did you hit her? Did you hit her?*—because a day or two earlier this weird video came out where she said that I hit her elbow and dumped a drink on her. I still have no idea what that was about.

"No," I said. "Ask her. She's right there." I pointed to Lindsay Lohan, who'd left the party shortly after we did. "Lindsay, tell them the truth."

She was walking with Elliot Mintz. People always referred to Elliot as my publicist, but he used to say, "My role is more what I would describe as crisis management." Our relationship was a lot like the Dragon Queen and the little guy in *Game of Thrones*.

"Paris would never," said Lindsay. "She's my friend. Everyone lies about everything. She's a nice person. Please, leave us alone. We're friends."

"You're friends?" they said. "Lindsay, you're friends?"

Elliot brought her over to the car and opened the door. To get her out of the rain, maybe? Or maybe to clear up any crazy rumors that might be flying around?

"She never did that," said Lindsay. "She's a good girl. A nice person. I've known her since I was fifteen. Please."

And then Lindsay got in the car, which was kind of awkward because I was driving a Mercedes-Benz SLR McLaren that had only two seats. She got in, and Britney kind of wedged up on the middle thing where, ideally, you would put your purse. On a video that captured this moment, there's a collective gasp, and then one of the paps says, "Oh, this is gonna be classic!" And they go at it, snapping their asses off, holding their cameras over the hood of the car. The raindrops on the windshield lit up like BeDazzled-time.

"Paris! Paris! Wipe the windows! Wipe the windows!"

I pulsed the wipers. Insane snapping frenzy.

"Thank you, Paris. Lindsay? Look over here?"

I put the car in gear, but the constant flashing on the rainy windshield was blinding, and I was always paranoid that someone would put their foot under the tire and claim I ran over them, because that's the kind of fucked-up thing people do in LA. Elliot stepped out in the street and waved me out of the parking space the way the guy with light sabers waves a private jet onto the runway.

"Let them out. It's raining," he said.

They shuffled aside, and we drove away. I don't remember where we went. Does it matter? All anyone cared about was that moment. The next day, the iconic shot of Britney, Lindsay, and me ran on the cover of the *New York Post* with the words BIMBO SUMMIT in gigantic type under our faces. I didn't love the wording, but my bangs looked super cute. How often can you nail that, really? Bangs are tricky.

The pap was right; it was an instant classic.

All these years later, I still see these pictures on T-shirts, posters, birthday cards, coffee cups, boxer shorts, glittery clutch purses—all kinds of merch. My favorite is the fold-out laminated sun shade that goes inside your windshield when it's hot.

Fifteen years later, Carter and I were honeymooning on a private island in the Maldives. We were busy ignoring the rest of the world, and when we finally sneaked a peek at our devices, every message app was blowing up with stuff about the fifteenth anniversary of the "Holy Trinity." I looked at the photo and laughed. We look like Charlie's Angels.

I appreciated Joy Saha's article in *Nylon*—"Paris, Britney, & Lindsay: The Triumph of the Bimbo Summit"—about why the mean-spirited *Post* headline hadn't aged well and how the It Girls of the aughts were reclaiming their narratives. I'd just gotten married and was running a massive media and lifestyle conglomerate. Britney had recently ended the outrageous thirteen-year conservatorship that exerted control over her finances and personal life. Lindsay had just gotten engaged and was working on a professional comeback. I was glad for her. We're not close, but I always wish her well.

I understand why the media wanted to pit us against each other. It sold papers. It generated clicks. That blizzard of flashing lights created a dozen or so versions of a classic photo—each with a slightly different perspective—and those images have generated millions of dollars in licensing and royalties.

Not for us, of course.

Britney, Lindsay, and I get exactly zero of those dollars. But somebody else bought a house with one of those pictures. Somebody put his kid through college. I understand what motivated them. I have a harder time understanding what motivated everyone who piled onto that headline with nothing to gain but the brittle satisfaction of a bully.

Joy Saha wrote: "In 2006, society had yet to grasp the concept of empathy, allowing for a broken system that thrived off incessant exploitation."

So, there was that.

I tried to stay out of the alleged "feuds" the tabloids were always whipping up. They constantly printed complete BS about my "bitter feud" with a friend I had no issue with or my "catfight" with some stranger I stood three feet from on a red carpet. Sometimes it was so ugly, it took me back to the roar of the Rap.

Pitting us against each other, Weaselmug drained our energy and stole our identities. That noise distracted us from some hideously real shit going down—shit that caused those boys to suffer and die. We did hear rumors about how they disappeared, but it was mostly in the context of a *don't go into the woods* kind of cautionary tale to keep us from running off. We didn't want to think about it. We were scared to think about it. And it was easier to not think about it when we had the Real Housewives of Running Springs to distract us.

In the years after my CEDU experience, the roar of the Rap was never far away. I tried hard to drown it out, but I couldn't party hard enough, couldn't drive fast enough, couldn't crank my music loud enough or vacuum up enough love to make it go away. Sometimes I fell back on that slay-or-be-slain mentality, and I'm not proud of that. I was fucked up, okay? And I drank a lot. Like, *a lot.*

The Rap was all about destroying people for who they are. People went for the most obvious target in the ugliest possible language. The N-word. The C-word. The F-word. (Not that F-word, the worse one.) I look back on some of the things I said in the years after I left Provo, in the throes of PTSD, and I'm mortified. Horrified. I'm grossed out, because that means those creepy people got inside my head. I never really left them behind.

Saying I drank to dull the pain—that's an explanation, not an excuse. Sometimes I was just wasted and being a fucking moron. I don't remember half the stuff people say I said when I was being a blacked-out idiot, but I'm not denying it, because coming out of the CEDU system, I had a severely damaged filter—except when I was buzzed and had no filter at all. My ability to trust people was systematically destroyed, so getting close to anyone made me feel vulnerable and raw. As a result, I said the worst things to and about the people I love most.

I'm a genuinely nice person. I try to help people whenever I can. I love to lift up my friends and fellow creatives.

Puffy and I were hanging out in our camp at Burning Man last summer, and he said, "We're the OGs, and we're killing it more than ever."

He's been there for me since those early hard-partying years along with a core group of good friends who always accepted me as I was in that moment: Puffy, Nicole, Kim, Brit, Snoop, Nicky, Farrah, Brooke, Whitney—looking at you, Allison and Jen—these people are family, and I'm grateful. I can't regret those party years, because they're all part of it. We lived for the nightlife.

My girlfriends and I had so much fun raging all around the world: LA, London, Burning Man, Ibiza, Saint-Tropez, Paris, Vegas. Sometimes they'd beg to go home. "Paris, please! Can we call it a night?"

I kept them out until dawn. I was afraid to be alone in the dark. No matter how far I traveled, in my dreams, I was back where I started, running down that mountain, slipping on mossy rocks, disappearing with the remains of the murdered boys.

10

After I tried to escape, I was seriously on bans: No one was allowed to speak to me or look at me, and I was not allowed to speak to or look at anyone else. I lost my phone privileges. Back in pinks. They took my shoes. Obviously.

Problem people had to sleep on the floor in the living room so a guard could watch us all night. The shower remarks were over-the-top filthy, and I got blown away every night during Rap. "Stupid spoiled bitch. You're not even trying to work the program. They're gonna send you to Ascent. You're gonna end up at Provo."

Kids who'd stayed at other CEDU sister facilities agreed that Ascent sucked. It was a military-style boot camp somewhere in Montana. Or Idaho. Montandaho. I don't know. Hard-core, middle-of-nowhere wilderness. You had to sleep in a tent and do hard labor.

They said all the kids were criminals and psychopaths and the staff people were even worse. The general take on Provo was a wide-eyed whisper: "Bad things happen there."

I sat through a few more Raps with a frozen Stepford smile. I was dying a million times inside, but I wouldn't let myself fight back; I had to conserve my energy. I planned to run again, using what I'd learned, but before I had a chance to try, the transporters came for me. Same as the first time, two people—a man and a woman—came in the middle of the night, grabbed me, and gave me the whole "easy way or hard way" bit.

This scene had already played itself out in my head a hundred times. I slept in my clothes, thinking about how I would handle it.

"Easy," I smiled. "I'm excited to go. I love the outdoors."

They were thrown off a little, but not really fooled by this. When they put the cuffs on me, they probably saw that I was shaking. The wife was a chunky middle-aged woman, not very tall, blond hair with gray roots. Her husband had a huge belly. I felt certain they'd never catch me if I could just make a break for it.

They gave me actual clothes to travel in—jeans and a T-shirt from the bag Mom packed. I'd lost a lot of weight, so the jeans looked baggy and sad.

On the way to the airport, I tried to chat them up and charm them, but Mr. and Mrs. Meathead sat in the front seat of the SUV, staring straight ahead. They kept the cuffs on me while we flew to San Francisco, where we were supposed to change planes. I was as sweet as I could be the whole way.

"Gosh, I can't wait to get to my new school. Do you think it would be okay to take the cuffs off before we change planes? It's just so embarrassing to walk through the airport like this."

"No," Mr. Meathead said flatly. "The paperwork says you're a runner."

But Mrs. Meathead sighed and gave him a look, so he took them off. At the gate inside SFO, I asked if she could please take me to the ladies' room, and she agreed. I went into a stall. She folded her arms, standing right outside the door.

"Don't try to lock it," she said.

I smiled and shrugged. "There wouldn't be much point."

I pulled the door shut and sat on the toilet without taking my jeans down, waiting, taking one deep, quiet breath after another, trying to think through what was going to happen next. After a while, Mrs. Meathead pounded on the door and said, "Hurry up."

I braced my hands on the toilet seat, breathing, waiting until I saw her eye at the crack in the stall door.

"What are you doing?" she said.

Here's the thing about dancing in a really crowded club: There's so little room to do anything, you end up basically jumping up and down for hours, which gives you the thigh muscles of a kangaroo. Without really thinking about it, I pulled my knees to my chest and kicked the door with both feet. She staggered back and fell to the tile floor, moaning sort of a wet, blubbery sound.

I just ran. Out the door. Down the concourse.

I heard her behind me, screaming for her husband, but I had a head start. By the time he started chasing me, I was halfway down the concourse. I bounded onto an escalator before I realized it was coming up, and I needed to go down. Too late to change lanes. I leaped out over the stairs, skipped like a stone, stumbled, found my feet, and kept pounding toward the one safe haven I could think of.

The Hilton.

Conrad Hilton was ahead of his time. In 1959, air travel was cutting edge, marketed with high fashion and art cross-promotions. Salvador Dalí and Andy Warhol did commercials for Braniff with stewardesses in Pucci uniforms. My great-grandfather turned travel upside down, building a luxury hotel right there at SFO. You could fly in, live your best life, and fly out again without ever leaving the airport. Papa was a young man at the time, and he loved that hotel, because it was always full of pilots, stewardesses, and jet-set people from all over the globe.

"The hotel lounge was the Tiger-a-Go-Go," he told me. "They had a team of dancing girls called the Tiger Kittens. Buzz and Bucky did a song about it. It was a big hit."

The song actually peaked at number 104 on Billboard, but it makes for a cinematic moment in my head: I see myself tearing down the concourse with Mr. Meathead chasing after me to the driving rhythm of Buzz and Bucky's surf rock anthem: "*Tiger! Tiger! Tiger-a-Go-Go!*"

The concierge looked up when I bolted past the front desk, screaming, "My boyfriend is trying to kill me! Get me in a taxi!"

A good concierge doesn't ask questions. He hustled me out to the curb and into a waiting cab. The baffled driver started to ask, "Where—"

"Just go! Just go!"

He peeled out.

Tiger! Tiger! Tiger-a-Go-Go!

As we sped away from the hotel, I peeked over the back of the seat and saw Mr. Meathead on the curb, looking like he was about to have a heart attack. The driver glanced at me in the rearview mirror. I was giggling and crying, high on adrenaline, and so happy to be free.

"Take me to the downtown Hilton, please." That felt as close to home as I could get. When he pulled up in front of the hotel, I said, "Be right back. I gotta run in and get money from my boyfriend."

"Yeah, right," he huffed.

I went in and crossed the lobby at a quickstep trot, trying not to look like I was running away. (Unicorn trot!) I ducked around a corner and took off running again, out the back door and up the street. I ran, walked, ran again, holding my hand against a stitch in my side. After a while, I sat on a bench. I had no idea where I was and had no money, but I was free, fighting tears of joy.

After a while, I went into a phone booth and toggled the switch under the receiver. When the operator came on, I gave her my parents' phone number.

"Mom! Mom . . ." I was crying before she had a chance to accept the charges. This was only the second time I'd heard her voice since I was taken.

"Paris, where are you? What have you done?"

"Mom, please," I sobbed. "You have no idea what's happening here. There's like—I got beaten up—they're crazy—I don't want to go to this place. Please, let me come home." As I pleaded for my life, I could tell she didn't believe me.

"Paris, calm down. It's all right."

"I'll never go out again. I won't lie. I won't go to clubs. I hate clubs! Mom, I just want to be home. I'll do good in school. I'll do anything you say. I'll be good, Mom. I'll be good, I swear."

"Paris, calm down. It's okay," Mom said. "Of course, you can come home."

"Thank you." I closed my eyes and slumped against the wall of the phone booth, desperately weary, desperately grateful. "Thank you, Mom. I'll be so good. I promise."

"Just stay on the phone with me. Stay right there."

I was happy to do that. All I wanted was her soothing voice in my ear.

"Everything's okay, Paris. Just stay with me while we figure this out."

It's cute how I kept forgetting that my mom is way smarter than me.

Apparently, after I ran the first time, my parents had a wiretap put on their phone, knowing that if I bolted again, I would eventually call, and they would be able to trace it.

I felt a firm hand on my shoulder and looked up to find a police officer standing there.

"You need to come with me, miss." He took the phone from me and said, "Mrs. Hilton? This is Officer—yes. I have her. Yes, ma'am. Will do."

I expected him to put me into the back of a cop car, but there wasn't one. He was a bicycle cop. He put handcuffs on me, got on his bike, and made me run behind him all the way to the police station, which was only a couple blocks, but *come on*. Fuck you, bicycle cop. Fuck you and your hideous shorts and the lame-ass gel seat you rode in on.

I waited on a bench at the police station until the Meatheads came for me. They were seriously pissed. Mrs. Meathead was holding an ice pack on her face. The front of her shirt was spattered with blood. While Mr. Meathead was at the front desk talking to the police officer, she bent down and burbled through her swollen lips, "Fuhtt you, you libble dwat. You're gomma be sowwy you did dat."

When the officer came to reclaim his cuffs, I begged him, "Please, don't let them take me. They're trying to kidnap me. They're going to beat me."

"We're her legal guardians," said Mr. Meathead. He showed the officer some paperwork. "As you can see, she's a violent offender."

It took me a beat to understand what that meant—and that it was true. Mrs. Meathead was really hurt. I did that, and I did not feel bad about it. Seeing myself that way made me feel even further removed from my real life. The Meatheads took me to the airport in cuffs, and I sat on the airplane, wedged between their sweaty bodies, feeling physically and emotionally crushed.

When we arrived at Ascent, a burly woman in combat fatigues strip-searched and groped me in full view of the staff and gawking students. There was a crew-cut-and-camo white-supremacist vibe to the place: a shack with a guard, a common area with wooden benches, a circle of tepees, a mess tent with a log for a table. The only sanitation was a pair of porta-potties. Instead of showers, you got a bucket of cold water with a cup and a bar of soap. Kids were required to strip naked and wash while staff watched.

In the morning, you had sixty seconds to pull on socks and shoes and bundle your sleeping bag into a backpack. If one person messed up, everyone was punished. The first day, there was a hair on my backpack, so they tore everyone's stuff up—probably just to make sure everyone hated me. Breakfast was a grainy cereal with milk that was obviously bad. I tried to drain off the sour milk, but the team leader said, "Eat it or I'll shove it down your throat."

Burly cuffed me on the back of the head. "Keep an eye on this one."

The program was similar to CEDU except the girls were called Otters and the boys were Tatankas. Boys and girls weren't allowed to look at each other. Another camp was being built nearby, so we spent our days hiking to and from that location, hauling logs, and digging holes. Every night, you washed your socks. If they didn't dry, you had to go without. It took me a few days to figure out a good method, so the backs of my heels were raw with weeping blisters.

Sometimes kids passed out, and we had to carry them back to the camp. Sometimes we never saw that person again, but a girl who came back after a brief trip to the hospital told me, "I was handcuffed the whole time. No one would speak to me in the ER."

Asking questions or voicing a complaint got you a slap across the face, and they made sure everyone saw it. Kids got punched, choked, and thrown to the ground, held facedown in the dirt with a staff person's knee on their neck. They kept us scared and hungry. If the milk was bad, and you couldn't eat your cereal, you had to carry it with you all day until you ate it.

Weeks went by. A blur of stiff, heartbroken misery. I was constantly scoping out the territory for any possible avenue of escape. I knew I would die if I stayed there, but traveling through the wilderness on my own—that didn't seem possible. Most of the other students scared me, but my tentmate seemed cool and was obviously as miserable as I was, so we bonded over that.

One night I said, "I don't want to leave you by yourself, but I have to get out of here."

She agreed, and we made a plan. Before we went to sleep, she went out to use the porta-potty, and a few minutes later, Burly called, "Hilton, get out here."

I went out, and she said, "What's going on? What were you two whispering about?"

"Nothing," I said.

"NO," she barked. "You tell the truth."

"Nothing's going on. We were just—"

Burly yanked me into the firelight and made me sit on a log while she paced and berated me.

This was a thing at Ascent. You had to sit on that log hour after hour while people took turns yelling at you, poking you, and smacking the back of your head until you confessed to something. Usually, I made up something that wasn't very bad, like "I dumped my cereal in the bushes" or whatever. That wasn't going to cut it this time. Burly kept me on the log all night. I was shivering cold and exhausted from the long day of manual labor, but I sat there and said nothing, because I didn't want to get my tentmate in trouble. It didn't sink in until morning that my tentmate had ratted me out.

When people woke up and found us still out there in this stand-off, Burly lost it. She had to show them she could break me. Everyone crouched by the opening of their tent, watching with huge, scared eyes as she slapped and strangled me, yelling with her hot breath on my face.

"If you fucking run—say one word about running—try to be a bad influence on other kids—I will make your life hell, understand? You are *never* gonna leave here. I will *bury* you here, and no one will give a shit. Your parents *hate* you. Get it through your stupid little bimbo head! *You belong to me*."

I can't even try to be funny about this or pretend I was a tough cookie. That chick scared the living shit out of me. I cried and begged her to stop, and every day after that, I did whatever she told me to do. I worked my ass off, ate whatever crap they put in front of me, and never ever said another word about running away. I played a familiar character: the stupid rich girl. The blond bimbo they expected me to be. I pretended to be all excited if I saw an elk and never said another word to anyone except when I was forced to participate in their insane rituals.

Years later, when I finally found the courage to google it, I was glad to see this place had been shut down. Kids had died there, and the lawsuits finally got to be too much. But other places just like it sprang up. It's infuriating how widespread this type of thing is—and that a lot of people have known about it for a long time.

In October 2007, Gregory D. Kutz, managing director of forensic audits and special investigations for the US Government Accountability Office, and Andy O'Connell, assistant director, testified before the House Committee on Education and Labor, presenting a report, "Residential Treatment Programs: Concerns Regarding Abuse and Death in Certain Programs for Troubled Youth."

Under the heading "What GAO Found":

GAO found thousands of allegations of abuse, some of which involved death, at residential treatment programs across the country and in American-owned and American-operated facilities abroad between the years 1990 and 2007. . . . GAO could not identify a more concrete number of allegations because it could not locate a single Web site, federal agency, or other entity that collects comprehensive nationwide data.

Burly wasn't lying. She really could have buried me there, and no one in any official capacity would have known or cared.

The report goes on to cite one agonized example after another:

- May 1990—Female, 15—died while hiking after reporting symptoms of dehydration for two days; left on dirt road for eighteen hours
- September 2000—Male, 15—held facedown in the dirt for forty-five minutes; died of severed artery in the neck
- February 2001—Male, 14—attempted to commit suicide severing artery with camp-issued pocketknife (knife was not taken away); hanged himself in his tent the following day
- July 2002—Male, 14—died of heat stroke exertion while hiking; staff member hid behind a tree to observe if he was "faking it"; checked for pulse after child lay motionless for more than ten minutes
- November 2004—Male, 15—forced to wear twenty-pound sandbag around his neck as punishment for being "too weak"; collapsed and died; autopsy revealed bruises over entire body.

This list goes on and on like a beatbox loop and doesn't even address the thousands of kids who suffered these horrific conditions and survived.

I've testified before House committees, so I know what it's like presenting information like this in a cold conference hall, facing a sea of men in dark suits. Most of them are there because they sincerely want to make a difference, but after a while, they look numb. It's impossible for them to see these statistics as *children*—but it's impossible for me to see these children as statistics.

I see that kid. I know that kid.

I *am* that kid.

After a couple of months at Ascent, I was as stoic and lean as the blade of an ax. The skin-crawling reality of the observed bucket shower had become normalized. I learned how to take a bitch slap. Go with the momentum instead of trying to duck. I no longer felt the sting when they talked about my parents hating me or told me I'd be a crack whore and die in a gutter and had no future. What did that even mean? The only future I could think about was surviving another day on that fucking mountain.

Haul another log.

Dig another hole.

Shiver uncontrollably through another night.

One day, they told us it was time to go on this thing called "Track"—or maybe "Trek"—that involved hiking over some mountains in Montana. They gave us some perfunctory survival training— how to pack our eighty-pound backpacks, pitch a tent in the snow, build a fire, find water—*Naked and Afraid*-type stuff, which would be hard even if you *wanted* to do it, and none of us did. Burly kept saying how life changing and awesome Track/Trek was, and I pretended to be excited about it, but inside I was like, *Nope.*

I'd been watching the way the moon came and went. Sometimes it was pitch black at night; other times the moon was so bright you could see your shadow on the way to the porta-potty. Sometimes in the morning, fog rose from the ravines so thick you couldn't see a tree ten feet away. I'd been weighing the advantages and disadvantages, the opportunity to hide versus the ability to cover the greatest distance as fast as possible. Counselors warned us about wild animals, but bears and mountain lions scared me less than these twisted people. I tried to find the courage to go alone, but at the last minute, I caved. Sometimes it takes more courage to trust someone.

There was a young girl who'd arrived recently and was having a bad time, mouthing off and getting slapped around a lot. (Let's just call her Tess.) One night, I whispered to her, "Let's get out of here. I'll tell you when."

Tess nodded, scared but resolute.

At two in the morning, we took off through the trees, down the mountain to a dirt road. She struggled to keep up, and I badgered her like a football coach.

"Keep going! You can do this! We can't slow down!"

After a while, we came to a small group of old mobile homes scattered around a cluttered field of junked cars and rusted machinery. We crept through the clutter, peeking in windows. Inside one of the trailers, a woman sat by herself, reading a thick book in the lamplight. She had a long, thick braid over her shoulder, jet black and steel gray, and a big dog curled up at her feet. A dog person. I thought maybe we could trust her.

When I knocked on the door, she opened it, not looking particularly surprised or curious. I babbled some made-up story in my baby-girl voice.

"I'm so sorry to bother you. Me and my friend were camping with some boys, and they're really drunk and tried to rape us, and we don't have anywhere to go," and on and on. I don't know if she believed us or not, but she didn't ask questions, so either she accepted the story on face value, or she knew the truth was something too terrible to tell.

"You must be freezing," she said. "Come in, come in."

She brought us inside, wrapped us in blankets, gave us water, grilled cheese sandwiches, and hot chocolate. She let us use her wonderful little bathroom with a real toilet and sink. When I stepped out of the private heaven of a hot shower, I found that she'd left clean clothes for me on the bed.

On the bathroom countertop, there was a little plastic basket with a basic assortment of moisturizers and makeup. I dabbed balm on my cracked lips and touched my lashes with black mascara. Looking in the mirror for the first time in several months, I hardly recognized my own face. Hardness. Sadness. You can see it if you compare photographs of me before and after all this happened.

When Tess came out of the shower, the sun was coming up.

"They'll know we're gone," I whispered. "We need to leave."

The lady let me use her phone to make a few long-distance calls to my friends in LA. One of my guy friends bought us train tickets, and our fairy godmother gave us a ride to the station.

"Good luck." She gave me a hug and drove away.

I still can't understand why she did this for us, but I'm eternally grateful. It's so rare to see someone just help without judgment. We tend to second-guess people when they're down. *What did that girl do to make her boyfriend beat her? Why doesn't that junkie just get a job?* Maybe that's how we reassure ourselves that we'll never be in that situation. Looking back, I see this woman acting on pure instinct. No hesitation. Just plain human kindness. Words can't express how much it meant to me. When I lose faith in people—when love feels impossible and it seems like anyone who isn't paid is going to abandon me—I think about that lady, and I know there's goodness in the world.

Tess and I stayed low, waiting for our train. This wasn't a busy station like London or Paris, where you can blend in with the crowd; this was a tiny little depot next to a bunch of hay bales. Maybe half a dozen other people around. The ticket agent kept glancing our way. Finally, our train came, and we hurried out to get on, but two crew-cut Ascent goons blocked us on the platform.

So, forget about goodness in the world. The world fucking sucks.

I gripped Tess's hand, and we were both trembling.

Back at the camp, they made everyone sit on logs. Strip search. Cavity examination. One of the guys who always watched me during soap and bucket time said, "Now you're gonna see what happens when you run away."

The creepy way he was smiling, I thought he was going to rape me right there in front of everyone.

Thank God, he just beat the shit out of us.

11

I don't know what happened to Tess, but I spent the next several weeks pretending I was *suuuuuper*, super sorry for running. I told Camo Goon that his beatdown really made me think about myself, and now, more than anything, all I wanted was to experience the life-changing awesomeness of Track/Trek. And I wasn't saying that because I thought I'd have another chance to run. They kept telling me I could go home after Track/Trek. They said that was how you "graduated" from Ascent, and I believed it, because kids who went on the Track/Trek that Tess and I ran away from—they were gone.

"It's a beautiful moment," Burly said. "You run that last bit, and when you get to the trailhead, your parents are there to celebrate with you."

I latched on to that image—the moment when I'd see Mom and

Dad. At CEDU, I thought constantly about home, about Nicky and my little brothers, and how wonderful it was at the Waldorf. Now I blocked all that out. It made me too sad. I worked my ass off for another shot at Track/Trek.

When it was time, I slayed the three-week hiking marathon, up and down snow-covered mountains, carrying my eighty-pound backpack. (Not exaggerating. They told us every day, "It's an eighty-pound pack, so use your legs when you lift.") We reached our encampment and built a sweat lodge—big branches lashed together into a roundhouse frame covered with canvas—and then the camo-squad led us in some bastardized version of a supposedly Native American ritual.

This vision quest thing lasted for days. We sat in a circle around a fire, allowed to leave the sweat lodge only to go to the bathroom—except we never had to go to the bathroom because we were given virtually no food or water and were sweating so profusely. We weren't allowed to sleep for seventy-two hours. If a kid passed out, we dragged them out in the snow to be revived and then trudged back in. It was our only breath of cool air, so I sat there praying for someone to keel over, even if it was me.

We were all crying. Coughing. Talking out of our heads. My eyes and sinuses burned from smoke and lack of sleep. I heard the voice of the operator.

Collect call from Star. Will you accept the charges?
Collect call from Star. Will you accept the charges?

And then my head bobbed, jerking me out of drifting half sleep. They made us say and do all these bizarre things—chanting, moaning, howling, beating drums, passing stones back and forth—I don't know. I didn't get it. It was beyond. If there is an authentic Native American ritual in which all these things mean something, please don't be mad. I'm not disrespecting that. Not at all. I'm just saying, we were in no condition to understand or appreciate anything like that, and the Camo Goons were in no way qualified to oversee it.

Anyway, I toughed it out, focused on that "home stretch" where Mom and Dad would be waiting.

When I got there, Burly was all *happy happy joy joy*. "You did it, Paris! You graduated!"

"I'm going home," I said. "Where are my parents?"

"They'll meet you in Redding and drive you to Cascade."

"Cascade . . . what . . ."

"You've still got another year to work the program," she said.

So—wow. Trying to find words.

At that moment, all that mattered was seeing Mom and Dad. I had to make them understand that they were being manipulated by someone who was even better at it than I was. Burly gave me some clothes, and I cleaned myself up as much as I could, but I still felt gross when I got in the car with Mom and Dad in Redding.

Dad was crisp and well groomed, as he always is. Mom smelled like a lavender patch in God's backyard. I just wanted to lay my head on her lap and die while she stroked my hair and told me how happy she was to see me. When she brought up the topic of this other CEDU program, I begged and cried.

"Mom, please, please, *please* take me home."

"You'll like this place," she said. "Look. It's really nice."

She showed me a brochure that featured happy students, green grass, and a stately lodge with a rainbow arcing across the sky above, with the words *The Cascade School*.

Again. Actual ad copy:

> *As a community, we acknowledge the true potential of*
> *humanity and the nobility of the struggle toward a sane,*
> *caring, and enlightened world.*

For fuck's sake.

"Mom, I can't," I said. "I'm literally going through hell. These places are insane. These people are lying!"

"Let's not spend our time arguing," said Mom. "This is hard for all of us. We have to be strong. We have one year left before you turn eighteen. This is our last chance to *save* you. We have to see it through."

She'd been primed for this conversation. If parents raised any doubts or fears, the counselors leaned into the CEDU script: *Don't believe anything your child says. She'll make up stories and say she's being abused. She'll say anything to go back to her old life—a life that will leave her dead or in prison. Tough love is the only way. You must be strong enough to save your child.*

They went hard on the idea of that two-year commitment. Your kid was "cured" only if your insurance ran out and you weren't wealthy enough to pay. They saw my parents as a deep pocket and used my escape attempts—especially the moment I kangaroo-kicked the door into the transporter's face—to convince my parents that I was on a dangerous downward spiral. I was supposed to feel lucky; no one pressed charges and I was going to a pristine mountain retreat instead of juvenile detention.

I didn't know what to do. I just cried. Mom stroked my hair, murmuring soft, comforting words. She kissed the crown of my head.

"My hair is so gross," I said. "My roots have grown out four inches."

"You could use a trim," said Mom. "These split ends."

I sat up, swallowing my tears, trying to look like a good girl.

I said, "Could we please stop somewhere? On the way to the school, I mean. There must be someplace we could go. If I'm going to be there for a whole year, I need to at least get the roots highlighted so it can grow out without looking totally jacked."

Mom agreed with that, and we found a place in Redding: a cute little salon situated in the hairstylist's house on the edge of town. Before we went inside, I hugged my father and said, "I love you, Dad."

"I love you, Starry," he said and held me tight for a moment. "I hope you know we're only doing what's best for you."

I smiled up at him and said, "I know, Daddy."

Mom and I went into the salon. I sat close to her until it was my turn, and then I sat in my smock, smiling and chatting while the stylist foiled my roots.

"I need to use the restroom," I said. "I'll be right back."

In the bathroom, I tore the smock off, jammed a magazine rack under the doorknob, and climbed out the window.

I ran like hell, dragging the foils from my hair and jamming them in my pockets. I saw a Greyhound bus station and dodged into the bathroom. The bleach on my scalp smelled pretty strong and was starting to sting, so I stuck my head in the tiny sink and cupped water over my burning scalp with my hand. I rinsed my hair as well as I could, forked my fingers through it, and twisted it into a tight bun on top of my head.

Counting the cash I'd swiped from Mom's purse, I scanned the bus schedule and calculated how long it would take to get to LA. Even though it wasn't the most direct route, I got on the first bus out of there and found a seat near the back, slumping down below the edge of the window until the bus rolled out of town.

The first stop was Chico, I think. A police officer got on and exchanged a few words with the driver, who laughed and shook her head. The cop got off, and we drove on, never going as fast as I would have liked. I scrunched down with my heart pounding. Eventually, I fell asleep with my knees pulled up to my chest, my arms covering my head. I didn't realize we'd stopped again until I felt a firm hand on my shoulder. I opened my eyes to find a cop standing there.

He said, "I need you to come with me, Miss Hilton."

"Where's my mom? I want to talk to my mom."

"She's pretty upset," he said. "One of the counselors from your school is here to take you back to campus."

I didn't bother begging. I went with a woman who looked a lot like Weaselmug. Same mousy hair and haggard expression. We drove for an hour or so, winding through a dark forest of fragrant pine trees, past a frozen lake, up into the jagged mountains. We stopped briefly at a set of big iron gates. There was a big rock emblazoned with gold letters: CASCADE SCHOOL.

The main building was another big log cabin/lodge-type thing. They gave me a rule book. Same CEDU deal as Running Springs: work, monitored calls, Raps, Propheets. I felt nothing when the male counselor told me to take off my clothes. I squatted and coughed and endured the cavity search without whimpering. I put on the pinks and followed my new "big sister" to our room.

She turned out the lights, and I waited until it sounded like she was sleeping. Only then did I finally allow myself to touch the slim roll of cash tucked under the bun on top of my head. The money was rolled tight, as slender as a skeleton key.

See, I had learned that these strip searches were about invasion, not investigation. It was a demonstration of their power over every part of your body, so they focused on the private parts—the parts you instinctively try to protect. Some of them obviously enjoyed it. They didn't even bother pretending. The cavity searches—like any sexual assault—that was about them, not the person they were doing it to. Once I understood that, it was easy to fool them.

I formed a strategy for keeping my money hidden while I waited for my next opportunity to run. It wasn't a lot. A couple hundred dollars. But it was mine. My sweet little money roll. Knowing it was there gave me a quiet fizz of happiness. Money meant hope. Money meant freedom.

Someday, I decided, *I'm going to work so hard and make so much money. Like a million dollars. And then I'll be safe and fuck trusting anyone ever again.*

I spent my days at Cascade working on a building site, trying not to be noticed. Weeks went by. Maybe a month. One day a skinny little girl came over to me while we were picking rocks. I don't remember her name; in my mind, she was always Mouse.

"You're going to run, aren't you?" she whispered.

I didn't say anything. Didn't look at her.

"Take me with you," said Mouse. "If I stay here, I'll die."

Fuck.

She was so skinny and small—barely up to my shoulder, maybe fourteen—and she cried a lot. She kept getting ripped apart in Raps for "tempting" her uncle and making him do bad things. She hadn't figured it out yet; you had to give them something to distract them. Like say, "Oh, I hate myself because everyone in my family is vegetarian, and I used to sneak out to Burger King." Let them all jump on that. "Bitch! Animal eater! Cow murderer!" Because, who cares if people tear you up for something that isn't true? I mean, it's annoying. It still hurts. But it's not as bad as people pouncing on the real you. If they get their claws into something real, shame takes hold of you from the inside, and you become your own worst enemy. (Apply as needed to internet trolls and gossip blogs.)

"Please, take me with you," said Mouse. "*Please.*"

Crap. This complicated things, but I couldn't leave her, knowing what it felt like to be left behind, knowing that the lady with the long black braid would have said "of course" and helped her without hesitating. I wanted to be like her, not like all the people who looked away.

On a night when the moon was good and bright, Mouse and I took off running. I dragged her down the mountain, gripping her skinny wrist in my hand. No mercy. No stopping. We had to get back to that Greyhound station. It was the only way out.

Finally, I saw a 7-Eleven.

Gotta love 7-Eleven. Open all night. Now it was almost morning.

"We need a disguise," I told Mouse.

I was being careful with my cash, but I bought some inexpensive brown mascara and used it to thicken our eyebrows into heavy unibrows. I feathered on mustaches and even gave myself a thin goatee. We slicked our hair back under baseball caps and hoodies from the clearance bin and got on a Greyhound bus, attempting to walk like b-boys. (Honestly, thinking about that cracks me up now.) We scrunched down in our seats and stayed silent through the long, winding ride. Ten or twelve hours later, we got to LA and disappeared into the city.

My friend let us stay at his place in Bel Air, just a few minutes away from the Jaclyn Smith house where we lived when I was little. For the first few days, I did nothing but sleep and eat and listen to music. Mouse and I sat in front of the TV for hours, soaking up all the interesting things we'd missed. When it felt safe to venture out, I went to the Whiskey Bar in the Sunset Marquis Hotel, where all the rock stars stay. I sat in the corner bobbing my head to the Cardigans' "Lovefool." I sang along, loud and joyful. I felt safe and fully alive, lost in the crowd.

Love me, love me, say that you love me
Fool me, fool me . . .

I created a character named Amber Taylor—because Amber Valletta and Niki Taylor. Supermodel vibes. I scrounged thrift stores for an appropriate look and bought five-dollar pieces on the street in downtown LA in the fashion district. Amber wore black, mostly.

Baggy skater clothes. Hot Topic style: long red wig, fake nose ring, a full sleeve of press-on tattoos. Amber was more than a disguise; Amber was a totally different person. A little vacation from myself. Amber had never been roofied or strip-searched or slapped around. She was sassy and smart, and I loved being her.

My money didn't last long, and I was afraid to stay in one place, so I called a friend of mine in New York—let's call him Biff—and he bought me a plane ticket to Connecticut, where he lived with his parents.

The only problem was Mouse.

"I'll fly you out," Biff said, "but you can't bring this little girl with you. It would be like kidnapping. She's a minor. I could seriously go to jail."

I put it off as long as I could, keeping my plan secret. The morning before I was to leave, I took Mouse to Denny's for breakfast. When the bill came, I gave her all my money and said, "Hang on to this. I need to use the restroom."

Without looking back, I went down a short hallway and, instead of going into the bathroom, I pushed through a door that said EM-PLOYEES ONLY. I hurried through a back area full of boxes and produce pallets, slipped out a back door by a dumpster, and ran as fast as I could down La Cienega Boulevard until I saw a city bus pull up to a stop. You could usually sneak onto a bus if the back door was open and a lot of people were getting off.

I crouched between the seats, fighting tears, forcing myself to focus on my strategy for getting through the airport. But guilt clawed at me.

It's clawing at me now. After all these years.

Over the decades, I've tried not to think about that skinny little girl in the huge, unforgiving city. When I think about the most likely fate of a kid like her, it makes me want to throw up. I was trying to save her, and I ended up throwing her to the wolves. I pray that she found someone who was better able to help her than I was. I hope she grew up okay and that she was able to forgive me.

Mouse, if you're out there, I just want to say I'm sorry I abandoned you. I was desperate and didn't know what else to do.

I didn't eat or sleep until I got to Connecticut. Sparing the details: It was a terrifying journey.

Biff's parents were cool with me staying at their house for a while, which I thought was amazingly nice of them. Biff's mom seemed a little bit put off by the Amber Taylor of it all, but she was very sweet to me. I stayed in their guest room for ten days, probably. Maybe two weeks. Long enough to catch up on sleep and watch a lot of television: *X-Files*, *ER*, *South Park*, and *Buffy the Vampire Slayer*.

One day, Biff said we should go into the city and have lunch. I was reluctant, thinking about the paparazzi who used to spot me coming out of the clubs late at night. I wasn't totally sure Amber Taylor would fool those guys, but Biff convinced me I was being silly. He took me to a diner on the Upper East Side. I was sitting there thinking how much I loved New York when my dad walked in, followed by a couple of transport goons.

Fuck.

I didn't say anything. Didn't move. Biff stared down at the table.

"Don't hate me," he whispered.

"I don't," I said. I figured it was karma for the way I dumped Mouse.

Another lesson learned: No matter what happened from here, I'd be better off alone. Always.

My dad stood next to the booth, blocking me from getting out. I breathed in the smell of his dry-cleaned suit, and I wanted to put my arms around him and tell him how much I missed him and Mom and Nicky and the boys. More than I'd ever wanted anything, I just wanted my dad to put his arms around me and take me home.

"Let's go, Paris." He said it quietly, not wanting to make a scene.

My throat felt hot and tight. I said, "My name is Amber. You must have me confused with someone else."

"Don't be ridiculous," he said. "I know it's you."

"No. I'm not who you think I am."

It's sad to think now how true that was.

"You don't know me," I said. "I don't know you."

I gripped the edge of the seat, but the transporter grabbed my arm and hauled me out of the booth. I started kicking and screaming. The goons stepped in with that "easy way/hard way" line, and I couldn't go the easy way, because I knew they were taking me to Provo. I went crazy on them, clawing and struggling. I didn't really expect to get away; I just wanted to make those dickheads work for it.

Hey—off topic, but not really—have you ever seen *Repo! The Genetic Opera*?

In 2006, I was looking to do something completely different. The producer Mark Burg, of Twisted Pictures, came to me with the weirdest idea I'd ever heard: an epic, gory, grand rock opera in the tradition of *Tommy*, *The Black Parade*, or *Quadrophenia*. Think *Saw* meets *Moulin Rouge*.

Repo! The Genetic Opera takes place in a dystopian world where the human race is plagued by genetic organ failure, so people have to buy transplant organs, and if they can't pay, the organs get repossessed by the fiendish slasher Repo Man, who's actually just a dad trying to protect his daughter Shilo. Meanwhile, Rottissimo, the heartless megarich titan who rules this nightmare world, finds out that he's dying, and he has to figure out which of his twisted children will inherit all his money and power: sadistic Luigi, insane Pavi, or beauty-obsessed Amber Sweet.

I spent several weeks studying the script and working on the music with Roger Love, the vocal coach who explained to me how being nervous manifests that baby voice I can't seem to get rid of. I auditioned for Mark and the director, Darren Lynn Bousman, who'd produced and directed three of the *Saw* movies, and they wanted me for Amber Sweet. It was an honor to be working with Paul Sorvino (Mira's dad, *Goodfellas*, etc.) who plays Rottissimo, and Sarah Brightman (*Phantom of the Opera*) as Blind Mag, who gouges out her own eyes and gets impaled on a fence. It's that kind of scene.

The script called for Amber Sweet to sing her face off—like literally sing until her face peels off the front of her head—so I'd have to continue my work with the vocal coach every day and spend hours in the chair getting prosthetics and makeup done. Several sick looks designed by Alex Kavanagh take Amber Sweet through a transformational arc from Rottissimo's bratty little girl to a raging transplant addict who trades sex for surgery.

After a limited theatrical release, the film went to DVD. There was a special screening at Comic-Con in 2010, and weirdly, it did really well in the Czech Republic. Lionsgate did distribution, and the film found a little niche of its own as a campy cult classic loved by a lot of the same people who love *The Rocky Horror Picture Show*. Goth girls dressed up as Amber Sweet for Halloween. I connected with a whole new fan base. I'm really proud of the vocal moments I found in that music. This soundtrack was insane—Rob Zombie, Guns N' Roses, Shawn "Clown" Crahan from Slipknot. We had so much fun on the set. Lots of fun memories.

Repo! is really a story about fathers and daughters.

One storyline is about a loving man who makes a terrible choice; trying to protect his fragile daughter, he imprisons her in a dark mansion. ("*She's been caged up like a monster by her overbearing father,*" the narrator sings.) The other storyline is about a terrible man who makes a loving choice; trying to empower his damaged daughter, he sacrifices his own vision of what her life should be.

In the Spirograph of memory and understanding, I see that my father and I embody both those stories.

Fathers and daughters. It's a tough dynamic. I don't know anyone who's gotten it 100 percent on either side. Ultimately, We the Daughters must accept that a father is more than the sum of his most difficult choices. I don't doubt my dad's love for me. I hope he knows how much I love him, how grateful I am for the advice and guidance he's given me, and how much I respect the role he played in our family's genetic opera.

At the end of *Repo!*, the Repo Man's daughter escapes, but everything comes to a disastrous end. In agony, he sings, *"Didn't I tell you not to go out?"*

"You did, you did," she answers, miserable, but not sorry.

"Didn't I tell you the world is cruel?"

"You did! You did!" sings the daughter.

But she knows the truth: being free and facing the world with all its monsters is better than being safe and leaving your life unlived.

There's a beautiful moment in the final act, when both fathers understand that the wild and beautiful daughters were never theirs to control. They could only teach by example. They could only love and let go. So they let go.

And it's okay.

I mean, it's awful. Terrifying. Bloody. Operatically tragic. But love endures. The fathers live on in their daughters. And in the end, Amber Sweet rules the world.

12

According to Mom, my parents didn't send me to Provo sight unseen. She says they went there, toured the place, and consulted with a therapist, and that there was never any talk of drugs, restraints, solitary confinement—none of that. Situated in a nice neighborhood near a golf course, Provo Canyon School appeared to be a conservative boarding school with pleasant grounds and well-maintained facilities. The tour didn't include the area where kids screamed in straitjackets, slept on the floor, and were locked in solitary confinement.

To me, it seems obvious that this place looked more like a prison or mental institution than a school. The classrooms were like an afterthought. But I do believe that my parents would never have sent me there if they'd known what was happening behind closed doors.

Remember, this was 1997. If you were cutting edge, you had dial-up internet that crawled out of a 56K modem. The guys who invented Google were still screwing around in a friend's garage. Troubled-teen facilities hid behind skillful marketing and daytime-TV endorsements. Thinking they were literally fighting for their child's life, parents signed over custodial rights and medical powers of attorney and agreed not to report suspected child abuse. Traumatized "graduates" were threatened and shamed into silence. The few who were strong enough to speak out had no way to connect or tell their stories until decades later.

Even now, with all the survivor stories pouring out on the internet, we don't hear many stories from the damaged families. Some parents are defensive and refuse to believe they could have been so wrong. Some parents are consumed by shame and guilt—especially parents who subsequently lost a child to suicide.

Mom and Dad had been through hell and back. I'm sure I don't know a fraction of what it was like or how it affected Nicky and my little brothers. The cover story to friends, relatives, and colleagues was that I was at boarding school in London. No one had any reason to doubt that. One of the heartbreaking aspects of all this is how isolating that must have been for Mom and Dad. I don't know who—if anyone—knew their secret. They were so distraught and exhausted by the time they got hold of me again, they weren't taking any chances. In their minds, Provo was the safest place for me: a lockdown facility. Kids went in and did not get out until they turned eighteen.

The transporters brought me to Provo in handcuffs. We went up in an elevator to a floor with an infirmary. Somewhere down the hall, someone was screaming. A girl was huddled on a bare mattress in the hall. Orderlies fell in step with the escorts and took me to a bare cinder-block room where a pig-faced matron waited with a creepy expression. Greedy. Hungry. A nurse who looked as small and nervous as a ferret said, "Face the mirror and take off your clothes."

Provo intake was a step beyond what I experienced at CEDU, Ascent, and Cascade. There was a full pelvic exam. When I tried to resist, Pigface said, "Open your legs for the nurse or we'll get someone to restrain you."

Nurse Ferret used a speculum to open me up and pushed gloved fingers inside me. I struggled to be still and not kick her in the face. Someone gave me faded sweats with the number 127 on the shirt. From that moment on, no staff member called me by my name. To them, I was 127, a numbered unit on an assembly line. They gave me the usual book of nonsensical rules and left me in an isolation room to study it.

The PCS rule book outlined a point system for achieving various levels where you could get weekly phone privileges and attend classes, but mostly it was an insanely long list of rules for absolutely everything: how to open a door, how to use the bathroom, how to stand up and sit down, how to speak and not speak, how to move and not move, how to trudge like soldiers to the cafeteria and stand in line like robots for meds. Failing to follow the impossible-to-follow rules meant corporal punishment, chemical or physical restraints, isolation in "Obs" (short for observation), or loss of privileges including visits and phone calls.

You started out in the hole with, like, five hundred IPs—Investment Points—and you were supposed to earn your way down to zero, but if you slouched, coughed, shuffled your feet, or got sleepy, someone would smack the back of your head and say, "Class ten!" which meant ten points got added. It took hours of sitting still to earn a few points, and they could take it all away in a matter of seconds.

I wasn't the only one sitting there with thousands of IPs. Failing to level up meant staying in Investment, so that's where I was almost the whole time. I don't recall ever being allowed outside. Eleven months without seeing the sky or breathing fresh air. I remember running around and around the gym, trying to help other girls keep up, because if one of us stumbled or slowed down, we were all punished. I scrubbed floors and cleaned toilets, trying to earn enough IPs to level up so I could call my parents or participate in group visits where boys were brought into the girls' area and we were allowed to sit at a table and talk.

Rebellious types slept on mattresses in the hall with the lights on and doors open. Staff came along once in a while to poke us to make sure we were breathing—or just because—so I never really slept. I just drifted in and out of this weird, twitchy state of semiconsciousness. My body was constantly on the alert, wired to wake up the instant someone touched me. If I dozed off, I went to a shallow nightmare place, haunted by an icky awareness of being watched.

Most people who worked there seemed to get off on degrading children and seeing them naked. They seemed to get a creepy pleasure from hitting, shoving, terrifying, and humiliating us. The few staff members who tried to be decent didn't last. Or their decency didn't last. I suppose they had to convince themselves they had no choice. All of them (as far as I knew) were Mormons, and most of them had gone to Brigham Young University, which—in their minds—was a big deal and somehow made them super-godly people.

That's so fucked up. People using religion—this holy thing—to manipulate and abuse people. Carter and I are both Catholic (officially), and I do believe in God, but churches give me anxiety. I'd rather just think about God on my own.

Instead of the chaotic Rap, Provo had "group therapy" where we sat in a circle—dry eyed and numb—and beat each other down with clumsy indifference. We were all so sedated, the screaming and weeping was minimal, but the objective was the same. We were supposed to tear each other down and tell on each other. Destroy any possibility of trust. Strip away any shred of self-esteem. It didn't matter if it was truth or lies; you got rewarded for being cruel. Turning us against each other kept us isolated and vulnerable. It was scary to see another person get slapped, choked, or thrown to the floor, but the shock was followed by a shiver of relief because it was somebody else. This time.

I cried a lot the first few weeks I was at Provo, but after a while, I didn't have the energy. Being observed in the shower, foul food, forced labor, endless screaming down the hall—this was my life now. Why fight it? I swallowed the pills and stared at the wall with the flawless mask of a runway model. Whatever they were giving me made me feel like my head was disconnected from my body. That scared me, so I figured out a way to fake-swallow it. When they made me open my mouth to show that I'd taken the pills, I tucked the capsules inside my lower lip and waited for an opportunity to discreetly spit them into a Kleenex.

That worked until some girl told on me. I saw her talking to Pigface. Pigface glanced in my direction. The girl scuttled off into a corner with that guilty *better you than me* expression on her druggy face, and I knew I was screwed.

"One two seven," Pigface said. "You think you're pretty smart, don't you?"

"I want to know what those pills are," I said. "I want to know who prescribed them and why."

"Obs. Twelve hours."

"You can't force me to take—"

"Twenty-four hours."

"Fuck you!"

When I turned to walk away, she picked up a phone and said,

"Dial 9 to Investment." Within seconds, heavy footsteps pounded up the stairs. I started to panic, because if a counselor did a Dial 9, you were immediately swarmed by orderlies. I've heard that a lot of these guys were red shirts recruited from the BYU football team. Some 250-pound running back would get injured and not be able to play, but he could still dominate a 98-pound kid with ease, and he needed money to replace his scholarship. If you resisted, one of them yanked your pants down, and Pigface jammed a syringe of "booty juice" into your butt cheek. I don't know what was in it, but I saw kids immediately go slack when it hit them. Within moments of the injection, they melted like cotton candy in the rain.

I tried to backpedal. "No, no! It's okay. I'm sorry! I'm sorry! It's fine. I'll be good. I don't need Obs."

"Take one two seven to Obs," Pigface told them.

"I'll be good! I'll be good! I don't need Obs!"

"Don't make it worse," she said.

I held up my hands to show the orderlies I wasn't going to struggle.

"You don't have to do this. I swear. I'll be good."

"Clothes off," said Pigface.

"No, no, *no, no, no, no!*"

Obs was an oddly shaped cinder-block chamber, not square, not circular—a hexagon maybe—about the size of a public restroom stall. There was nothing in there except a bucket and a roll of toilet paper on the cement floor near a drain hole. In the light of the open door, I saw blood and feces smeared on the wall. When the door slammed shut, the only light filtered through a small window with wire mesh inside the glass.

It was freezing cold. I read somewhere recently that they keep it between fifty-five and sixty degrees, but it felt as raw and frigid as a meat locker. They took your underwear and bra when you went to

Obs so you couldn't use them to kill yourself. Sometimes they gave girls shorts and a tank shirt made of a sort of gauzy muslin. Other times not. I don't remember having anything on that first time.

I paced, rubbing my arms, trying to warm up, staying close to the little light of the window. A girl in another room screamed and screamed for what seemed like a long time. She screamed herself hoarse and then fell into a rhythmic moaning that rose and fell like the sound of the ocean. I was reluctant to sit on the floor. It felt like ice under my feet, and a sickly crap smell lingered around the drain hole.

When I couldn't pace anymore, I scrunched down in a corner and put my arms around my folded knees, rubbing my legs. My hands and feet were numb. My core clenched in a hard knot. I couldn't even cry. I just *meep*ed like a baby bird who fell out of the nest. Stunned. Featherless.

And that's how you make someone want to kill herself with her own bra.

Shutting any kid into a cell like this is child abuse. For a kid with ADHD, it is straight up torture. And I'm positive most of the kids in these places are there because of ADHD behavior issues.

Eventually I was on the floor in a fetal position, my teeth chattering, my muscles screaming, my mind stuck in an endless loop: *This is so fucked up. This is so fucked up.* There was no doubt in my mind that I was going to die of hypothermia and my soul would be trapped in this shit-infested cinder-block tomb forever.

Time slipped out of joint, like a dislocated shoulder.

Silence.

The darkness was so all-consuming, the only way I could stay alive was to find a source of light inside myself. I don't know how else to explain it.

I fell inward, and I found a beautiful world.

I built a beautiful home.

I created a beautiful life.

This wasn't a nebulous daydream; it was a mechanically specific vision. I plotted logistics, built a Rolodex of possible allies, inventoried assets, and weighed liabilities. I made conscious decisions about playlists, puppy care, the boning of a corset, the citrus note in a floral fragrance. The minutiae took me in. The details comforted me. This architecture of love, music, roses, and all good things was as real to me as the Waldorf-Astoria was to my great-grandfather.

I didn't lose my grip on reality—I found it.

My nightmare life at Provo Canyon School was based on lies and mind games. My beautiful world was organic and sustainable because it flowed from the real me. My real life had nothing to do with the twisted existence these strangers manufactured for me.

Here's what I believe: Your reality is totally up for grabs; if you don't create your own life, someone else will create something based on their own agenda and project that on you. Don't let them do it, my loves. Don't let them tell you that their *something* is bigger than your *everything*.

Think about that famous René Magritte painting that shows a pipe with the words *Ceci n'est pas une pipe*. ("This is not a pipe.") Back in 1929, people looked at it and said, "Erm, I know what a pipe is, mate, and that's a pipe."

But it isn't a pipe. It's a *painting* of a pipe.

Magritte wasn't asking us to pretend that the painting is a real pipe; he was daring us to accept the smoking-hot *realness* of art.

The name of this painting, BTW, is *The Treachery of Images*, which is a perfect description of social media, isn't it? I love creating and consuming content, but it's possible to lose yourself if you forget that *life* and *images of life* are two very different things.

In 2017 I collaborated with a handful of brilliant people on *The American Meme*, a documentary that tries to unpack the difference between fifteen minutes of Vine fame and a sustainable, meaningful career as a performance artist.

Fun fact! The director, Bert Marcus, is the guy who kissed Nicole Richie in that sixth-grade game of Spin the Bottle back in chapter 2. See how the Spirograph keeps going? Past, present, and future always connecting.

But getting back to *The American Meme*: Some people say I opened the door on influencer culture the way Pandora opened the forbidden box. I'm willing to own the "OG influencer" thing, and I'm not saying everything about it is awesome, but it has been democratizing in both artistic and economic spaces. It's liberating for a lot of people who couldn't get past the old-style gatekeepers.

Disruption is scary for people who lack imagination, and *terrifying* for people who hold on to the old-school power structure. They don't like the idea that the future belongs to those of us who happen to be a little bit mad.

I couldn't have put this into words when I was seventeen, and these days I'm too busy to sit around contemplating the nature of reality, but I've always, on some level, rolled with Magritte's expanded definition of what *real* means. When I heard my father and grandfather talk about huge amounts of money involved in real estate, I knew they weren't talking about a physical truckload of cash. I grew up understanding that intellectual property is a tangible asset just as much as a hotel is. The only difference is that real estate is defined by boundaries; a creative mind is a limitless empire.

When VR came along—crypto, NFTs, the metaverse—I jumped in without hesitation. I couldn't understand why so many people resisted. A few months before I got married, I was on *The Tonight Show*, and Jimmy Fallon said, "I didn't know how into NFTs you were. Do you guys know what that is?" he asked the audience. Spattered applause indicated that a few people did.

"Like twelve people know," Jimmy said. "I barely know. Can you explain what an NFT is?"

"It's a nonfungible token," I said, "which is basically a digital contract that's on the blockchain, so you can sell anything from art to music to experiences, physical objects . . ." I suggested that he could sell a joke.

"Are you kidding?" he said. "I can't even do that to my audience tonight."

He got a good laugh, so let's use that as an example: Jimmy Fallon offers a joke and receives laughter in return. It's a transaction, one thing exchanged for another. The audience wants to experience the feeling they get from laughing; Jimmy wants the audience response that raises his stock as a comedian. So, the joke and the laughter both have real value. I love me some cash, but *value* doesn't always mean *money*. Diamonds are expensive, but time is far more precious.

Time is the most valuable natural resource we have.

Provo Canyon School robbed me of that precious commodity—my time—especially during those terrible hours in Obs. They took everything from me: light, space, comfort, my clothes, my name. We weren't allowed to dance, sing, or even hum. I had no canvas to paint, no clay to sculpt, no way to write, sketch, sew, collage—nothing.

But they couldn't take the core of who I am as a person.

As a creative.

My mind was my medium. Within myself, I had unlimited supplies of rhythm, color, and style. No rules. No limitations. No laws of gravity or physics.

I created a future world, a future self, a future life without boundaries.

That's how I survived while so many other kids were just gone.

Checked out. Someone was always screaming in a straitjacket or confined on suicide watch. Some ex-footballer orderly was always staring at me with his disconnected stare. Every time I ended up in Obs, I was terrified I'd come out like one of the zombie kids—lights on, nobody home—or like the soul-dead staff who were too jaded to feel anything.

I tried not to think about my family. I missed Nicky's voice and her commonsense take on everything. I was afraid my little brothers wouldn't even remember me. When I thought about my parents, I felt so deeply angry I hardly recognized myself. I didn't know it was possible to simultaneously love and hate someone as hard as I loved and hated my parents while I was huddled on that cement floor, freezing, starving, feeling chunks of my soul slip down the drain hole.

I focused on my inner empire.

What I would create. Who I would become.

My life after Provo would be everything. Instead of numbered sweats, I'd curate a designer wardrobe and never wear the same outfit twice. Instead of bloodshot eyes and a bruised face, I'd have lush fake lashes, a seamless spray tan, and a touch of glitter on my cheekbones. Instead of shame, I would wrap myself in audacity, and I would make so much money and be so successful, no one could ever have control over me again. Fuck trust. Fuck entitlement. Fuck inheritance. I would never take another dime from my parents. My belongings, my well-being, and my body would belong to me and me alone.

I kept my eyes on that small keyhole of light: February 17, 1999. My eighteenth birthday. Legally, I'd be an adult. More important: I'd be free.

Mom says I was at Provo Canyon School for eleven months: spring 1998 until January 1999. I know I was there that Christmas, because my family was allowed to visit, and my father shot some awkward home videos.

"Here's Starry's room," he says on the grainy film, working hard to sound like everything is okay. My little brother darts past the camera, bored silly, the only one honest enough to say he just wants to get the hell out of there.

Nicky stands awkwardly in the cramped space between the beds, towering over me with her chunky heels and supermodel posture. It's shocking to see us side by side. She's the picture of a vibrant, well-loved teen. The healthy smile of a California girl. The healthy confidence of a native New Yorker. I look like a goldfish out of its bowl: beaten down, emaciated, and shy, with dishwater brown hair and a forced fake smile. Baggy jeans and an Abercrombie shirt hang on my body, clothes bought for someone my family used to know.

My mom looks pinched and sad. She touches a plush toy bunny she'd sent to me the previous Easter, not understanding that this was the first time I was seeing it. The bed she was sitting on had been hastily jammed in next to a set of bunk beds so my parents wouldn't know I usually slept on a mattress in a hallway.

Pigface lingers in the shadows outside the open door.

This was just a couple of months before my eighteenth birthday, but I was so desperate to leave this place, that matter of weeks felt like an eternity. As my parents were set to go, I put my arms around my father and whispered in his ear.

"Dad, *please*. Get me out of here. You don't know what—"

"Starry, you need to finish what you started."

I leaned in close so Pigface wouldn't hear me. "*Get me out*. If you don't believe me when I tell you this place is fucked up, believe me when I say that I will leave here five seconds after I turn eighteen, go to the *Wall Street Journal*, and tell them everything. *Every. Thing.* I am not fucking kidding."

He drew back, looking a little stunned. But then he squared his jaw and said, "Merry Christmas, Star."

He hurried down the hall to catch up with Mom, who had Barron on one hand and Conrad on the other. Nicky glanced over her shoulder. It bothered me that I couldn't tell what she was thinking.

I think it was a couple weeks later when Pigface told me I was going home. She didn't look me in the eye, didn't say "good luck" or "go screw yourself"; she just walked away, in the anticlimactic couldn't-care-less way a bully would walk away after kicking down your sandcastle.

My parents came and got me a few weeks before my eighteenth birthday, and we all left together as if everything was hunky dory. We didn't talk about why I was getting out early, and I didn't care. It was one of the happiest moments of my life.

"It killed us to leave you there," Mom says now, "but we kept thinking—kept saying to each other—we have just a few months before she turns eighteen. After that, there's nothing we can do to save her."

Mom says they heard the rumors about stuff that went on at other emotional-growth boarding schools, but they assumed that sort of horror show was only at the low-rent places. They were paying top dollar, so it must be fine.

"Had we known," Mom says, "Dad and I would have been there in one second." And I believe her. It doesn't change what happened, but I do believe her, and I hope that brings them some comfort.

Twenty years later, the truth about Provo and the CEDU sister schools began to seep out on the internet. Brave survivors started telling their stories. It took me a long time to find the courage to open up about it, and when I added my voice to the growing survivor community, it was difficult for my parents to hear. They've taken a lot of flak for their decision to send me to CEDU and Provo. Industry gossip. Twitter. Social media. Some of it has been brutal. There were times when Mom felt so overwhelmed by it, she couldn't get out of bed. So it's important for me to acknowledge here that my parents also deserve some credit for my survival.

Rick and Kathy Hilton didn't raise a fragile little Fabergé-egg rich girl; they raised a badass kid who kept fighting, climbing, running. We've actually laughed about it a little.

"You were like Houdini!" Mom says. "Anywhere we put you, they'd call and say, 'She's gone!' and off we'd go again."

My stubborn streak, my staying power, compulsive work ethic, and creative vision—all that was in my bone marrow. I inherited determination and a love of life from my mom and dad. They gifted me with a spine and the idea that I was entitled to good things. I refused to accept that I was a worthless piece of garbage, even when a grown man twice my size wrapped his hands around my neck and squeezed off my windpipe, screaming in my face, "*YOU ARE A WORTHLESS PIECE OF GARBAGE.*"

I knew it wasn't true.

I knew I was a Hilton.

PART 3

*I'm a girl from a good family
who was very well brought up.
One day I turned my back on it all
and became a bohemian.*

BRIGITTE BARDOT

13

The year 1998 was basically a giant hole in my life—no music, no TV, no clue about pivotal changes in communication and technology or anything else going on in the world. In January 1999, I was released from Provo Canyon School, and Britney Spears dropped her debut album, . . . *Baby One More Time*. I couldn't get enough. The rebellious energy. The new way of mixing and editing music. She wears the music like a catsuit on that album. I was instantly dying to know: *How did they do that?* The shift in technology maybe wasn't so noticeable for some people, but I'd been music deprived for most of the past two years.

The video for the title track on . . . *Baby One More Time* starts out with Britney sitting in class, flicking her pencil and bouncing her foot as the agonized seconds click by. Then the bell rings. She's free.

That was so me.

That impatient schoolgirl dying to be free. And then she is. And she transforms and becomes herself. I loved the idea that a girl could own her sensual self like that and just enjoy it without shame or fear. But then there's that line that keeps repeating: *My loneliness is killing me.* Because a girl who doesn't conform, a girl who's disobedient and bold, a girl who shows her strength and sexuality—that girl is on her own, no matter how many boys dangle from her charm bracelet.

For two years, I was starved for music, for art, for food—everything that makes life beautiful or even bearable—but mostly I was starving for love. From the night I climbed out the window to kiss the pedophile, I had felt cut off from my family. That was the most brutal part of everything I'd been through. It wasn't the physical miles that separated us; it was layer upon layer of shame, lies, and denial.

To be a good "graduate" you were supposed to say that CEDU and Provo saved your life. They programmed us to believe that if you talked shit about the school, the school would talk worse shit about you—to your family, to potential employers, and in my case, to the tabloids. It was a powerful muzzle. Most survivors—including me—just wanted to get on with our lives and never think about those places ever again.

I recently asked another survivor, "How did you cope with things that first year after Provo?" and she said, "I drank until I was blind."

Self-medication is common among survivors. So is self-harm. It makes total sense. It takes a lot of effort to fake it in a world you no longer recognize, and advanced imaging shows that childhood trauma affects the brain: the nucleus accumbens, the pleasure center where addiction clicks in; the prefrontal cortex, where impulse control happens—or doesn't happen; the amygdala, where fear lives.

Nicky was the bright-yellow pool noodle who kept me from drowning during my first few months of freedom. While I was away, she had evolved past that knobby, pony-legged stage tall girls go through in junior high. At fifteen, she scored a sweet internship at a major fashion magazine and was dreaming of her own design empire. Elegance radiated from her skin, her hands, her feet, the set of her chin, everything about her. She had Dad's slender height and Mom's flawless social instincts. Nicky always knew the right thing to do, and she did it, but not in a prissy or fake way. She knew how to pull it off. She has her wildly creative side, but her overall vibe is wise, keep-it-classy virtue with an edge of cool intelligence—like Audrey Hepburn in *Funny Face*.

Nicky grew up with normalcy and nurturing. She thrived in the healthy school environment at Sacred Heart, learned from exposure to the rarefied social atmosphere of New York, and slept in a quiet room where she felt loved and protected. I was never jealous of my sister, but I was envious. While I was locked up, Nicky and I sort of switched places; she moved forward while I stood still—or was dragged backward. When I came out of Provo, she was fiercely protective of me, and I looked up to her, as if she had become the big sister and I was the little sis, always trying to catch up. I still feel that way today.

I wasn't that surprised to find that Nicky and my little brothers, my aunts and uncles, my grandparents, family friends—even Wendy White, who always knew everything—had no clue where I really was between summer 1997 and January 1999. The whole thing was an ugly little secret shared by Mom, Dad, and me. We didn't discuss it. It was like the previous seventeen months never happened.

Mom had a whole elaborate story I heard in bits and pieces when friends, hairdressers, and anyone else wondered why I disappeared so completely and reappeared so suddenly. Somebody called to interview her for a magazine article, and when they wouldn't accept her vague responses, she defaulted to prank-call mode.

"Well, Paris and Nicky interviewed at Sacred Heart. Nicky's about to graduate. It's been a wonderful experience for her. But Paris said, 'Mom, no way am I going to an all-girl school.' And so, she went to the performing arts high school, and she had a 3.8 GPA. She's very smart. But you know how that is with the serious ballerinas and the—the—anyway, she went to Dwight and just didn't bond with anyone there. Teachers. Students. It was just . . ."

She frowned, gripping the phone in her fist.

"Run away? Of course she didn't *run away*. That's—that's just one of those crazy . . . no. There was a stalker. Stalking her."

(The stalker part was true. That really did happen.)

"It was the most frightening thing I've ever been through. Here's this attractive girl being followed. Being stalked. We were getting bizarre things in the mail. We did everything to protect her. It was her senior year, so she graduated with homeschooling. In London. So, now, in addition to the Waldorf security, we have private security tailing them, watching every move they make. We see everything. Who, what, where, when."

I took my cue from Mom and stuck to that story. I was happy to cast her and Dad as vigilant, fully present parents. That's who they wanted to be. That's who they *are*: the parents who would go to the ends of the earth for their children. Only in my case, they went to the wrong end.

I no longer knew how to be myself around them. I was walking on eggshells, trying to say what I thought they wanted to hear. Pigface had warned me that, even after I aged out of Provo, my parents could commit me to a mental hospital anytime they wanted. I didn't really believe it at the time, but years later, I saw what happened to Britney—how her dad legally took control of her personal and professional life—and it shook me. My parents did their best to bring me back into the family dynamic, but there are some lessons you can't unlearn. Underscoring everything they did to show me how much they love me, there was this idea that had been drilled into me by my keepers at CEDU, Ascent, and Provo: *They sent you away. They couldn't stand you. You're an embarrassment to everyone you love.* That message played on steady repeat like the jagged edge of a jigsaw, etching a deep groove.

In my mind, love was conditional and couldn't be trusted. Love was something I didn't deserve but could manipulate if I kept it at a safe distance.

My little brothers were so funny and sweet. Barron was ten now and deliriously happy to see me. He just wanted to hang with me at the park; he didn't know many other adult(ish) people who were happy to go on the swings and slides and teeter-totter with him. Conrad was five and full of questions about bugs, animals, space, and science. They were both bright and adorable. I loved them to the moon and back, but there was a blank space in those relationships, and it would take a long time for us to fill it.

In any family where there's a big age difference between the oldest and youngest, it's almost like two different families. But this was more than that. Conrad had no memory of the time before I went to live with Gram Cracker. Between Palm Springs and CEDU, I was an agent of chaos, in daily conflict with my parents. Now I was back, and the tension was like a persistent ringing in my ear. I didn't want to be separated from my family again, but the minute I set foot in my family's apartment at the Waldorf, I knew I couldn't live there.

I was afraid to go to sleep in the room where I'd been abducted. I sat up doodling and sketching, listening to music, making lists, thinking about ways to make money and leverage the assets no one could take from me: my face, my name, my legs, modeling contacts, and experience on the runway—none of which would mean any-thing if I wasn't willing to work hard. And I was willing. I knew I could work like a rock hauler.

I tried, briefly, to finish high school at Canterbury, a Catholic boarding school in New Milford, Connecticut. They didn't torture children—props for that, Canterbury!—but Catholic school didn't work for me. One good thing: I got to play ice hockey. I always loved the Rockefeller Center skating rink as a kid. I was fast and fierce on the ice. Now I had a lot of aggression to work out, and hockey's great for that. I flew around swinging my big stick. I loved the fresh, cool air in the arena and the fresh, cool girls on the team.

I made a few fun friends who were happy to sneak out with me and go clubbing. Usually, we took the subway into the city, but one night, I treated us all to a limo. I told the driver to wait outside cam-pus, but he rolled up like, "Yes, I'm here for Paris Hilton." This was not well received. And it was the last straw. I'd been cutting classes and failing everything, so they kicked me out.

In 2007, Canterbury's director of finance told the *Danbury News-Times*: "Her goals and priorities were not the goals and priori-ties of the school."

I'll agree with that.

I went to Storm King, a wonderful place for rich fucked-up kids, but I got kicked out for the usual reasons, plus keeping ferrets under my bed. My last resort was Beekman, a tiny school a few blocks from the Waldorf, and I was just so bored, I was like, "Forget this."

There was nothing wrong with any of these places, but I had ex-actly zero transferable credits beyond ninth grade at Palm Springs. This was a rude surprise for my parents, who'd bought into CEDU's "integrated arts and academics" pitch. CEDU had an elaborate "graduation" ceremony where they handed out fake diplomas; Provo Canyon didn't even bother. So now, at age eighteen, I'd have to enroll as a tenth grader in any properly accredited high school, public or private.

Hard pass.

This whole shit storm had stolen two years from me, and that's like—what is that? Like 10 percent of my life at the time? No! More like 20 percent, isn't it? Because, like, two years would be a fifth of your life if you're twenty, and I was only eighteen, so—*ugh*. Forget it. I can't do math. *Math* got robbed from me, along with geography, algebra, socialization, healthy flirtation, how to conduct my body and value my soul. Everything a kid is supposed to get from high school—homecoming, prom, the whole Brat Pack sizzle reel—I got screwed out of all that. My education was how to scrub toilets and haul rocks, how to fight for my sanity, how to hurt people before they had a chance to hurt me. I was great at all that. Algebra, not so much.

I can't let myself think about it. It still pisses me off.

Bottom line: I wasn't made for school. Grinding away at it would only slow me down and make me feel worse about myself than I already did. I figured I'd get a GED someday if it ever became an issue.

I did my best to reconnect with my childhood friends, but I felt weirdly shy around them. When I was a kid, my bashfulness translated to silliness and overcompensation—constantly trying to make people laugh and show how brave and cool I was. I came out of Provo burdened with my natural shyness plus layers of trauma, degradation, and anger. I was locked into the London boarding school story, trying to avoid detailed conversation about it, and you know how it is when you're being dishonest; you second-guess everything. You question what other people think of you, because you don't know what to think of yourself, which makes you paranoid, and then you just want to run and hide.

That summer, I saw the movie *Big Daddy*, an Adam Sandler rom-com about a guy who—through a series of events that could only happen in an Adam Sandler rom-com—becomes the ad hoc father figure to a five-year-old boy. There's a great moment where they're walking down the street together, and Adam is telling this little boy that he'll have to get used to a new person who (Adam hopes) will be a big part of their life.

The little boy says, "I'm scared. What if she's not nice?"

Adam digs a pair of sunglasses from his pocket and says, "See these right here? These are magic sunglasses, okay? If you're afraid, you put 'em on, and they make you invisible. Keep those on and no one can notice you until you decide they can."

I was immediately like, *yes*. That works! That's why I always need my sunglasses with me, night or day. And that's what was in my heart when I did a line of Y2K-inspired sunglasses with Quay—a brand led by women—with a big chunk of the money going to Project Glimmer, a nonprofit dedicated to instilling confidence in forgotten girls. Girls in the foster and congregate-care systems. Girls with special needs. Girls who need to be seen, even when it's scary. I want them to know: *I see you—if that's okay with you*. It sounds silly, but that little magic-sunglasses coping mechanism made it possible for me to stand up and start my real life.

My first and best source of income was modeling. I knew how to walk and still had some connections, so my first move was to renew relationships with designers and several different modeling agencies in the US and Europe. The unfortunate trend at the time was the whole "heroin chic" thing—stick-thin body, sunken cheeks, and big, hungry eyes. After seventeen months of malnutrition, I was as thin as a blade of grass. I wasn't trying to be a size zero; I was a kid who'd been living in a state of near starvation. After several months of that, food was an afterthought. When I needed sustenance, I drank a Red Bull and kept on dancing.

In a way, 1999—that first year after Provo—felt a lot like skydiving: After a prolonged period of terror, self-doubt, and confusion, I launched into the sky, and this free-falling, high-speed gravity-rip took over.

The whole world was picking up speed.

Euros had become a thing. The new iMac said "Hello" and came in a selection of Easter-egg colors. Everyone had email now. And cell phones! When I lived in Palm Springs, Gram Cracker had a "mobile phone" the size of a submarine sandwich with an antenna sticking out the top. Now, everyone had these adorable little Nokia phones. I couldn't wait to get my hands on one.

Trying to reorient myself, I consumed movies, music, and television: *The Sixth Sense*, *The Matrix*, *Notting Hill*, *Austin Powers*. The Goo Goo Dolls and Eagle-Eye Cherry were still huge, but grunge was on the way out. House music had grown by galaxies with the advent of computer mixing and editing. Pop music was cleaner on the tech side and dirtier in the lyrics department.

Think Ricky Martin's "La Vida Loca":

*She'll make you take your clothes off and go dancing in the
     rain
She'll make you live her crazy life, but she'll take away your
     pain
Like a bullet to the brain.*

It was liberating and terrifying, and I was so there for it.

The first thing I did was dye my hair back to a Barbie platinum. (I'm a natural blonde, if you don't count hair color.) Feeling golden, I raided Nicky's closet and hit the clubs. If anyone asked where I was going, I said, "Out." I was eighteen now; no one could tell me what to do, what to wear, or how to feel. All I wanted was to recover some shred of happiness and lay the foundation for my independence. When I was out at night, rocking my magic sunglasses, all I felt was joy.

Euphoria—the emotion, not the show.

But can we talk about *Euphoria* the show for a minute? I mean, first of all, Zendaya is everything, but that show so gorgeously captures the thrashing, beautiful, frustrated, sensual, stupid, fun, crazy, sexy, dangerous, dazzling meaning of young adulthood unleashed. I hope people watch it and go, "Oh, yeah, maybe my kid's not as out of bounds as I thought she was. And maybe the world my kids are growing up in is a bit more complicated than the Blockbuster Video family-friendly aisle I grew up in."

Anyway. Euphoria. I was literally euphoric leaving that hellhole.

There was no time to rest or decompress. I had to do everything, now, before any more time was taken from me. I needed a team of people I could trust. This was a challenge, because my ability to trust anyone had been pretty much murdered. I could count on my dad's secretary, Wendy White, for honest bookkeeping and logistical support. I was angry at my parents, but I could count on them for candid, expert advice in matters of money, which also gave us a safe topic to talk about.

I also had Papa, who knew more about business than the collected faculty of any MBA program. Papa was overjoyed to answer questions about indemnities or the difference between Delaware corporations and LLCs. At the mention of profit-and-loss statements, he got a moonstruck "hello there!" look on his face and didn't stop talking for an hour. I didn't fully appreciate it at the time, but this was a super solid foundation on which to build the first phase of my business life.

When I told Papa I wanted to make a hundred million dollars, he didn't laugh or pat me on the head. He asked, "What for?"

"The usual stuff," I said. I didn't have a spreadsheet mentality about it, but I was fixed on that goal. I thought a hundred million dollars would make me feel safe.

"You can do it," said Papa. "Don't let people say you can't. When I was your age, I was a photographer for the US Navy during World War II. Learned to fly. Got my twin-engine rating at age nineteen. Came home from the war and started an aircraft leasing company."

Papa came up with twenty-five grand of his own to invest—against his father's advice—in a football franchise, which he cashed out of years later for ten million dollars. He founded the American Football League and bought the Los Angeles Chargers—all that and a lot more before he took the Hilton Corporation to the next level in Vegas with the Flamingo and the Las Vegas Hilton, where Elvis Presley played 837 consecutive sold-out concerts between 1969 and 1976. Like me, Papa was a tech nerd. He changed the casino business forever, pioneering "eye in the sky" visuals that made the pit a lot safer for visitors and less susceptible to cheaters, gropers, and other problematic people.

Vision. Maybe that's what I inherited from Conrad Hilton.

To be an agent of change, you have to get there first. Can you *see* it? And are you willing to trust your instincts?

When I moved back to LA in 1999, I felt like I'd missed so much. I had a huge appetite for fun, music, laughter, clothes, people, places, and just a lot of everything.

MUSIC CUE: Ultra Naté, "Free"

This was my anthem after I left Provo. Go listen to it. Right now. And dance. Seriously. Your soul will be changed.

To this day, when I play it in a show, the iconic opening chord progression brings tears to my eyes. I'm instantly back in New York, dancing at a club where they projected the video on the wall—a bigger-than-life image of this stunning woman in a silver straitjacket. She stands in the middle of a cold, clinical environment that felt horribly familiar to me.

Then comes the unstoppable pulse of the music.

At first, there's sorrow in the lyrics:

Where did we go wrong?
Where did we lose our faith?

The despair is undeniable, but as the song evolves, joy takes over.

You want it, you want it, reach for it

Euphoria.
Ambition.
Possibility.

It made me feel giddy and elated, like I could do this—all this, everything I had to do—I could do it.

Do what you want to do . . .

Months of visualizing and planning distilled to a driving ambition that powered me the same way the bass line powers that song. I went out, telling Dad it was "networking"—and it was—but mostly I just wanted to have fun and feel happy.

My love-hate relationship with sleep kept me going. No matter how exhausted I was—literally nodding off in the cab at three in the morning—as soon as I lay down in bed, I was wide awake. I couldn't sleep with the lights on, and I couldn't turn the lights off. Because in the dark, they came for me.

In the dark, I heard hushed voices in the stairwell.

Water dripping in a metal sink. Footsteps. Down the hall. Like distant thunder. Closer. Coming closer. Right outside my door. And then—

Hands.

Grabbing the back of my neck.

Clamping down on my mouth.

And then I was back in that dank cement cell. Or running through the woods where the dead children were buried. Or staring at a wall, paralyzed by fear, aching to wake up, trying to force myself to scream, and when the screaming finally came out of me for real, it jolted me wide awake. Heart pounding. Cold sweat tickling the back of my neck. I sat up in bed, and I knew I would have to stay there, knees pulled up to my chest, even if I had to pee, because if I set my foot on the floor, a hand might reach out and grab my ankle.

this is not real
this is not real
stop being stupid
this is not real

I coached, berated, and trained myself not to think about those things that had happened. And those other things that had happened.

They called it a "medical exam." And because I wasn't ready to call it "digital rape," I called it a medical exam, too. Before CEDU/ Provo, I'd never been to a gynecologist. I was a kid with only a vague idea of what that even meant.

The staff at Provo had their favorites. Always pretty girls. But I don't think it was about pretty. I think these were weak people in the outside world, men and women who got off on the power they had over us. They took us to the infirmary and made us lie on the table. Made us open our legs for their stubby fingers. If we resisted, they had the booty juice ready. There was always a tray with syringes.

One of the girls who, like me, got taken to the infirmary on a regular basis—I'm just going to call her Needles—came to me and one other girl while we were cleaning the bathroom and whispered, "If they come for us tonight, I'm getting out."

I was immediately interested. "How?"

"We get his keys. Whoever's on the table closer to the supply cabinet—grab the syringes and stab him."

"What if it's too much?" the other girl asked. "What if he dies?"

"What if *we* die?" said Needles. "Paris, c'mon."

Needles made the point that I was tallest and could get him in the neck.

"I'll grab the keys," I said, "but I can't stab the guy. Seriously. I can't."

But I was kinda thinking, *Could I, though?* That's how far I'd turned.

It didn't matter. The other girl immediately reported the conversation to Pigface, and Needles threw me under the bus, claiming the stabby part was my idea. I didn't blame her. I understood the *say anything* desperation she must have felt when Pigface confronted her. Pigface gleefully sent me to Obs, and as soon as I got out—what a coincidence—it was time for another late-night gynecology exam.

After I got out of Provo, I thought of myself as a grown woman, and I wanted to have grown-up relationships with men, but the thought of going to a gynecologist for an exam and birth control terrified me. I couldn't separate that word from what those Provo people did. Those perverted fucks with their gloved thumbs and sunken eyes and this very specific kind of creepy laughter. The kind of laughter you'd hear from a kid as he pulls the wings off a baby bird or tortures a squirrel in a homemade trap.

I tried to smother the memory of that laughter with alcohol, Molly, and music, but even if I fell into bed, danced-out and drunk as the sun came up, I always woke up within an hour or two, sweating and screaming. I found more meaningful rest in cars, airplanes, makeup chairs, or even a dark corner with the comforting chaos of a party going on around me.

The only way I could sleep in my own bed—alone or otherwise—was if I had my dogs with me. Back then, I had two sweet teacup Pomeranians: Sebastian (named after Ryan Phillippe's character in *Cruel Intentions*) and Dolce (self-explanatory). They weren't trained as such, but these were therapy dogs in the truest sense. All that CEDU "emotional growth" BS left me with an abiding fear of human therapists, and I thought I'd die if any of my friends or cousins knew what had really happened to me. My dogs were my support network.

Dolce and Sebastian didn't question my choices or prod me to talk about my feelings. They didn't try to unpack or understand me. They were just there, following me when I paced in circles or piling on top of me when I curled up in a corner on my closet floor.

Dog love has always been my sanctuary.

My current cutesy crew—Diamond Baby, Harajuku Bitch, Slivington, Ether, and Crypto—live in their own mini Dream House in my backyard. It's big enough that I can crawl in there if they need me. Or if I need them. A mini Dream House is not over the top at all when you consider that my dogs surround me with a fortress of love.

Mornings were usually pretty rocky for me. I was grateful for an hour or two of dreamless sleep, if it finally came, but I usually got up feeling like I'd slammed my head in a car door. My stomach churned, empty and tight. My jaw throbbed from clenching my teeth. I forced my forehead to relax, because I didn't want to develop a line between my eyebrows.

By midafternoon, I was ready to chow down on whatever fast food was available. I lived for McDonald's and Taco Bell, and I could eat a gross amount of fat and calories, because I never sat still. I was constantly trotting, skipping, hustling, hopping, and dancing. I never sat down while I checked my messages, returned calls, and paged through the papers, soaking up the gossip and planning my evening. At night, I came alive.

There's nothing like that LA nightlife anymore. Back then, we didn't have to deal with any of the exposure and distractions that consume people now. Twitter and Facebook hadn't been invented yet. Netflix was a thing where you literally received a physical disc in a bright red envelope via snail mail, played it in a DVD player, and then mailed it back to Netflix in the same envelope with a little flap torn off. If you wanted to see people, engage in conversation, hear music, and develop a network, going out was a way of life. You were never troubled by the idea that someone was going to film you doing something idiotic, and if they did, so what? Who were they going to share it with? There was no YouTube, either.

I had no stylist, no agent, no managers, no publicist. My friends and I were just out there every night, wearing whatever we felt like wearing, finding our own style and having fun with our hair and makeup. Some of my looks back then were way over the top, but my childhood had been stolen from me before I was done playing dress-up; I earned all that extra.

Mom and Nicky shopped for the big labels at Henri Bendel, but I was a downtown girl. My favorite boutique was Hotel Venus, a rave store owned by Patricia Field, the costume designer for *Sex and the City*. I went in there with my mom's credit card and loaded up on platform boots, micro-minis, and several sick outfits my mom hated. When the bill came in, Mom thought I'd spent the money at an actual hotel, and she called them up demanding to know what the hell her daughter was doing there.

Nicky and I both wore a lot of Heatherette and walked in a lot of Heatherette shows. This adorably campy brand was founded in 1999 by Richie Rich, a performing artist with Club Kids, and Traver Rains, a Montana farm boy who somehow ended up in the New York fashion world. I read somewhere that they named the brand after their friend Heather, an opera singer with one leg. Clearly, it was destined for out-there greatness.

I lived for Heatherette's rave tanks—glittery, glammy, heavily bedazzled tops worn by Britney, Madonna, and Gwen Stefani. I think one of those little tops made an appearance on *Sex and the City*, which was a serious style barometer at the time. You could pair these little tops with jeans or a little skirt or just about anything, and because they were designed by a dancer, you could rage all night, look great, and be comfortable. They also made the sickest, sparkliest little dresses.

Oh, come back, Heatherette! I miss your crazy charm.

My calendar was jammed with events at various clubs, private homes, and Avalon, a huge event space in an old building on Hollywood and Vine. I made a point of attending events thrown by Brent Bolthouse, my old friend who had planned my sweet-sixteen party, and learned a lot from the way he curated parties based on the right mix of talent and experience rather than fame and money. There were no random people, no crashers, no desperados. It was all people you knew or wanted to know—interesting people having interesting conversations about art, music, and movies.

People trusted each other. I felt safe, even when I drank too much. It was all so much fun. (Remember *fun*?) There were signs: NO CAMERAS. Purses and pockets were checked at the door to make sure no one brought in those little disposable cameras we used before smartphones were a thing. Now you can't keep the cameras out because no one wants to give up their phone. You'd get less resistance if you asked them to donate a kidney at the door.

I'm not judging. I'd give up the kidney in a heartbeat. My phone is like my jet pack. I have five dedicated phones, separate numbers for work, personal, Europe, prank calling, and one more with a number I give out if people ask me for my number but I don't feel totally comfortable giving my *real* real number and I don't want to be mean, because I'm a pathological people pleaser. Even Carter can't get me to part with more than two of these phones, and believe me, he has tried.

Kids who grew up with smartphones, Facebook, and Instagram never got to experience a club or house party where they were totally free to be themselves without feeling like they were constantly on guard.

My friend Holly Wiersma, who later produced *Dallas Buyers Club*, produced a doc called *Guest List Only*—a character study of people on both sides of the velvet rope—starring club promoter Sarah Uphoff (everyone called her "Pantera Sarah") and me along with other regulars at Opium Den, Dublin's, and Vinyl—all my favorite LA hangouts. I remember Sarah running the door, selecting who was in and who was out. People loved to come out with me because I was always in, and I was always in because I always had an amazing group of cool people with me. I was curating an incredible circle of friends—and not just the famous people you already know about. I'm talking about wonderfully strange, creative people whose names you may not recognize, even though they made LA the wonderfully strange, creative place it was. I loved hanging with artists, poets, musicians, filmmakers, writers, and technology geeks.

A friend asked me to be in an indie film called *Sweetie Pie*, which was beyond lame, but to me, it was a big deal. I was in the movies! Seriously, it was a great way to start learning about the process. That's the kind of education that works for me. I need to be on my feet, asking questions, part of the action.

I started learning my way around the recording studio the same way. I met a producer who'd worked with Jessica Simpson and Kelly Rowland, and we collaborated on the early recordings that would eventually grow into my first album. The studio was heaven to me, combining two things I love almost as much as I love my own skin: music and technology. The migration of music into the computer world—we take it for granted now, but back then, it was this rush of freedom and empowerment. Creators didn't need permission anymore; before GarageBand, before Logic Pro, there was just good old Logic—democratizing software that opened the garage door and let everybody in.

The paparazzi were evolving with digital cameras and lightweight video equipment that made it possible for them to get airable walk-and-talk film footage and crisper, higher-definition photos with virtually any kind of lighting. Going out almost every night in LA and New York, I was getting a lot of attention, which I loved. It made me feel like a star. After that long period of never being allowed to look in a mirror, I enjoyed feeling beautiful.

Instead of cussing or avoiding the paps like a lot of people did, I waved and called out, "Hey, boys!" and made sure they got all the good angles of me struggling with my shopping bags or getting frozen yogurt and being all Marilyn Monroe on the subway grate. They could get more money for candid shots. Unlike a red carpet, where dozens of photographers are all taking essentially the same picture, the candid shots were unique. Tabloids craved photos of a celebrity in an unguarded moment, eating a burger or walking the dog, as if they were a real person. The paps weren't allowed to come inside a club and bother people, so they camped outside, waiting for us to come out.

I bought some adorable sneakers at a little place on Melrose. Roller skates popped out of the bottom when you pushed a button on the side. Those were my favorite clubbing shoes of all time. I zoomed all over the place. If a pushy guy hit on me, I zipped off across the dance floor. It made for good video—me zooming up and down the street, in and out of parties and night spots. People started calling me "Roller Girl," which I loved. They might have been referring to the Roller Girl porn star in *Boogie Nights*, but that movie came out while I was at Ascent, so I didn't know anything about it until years later.

The Penfifteen Club did a song called "Ms. Hilton" that kinda says it all:

Ms. Hilton, you must be worth a trillion bucks.
Get the feelin' that you really don't give a fuck.
Ms. Hilton, I like the way you push and glide.
Roller skates on a social butterfly, woo!

A few years later, this song was on the *Simple Life* soundtrack, but it was written back when I wasn't famous, just starting to be known a little. Even then, I knew I wasn't trying to build an ordinary career; I was building a brand that would eventually turn into multiple income streams—but that sounds way more calculated than it was. Looking back, I see the mechanics of it falling into place, but at the time, I was just a teenager, having fun without apology, without inhibition. That made fun people want to hang out with me, and when I showed up at a party with a crew of models, actors, and socialites, the paparazzi always followed, so pictures would show up in Page Six or *People* or the early online gossip blogs. Event planners *really* wanted me at their parties.

I'm not talking about the Lipschitz wedding or your cousin Jill's living room hang; I'm talking about gallery openings, film premieres, and product launches—business functions and nonprofit-organization galas—parties with a purpose. There's a lot at stake in those red-carpet events. People invest a lot of money sponsoring them. You see how all those red carpets are stretched out in front of a wall covered with logos, right? If nobody interesting shows up to stand in front of it, that's a stupidly expensive lost opportunity. They need beautiful people on that red carpet to draw the attention of the paparazzi. When my picture appeared in Page Six, *WWD*, tabloids, entertainment sections—wherever—that sponsor got the exposure they were hoping for, and the pap got paid for licensed use of the image. So I started thinking: *What's in it for me?*

I was having fun, but I was bringing a lot to the table. Why shouldn't I get paid to show up at that party and magnify that brand?

It's kind of hilarious to me when people assume I was putting myself out there because I craved attention like a pound puppy. I loved feeling special—of course—but I started making real money when I realized that I was an amplifier and attention was the power cord. I transformed attention into a marketable commodity to benefit brands I believed in—including my own. I always knew, on some level, that there was a difference between that kind of attention and love. But sometimes, when love didn't come along, the constant clicking was an okay substitute.

Before Carter and I got together, he and his brother, Courtney, wrote a book called *Shortcut Your Startup: Speed Up Success with Unconventional Advice from the Trenches* (Gallery Books, 2018).

If that book had been available when I first started building my businesses—oh, wait. Never mind. I wouldn't have read it. I wasn't really in book-reading mode. Now, I'm kind of a business-book addict. I make Carter drag an extra carry-on so I can load up before a flight at the airport bookstore. Back then, I was just living my life moment to moment, but I was doing things that hadn't been invented—like taking selfies. I didn't stop to wonder what to call it or if it added up to some kind of strategy.

Anyway. *Shortcut Your Startup.*

In their book, Carter and Courtney pose "three key questions before you start anything":

1. What does success look like for you?
2. Why has no one else done this?
3. Why you, why now?

Looking back on the start-up I didn't even know I was starting up:

1. Success, for me, looked like a grand ballet of security, respect, and the ability to help other people. I wanted to bulletproof my independence, show the world what I was capable of, and facilitate brands and artists I believed in. That's still what success looks like for me, even now. My core vision has never changed, and while it does involve raking in as much money as I can generate, it's never been about money for money's sake. It's always been about how I wanted to feel, not what I wanted to get.
2. I think no one else had ever done what I did, because no one has ever been me before: a specific girl, born at the dawning of the Age of Aquarius, with my unique

combination of advantages that lifted me up and disadvantages that forced me to grow. I'm sure I wasn't the first socialite to do the math on the party equation, but my experience and resolve gave me the nerve to ask. Making the ask is where so many entrepreneurial endeavors die. Pride gets in the way. Or the lame idea of "that's not how it's always been done." My pride had been taken from me, and I didn't know or care how things had been done in the past. I was doing everything in my power to burn my past to the ground. So, I made the ask, and like Jesus said: "Ask and it shall be given unto you."

3. Why me? Because I didn't trust anyone else. And why now? Because now is all there is. Now is all that matters. This may be my ADHD talking, but *now* is the only universe worth living in.

New Year's Eve 1999, I partied like—well, you know.

Some people were weirdly freaked out by the idea of Y2K, but I gladly turned the page. New year, new decade, new century. Embracing the idea that this would be my best millennium ever, I launched into a lifestyle of constant work and travel that continued for the next twenty years.

14

The first step to self-reinvention is inventory. Give yourself credit for everything you've got going for you. Whatever's going against you, figure out how to use it to your advantage.

I turned nineteen in February 2000. I knew what I had going for me, and it was a lot. I was strong. I was beautiful. I could make people laugh. I knew where to go and how to be seen. I signed with a major modeling agency, I continued to build my side business—getting paid to party—and I started paying closer attention to conversations about real estate and investing. It was an interesting moment for Hilton International. There was talk about a hotel on the moon, but Papa was still chairman of the board, and his feet were firmly on the ground. Hilton acquired Doubletree, Hampton, Homewood, and Embassy Suites. They already had Bally's and Caesars in Las Vegas.

I told Papa, "I think I want to have my own hotels someday."

Most people would have looked at me like I was suggesting a hotel on the moon, but my grandfather was like, "Of course. You should totally do that." He didn't offer to help me, but he and Dad answered questions and coached me through some early dealings. I knew I needed a manager, but I didn't know who to trust, other than Dad and Papa. I hated the thought of giving up a percentage of my earnings, so I created a fake manager with her own email and her brusque, smoky voice on the phone.

"Yes, I received your offer and confirmed availability for Miss Hilton. If we can compromise on that back-end percentage and do another ten K up front, I think we have a deal. Yes, I'll fax you her signature."

I don't remember the fake manager's name, but she was like a grown-up version of Amber Taylor. She negotiated for me like a pit bull. Even after I signed with a major modeling agency, I kept her around for odd jobs.

In May 2000, I went to the Cannes Film Festival for the first time. I dragged way too much luggage with me, because every day had at least three or four looks: breezy walk around town bumping into movie stars look, tasteful lounging by the pool like Marilyn Monroe look, stunning evening out at the art films look. I put a lot of work into my look for a lunch with one of the most powerful men in Hollywood. I wanted Harvey Weinstein to see a woman who belonged in the business: classy, beautiful, castable, and different from all the other nineteen-year-old girls with big movie star dreams. I was with a producer friend who was trying to pitch a project. This was an amazing opportunity for both of us, and we wanted to make a good impression.

The lunch was not a success. The producer sat there cringing and saying nothing while Harvey made pervy, weird comments about me and my potentially huge future in his world. He was as creepy and aggressive as a person could be over lunch in a crowded restaurant. We left with very little hope for my friend's project.

The next night I attended an amfAR (American Foundation for AIDS Research) event. Harvey saw me across the room and called out to me; I tried to pretend I didn't see him and walked away. He followed me.

I walked faster.

He walked faster.

I headed for the ladies' room with my unicorn trot and locked myself in a stall before he came in. He pounded on the stall door and yanked on the handle, yelling gross, drunk nonsense like "Ya wanna be a star?" and I was just trapped in there like, *Where the fuck is a bathroom window when you need one?* until the French security men came in and forced him out of the ladies' room. He was yelling, "This is my event! I'm Harvey Weinstein!" but they didn't understand—or didn't care—and literally dragged him out.

I told no one, because that's what you did back then. It was like the bucket shower thing; if you wanted to survive, you just accepted it. Years later, when the scandal happened and the Weinstein power structure started to crumble, reporters kept asking me, "Have you ever had a Harvey Weinstein thing?"

And I said, "Nope."

I was embarrassed by it, and I have a pathological fear of embarrassment. I was afraid that if I shared that story, the next question would be, "Why didn't you speak up at the time?" and I had no answer for that. That's one of those questions that shifts blame onto someone who shouldn't have to own it.

Like "Why didn't you scream?"

Or "Why didn't you kick him in the balls?"

There's no answer to these questions other than, "Why don't

you go fuck yourself?" I admire the courageous women who stepped up and called him out, but every woman who went through something with him—and others like him—has the right to process it in the way that works for her. No woman should be shamed for taking care of herself.

That year at Cannes, the Palme d'Or went to the Björk movie, *Dancer in the Dark*, about a factory worker who's going blind. At a sad point in the film, she says, "I've got little games that I play when it goes really hard . . . I just start dreaming, and it all becomes music."

That's a good description of my coping skills back then. And now.

I was walking a lot of red carpets, feeling long legged and strong, figuring out my own style. Having missed a pivotal year of pop culture and style influence, I had no choice but to invent my own. It made me feel insecure, and it shouldn't have, because inventing your style is liberating. If you follow the crowd, you're too late; whoever blazed that trail has moved on, so you may as well blaze a trail that suits you, even if other people don't understand it.

Fashion reporters frequently mentioned my "distinctive walk" on the runway—some loving it, some hating it—but I didn't know what that meant. Now, when I see pictures from those first two years after Provo, I see a weight on my shoulders. I carried so much anger, hurt, and shame in my posture. I guess it came off as nonchalance. Coolness. No fucks given. But it was actually the walk of a girl interrupted, always in a hurry to catch up with herself.

"The Real Slim Shady" was the song of the moment, and we danced, doing a wide one-arm wave, that flat refrain repeating with the strobe lights:

please stand up
please stand up

In my mind, it was a song celebrating imposter-hood—the way we all posed and pretended to be tough—the only thing we all had in common.

One night, Nicky and I were in a club, doing karaoke, and we noticed a guy staring at us. He was hot—or maybe just projected that self-assurance that makes people believe you're hot. If you know in your heart that you're hot, you are hot, according to the laws of hotness physics.

This guy was older than me. Coarse. Arrogant. The overconfident "bad boy" from central casting, the perfect guy for a girl going through the most self-destructive moment of her life. I wasn't looking for Mr. Right; I was looking for Mr. Spite. His nickname—which he loved—was "Scum." I thought that was so badass.

We started dating, and I have to give credit where credit is due; he was every bit as charming as Mr. Abercrombie. It was all very thrilling and naughty—a whole new brand of adrenaline. I was obsessed.

I don't remember that much about the night he wanted to make a videotape while we made love. He had often said it was something he did with other women, but I felt weird and uncomfortable about it. I always told him, "I can't. It's too embarrassing."

He kept pushing. I kept making excuses: I was tipsy and tired from a long night of partying. The lighting wasn't good. My hair and makeup were beyond. He told me I always looked gorgeous no matter what and that it shouldn't matter anyway, because this wasn't a performance. It was just for us. No one else would ever see it. And then he told me if I wouldn't do it, he could easily find someone who would, and that was the worst thing I could think of—to be dumped by this grown man because I was a stupid kid who didn't know how to play grown-up games.

The truth is, I wanted to be alive in a sensual way. I wanted to feel like a woman who's comfortable in her own skin. I was struggling to understand my sexuality; there's no way I could have explained it to anyone else. I had no language for it. I'd never heard the word *asexual*.

I know, right?

The world thinks of me as a sex symbol, and I'm here for that, because *symbol* literally means *icon*. But when people saw that sex tape, they didn't say *icon*, they said *slut*. They said *whore*. And they weren't shy about it. The ironic thing is, because of the abuse and degradation I survived as a teen—and maybe partly because of the way I was raised—I feared sex. I hated the idea of sex. I avoided sex until it was absolutely unavoidable.

Tabloids created this narrative about me sleeping around with a hundred gorgeous guys—not the truth at all! I longed to feel close to someone, to be intimate. If a guy was kind and took his time, I could go on kissing and snuggling forever, thinking, *Okay, maybe this time. This time it could happen.* And then I would freak out and be weird, and the situation became awkward, leaving me with two shitty options:

A: I could cut him off and have him dump me and tell everyone I was "frigid" or "a cock-tease" or "a dyke."

B: I could fake it—and I was good at faking it, but it felt like getting run over by a minibike a hundred times.

My friends were like, "Oh, it's so good"—like orgasms all the time. And I was thinking, *Sure. That doesn't even exist.* I thought it was something in the movies. I didn't even believe it was real because that free, playful part of me was completely closed off. I thought orgasm was something faked so sex could be over. I kept trying to make it work. Part of the princess brand is a prince, right? But it was pretty rare for a guy to get past the make-out stage. Some of them waited for months or even a year.

I called myself the Kissing Bandit.

They called me Princess Blue Baller.

Mom always said, "Don't do it till you're married. The guy will be obsessed with you if you don't do it." That might have worked on *Happy Days*, but it didn't work on any guys I dated. They'd be like, *What the hell?*—and then they'd cheat, and I'd find out, and then drama, drama, drama, breakup. It was a vicious cycle. Like *Groundhog Day* without the adorable groundhog.

I hope this isn't TMI. It's weird to talk about it, but I don't think I'm the only girl who's gone through this kind of thing. I appreciate how the conversation around sexual identity has evolved to take in all kinds and to recognize that sexuality is fluid. People grow and change. Healing happens, but damage runs deep. I don't know if I'll ever be fully healed or fully who I might have been.

Did I mention Carter has a degree in psychology?

He does. And it comes in handy.

Sex is a thought process for me. It has to start in my brain, or it's not going to work. Carter gets that, and he lets me know I'm worth the effort. He's going to be so embarrassed that I'm talking about this—and *I'm so embarrassed*. Oh, my god, this is so fucking embarrassing! But I promised myself I would be truthful, and I know there's someone out there who needs to hear that they're not weird or frigid or dead inside—they're just who they are at this moment: an asexual person in a hypersexualized world.

The thing is, Mom was right.

(Did you hear that, Mom? I said it. You were totally right.)

Making guys wait, protecting myself, and not giving it up all over the place actually did work better for me in the long run. If I'd been fucking around as much as the tabloids made it seem, what little self-esteem I had left would have been chewed to bits. It's true; we all want what we can't have. And back then, this is the thing I couldn't have. My sexy clothes, music, videos—the whole Carl's Jr. burger-eating routine—that was my way of reclaiming a healthy sexuality that had been robbed from me. It made me feel alive and playful in a way I wish I could have been when I was in bed with someone I cared about. I have that now with my husband, and I cherish it. At nineteen, all I could do was pretend.

I wasn't capable of the level of trust required to make a videotape like that. I had to drink myself silly. Quaaludes helped.

But I did it. I have to own that. I knew what he wanted, and I went with it.

I needed to prove something to him and to myself, so I got hammered, and I did it.

Despite the age difference and the logistics of my high-mileage work life, the relationship with this guy went on and off for a couple of years—which is a long time to a teenage girl. Eventually, I got bored and pissed him off. One night, my girlfriends and I were out for karaoke, and ran into Nicolas Cage, who invited us to an after-party. We didn't go because it was Nic Cage. We would have gone to an after-party at Billy Bob Nobody's house just as readily. Because *after-party*! Bring it. So we went to this house where there was a car and a motorcycle in the living room and a shrunken-head collection upstairs, and a good time was had by all.

When I got back to my house, the on/off boyfriend was there, upset that I had not been returning his calls. There was a bit of drama, and that was that. This is actually how most of my relationships ended over the years. I hate confrontations, so I always tried to ghost the person. Sometimes they got the message. Sometimes they got mad. This was definitely not the ugliest scene resulting from that MO. For a long time, I thought that if someone got so jealous they threw a phone at your head or grabbed you and shook you till your neckbones rattled—well, that must mean they *reeeeeeally* loved you, right?

Ugh.

One weird footnote to the shrunken-head party was that some woman came over to me at a club a few days later and threw a glass of red wine in my face. Not sure what that was about. I'd already moved on.

That videotape never crossed my mind.

Why would it?

There was no YouTube back then, no way for a regular person to upload something like that onto the internet. The technology for humiliating someone on that level hadn't been invented yet.

On New Year's Eve 2000, I celebrated with a trip to Vegas, where I went into an exotic pet store and came out two hours later with several small animals including two ferrets and a baby goat. When I got to the airport with all these pet crates and supplies, the gate agent told me, "This is not a traveling zoo." I had to rent a limo and travel through ten hours of New Year's Eve traffic back to LA by myself with my new animal friends crapping all over the seats. I spent the first few hours of 2001 drinking champagne and helping the driver clean it all up.

Thus, the aughts were defined as the decade of *extra*.

15

I loved the early 2000s party vibe even more than the late 1990s; you were encouraged to be out there and be extra. *What Not to Wear* wasn't until 2003, and *Fashion Police* didn't come into play until 2010, after Twitter had gotten a choke hold on everyone's ability to think for themselves. I don't know why there's never been a show celebrating style that's unique and fully individual, but you know what? You don't need permission to be an icon.

Madonna's tulle skirts with biker boots.

Sarah Jessica Parker's circle skirts and fascinators.

Gaga's elevator boots and meat dress.

Somebody had to do it first, right? It doesn't matter if the people around you don't get it right now; one beautiful thing about the internet is that the moment lives on for all time. Björk's Marjan

Pejoski swan dress at the Oscars got laughed at in 2001. Now it's iconic.

The reverse is true, too, of course. The bad moments also live on and probably get more retweets. But the takeaway is, *wear what makes you feel good.* When I share looks, ideas, and products as an influencer, my goal is not to teach you how to please other people; I'm encouraging you to please yourself. Even if the particular look doesn't stand the test of time, the memory of that good feeling will. And who knows? The look might experience a moment when the time is right. Papa used to say, "Even a broken clock is right twice a day." Style goes around and comes around: Spirograph, not Etch-a-Sketch.

I moved into a huge house with two other girls—Playboy bunnies Jennifer Rovero and Nicole Lenz—who were always ready to party and had standing invitations to anything happening at the Playboy Mansion. We each had our own floor with big bedrooms, bathrooms, and spacious walk-in closets. The mid-mod wallpaper and furnishings—boomerang coffee tables, papasan chairs, and glass bricks—reminded me of *Austin Powers: The Spy Who Shagged Me.* We called the landlord Mr. Furley because he reminded us of the vaguely creepy old landlord played by Don Knotts on *Three's Company.*

The neighborhood was quiet and full of flowers, a perfect home base for me. You don't find a house like that in LA for the money we could afford, so at first, we couldn't believe our luck. We were like, "Oh, my god! How are we renting this giant house for so little money?" Then we realized Mr. Furley wasn't moving out. We moved in, and he stayed in his room on the top floor. That was the catch. He swore he wasn't spying on us, and we never saw any signs of it, but we figured he could easily have had peepholes.

But it was a really, really great house!

Obviously, I wouldn't accept this as okay for any nineteen-year-old girl now, but Jen and Nicole were a couple years older than me, completely comfortable in their own skin. They had a lot of experience handling all kinds of iffy situations. They didn't love Mr. Furley haunting the place, but it wasn't a deal breaker either. We figured we could keep an eye on Mr. Furley, and as long as he didn't try anything, it was worth letting him feel like he was Hugh Hefner's Mini-Me living in a house with a bunch of beautiful girls. And he never tried anything.

To be honest, I didn't really care. It's sad, but I was basically desensitized about being seen naked. I'd love to say this was because I was empowered with free and full ownership of my body, but the truth is, modesty is one more thing I'd been robbed of. Modesty was a luxury I learned to do without. How else would anyone be able to stand that invasive shower observation day after day? Some girls slowly died inside. Not me. I just became numb to it. After a while the gross comments just bounced off the wall. When they stared at me with their greasy little eyeballs, I stared back, thinking, *Eat your heart out, fuckface.*

Creepy behavior is about the creeper, not the person being creeped on.

The mind has powerful coping mechanisms; almost anything can be normalized or compartmentalized if the alternative is to go crazy. I'm not saying it's great, but it made me stronger and forced me to get over myself in terms of how other people think about me. After going through that, I was tough enough to withstand anything internet haters dish out. You can't internalize the hate and judgment and degenerate Twit-spew. It's a poisonous wild berry cooler of crap that paralyzes you and gives the anonymous all the power.

These days I really do feel empowered by free and full ownership of my body, but that's something I grew into. It took me years to understand that I'm a performance artist, and my body is my medium—like a blank canvas or an empty stage—and I'll never create anything meaningful if I come to the work from a place of shame and cowardice. It's not about how much skin you show; it's about who owns the moment.

Modeling and acting, you have to be cool with being looked at—objectified, even—but you have to own it. You're not there as a prop for someone else's art; you're there as a collaborator, breathing life into a shared vision, taking that idea to a whole different place because of your own creative input. No one has the right to take it anywhere you don't want to go. The greatest photographers are the ones who understand that. They get you to go above and beyond by bringing you into the vision.

This was pre-iPhone, but I kept my old-school beeper with me at all times so I could take advantage of any opportunities that came up. One day I got a call to fill in on an ad campaign for Iceberg jeans. It was great money, and more important, the photographer was David LaChapelle. This was huge.

As a teenager, David was a protégé of Andy Warhol. When his first book, *LaChapelle Land* was published in 1996, *New York* magazine called him "the Fellini of photography" because he created huge controversy with images that basically microwave everything you ever thought about constructs like *pretty* and *art* and *weirdness*. Naked people piled up in a Plexiglas box. Children destroying a fancy dinner party. The environments are colorful and iconic.

Like Herb Ritts or Annie Leibovitz or Richard Avedon, David has an unmistakable style. You recognize his work the second you see it. I'd never seen anything like the pictures LaChapelle was doing back then. The faces are breathtaking. No fear, no hesitation, no inhibition. I wanted to feel what those people were feeling. I wanted to be a work of art like that.

David just wanted someone who was available. That morning,

they had set up the Iceberg shoot and discovered that the model he'd chosen didn't fit the designer's sample size. So he beeped me. It was crazy for a minute because I'd been out partying every night that week—dancing my ass off at a series of parties and raves, living on catnaps and French fries—but I was not about to miss this opportunity. I zipped over from my house in LA, careful to avoid my mom, showered, changed, and threw myself together in record time. I was at that shoot literally forty-five minutes after he beeped me. I was dying of excitement.

It went fine. Nothing extreme. He did a lot of standard commercial campaigns back then, and this was one of them. Cool, but appropriate for a mass audience in print.

I wanted to be in one of those iconic David LaChapelle shoots with the bizarre setups where it feels like a still from some NC-17 arthouse movie that exists only in his mind. Participating in those photos was more than modeling; it was performance art. I *was* glad for a chance to show him how hard I was willing to work, and I hoped it would go somewhere.

His second book, *Hotel LaChapelle* (Bulfinch, 1999), reimagined Madonna as Krishna, Leonardo DiCaprio as Marlon Brando, and Marilyn Manson as a school safety officer. He posed Barbie with a little gun shooting Ewan McGregor in the face as he breaks into her Dream House.

That book came out right after I left Provo. As I relearned New York, I saw it in every bookstore window, and I tried not to get stuck on the idea that I might have been in it if I hadn't disappeared. I wondered if he'd heard the London boarding school story or if he even noticed I was gone.

I try not to think about how easily I slipped through a crack in the floor. It's like, if you were walking down the street with your friends, and suddenly one of them slipped down an open manhole, you'd notice, wouldn't you? I certainly would! I mean . . . I think I would. I *hope* I would. Or maybe we're all so focused straight ahead, people slip away when we're not looking.

Shit. Let's all take a sec and check our people. Make sure no one has slipped down a manhole.

If I didn't notice you slip down a manhole, I'm sorry. And if you didn't notice when I slipped down the manhole, please, know that I'm not mad about it.

Anyway, I reconnected with David at a party and told him I'd love to work with him again. (Networking, always networking.) I didn't tell him about everything that had happened to me during my lost years, but he could tell it was a lot. I think this is an important aspect of his genius. He sees. I wonder if maybe he recognized we had something in common; we'd both sustained some damage during our teens.

We talked about Andy Warhol's muse, Edie Sedgwick, the intriguing idea of the "It Girl," and how celebrity worship mimics religious ecstasy.

"Throughout history," David said, "you always see the *celebrated* ones—queens and kings, aristocracy, entertainers—seemingly above all others, God-like to the people who celebrate them. People cried at a Beatles concert the same way they cried over a vision of Mary. It's the same well of tears."

Like me, David was raised Catholic, and he was very into it. His work is soaked in spiritual influence—transcendence, forgiveness, enlightenment—and full of religious iconography. In the late 1970s, he dropped out of school after ninth grade, ran away from home, and worked as a busboy at Studio 54, surrounded by innovators like Grace Jones, Freddie Mercury, and David Bowie and legends like Andy Warhol, Diane von Furstenberg, and Salvador Dalí. I totally get how a kid would come from that experience with a different vision of the world. My own worldview was influenced by the music and intensity of club life, and I'd grown up surrounded by my mom's circle of fabulous friends, including legends like Paula Abdul, Michael Jackson, and Wolfgang Puck.

David was just seventeen when he started working for Andy Warhol at *Interview* magazine in 1980, and he worked on every issue until Warhol died, in 1987. Warhol was like, "Do whatever you want. Just make everyone look good." David LaChapelle is what happens when someone is wise enough to give a creative kid a broad directive and then trust the result.

Go. Do your thing. I trust you.

I imagine those are the hardest words for a parent to say. Maybe it has to come from a godparent first. In my role as fairy godmother to my Little Hiltons, I take that message seriously and keep it in front of them all the time. That's not something said very often to girls, by kids questioning gender and sexuality, by artists or adventurers, by anyone who dares to be different. Different scares the people who love you. Purely on instinct, driven by fear, they try to protect you. Like my parents tried so hard to protect me. I promise, it's coming from a place of love. Try not to be mad. If you need to hear someone say it and the people in your life just can't—I've got you:

Go. Do your thing. I trust you.

In spring 2000, David and I started shooting, experimenting, getting together whenever we could find time, coming up with weird ideas and juxtapositions. And with every edgy thought he had, I was like *yaaaasssss*. He always had the vision, but within that vision, he gave me a lot of freedom. Most of the wardrobe was random, inexpensive clothes I pulled from my own closet mixed with key designer pieces that I borrowed from Nicky and Mom.

There was no expectation as far as publication, so there were no boundaries. The images David created are all about contrast—

glitzy meets gritty—which is the soul of Los Angeles, really. He shot Nicky and me in front of the Grand Motel, an infamous "nuisance motel" on La Cienega near Pico Boulevard where people were constantly getting arrested on drug and solicitation charges. The cops were called to the Grand so often, the owners ended up getting sued by the city attorney's office for being a "drain on police resources."

Nicky and I stood in front of a pink Rolls-Royce parked next to a rusty phone booth, arm in arm on the stained pavement. She looks sweet and sophisticated in a black-and-white-striped Missoni cocktail dress. Her only accessory is a polka-dot Dolce & Gabbana purse. I'm standing there in Roberto Cavalli short shorts and jacket with no shirt, my legs and lips open. A long Lady Godiva wig cascades over my shoulders, along with assorted bling, including a necklace that spells out the word RICH.

It's not as simple as good girl/bad girl; the black-and-white stripes are at the center of the photograph, and complexity ripples outward. It was shot in the cool evening hours when traffic was slow and the streetlights were coming on. Nicky and I look fresh and clean. There's no *walk of shame* vibe. This isn't a picture of two girls stumbling home when the party is done with them; it's two bright fairy lights who just popped in to see what condition your condition is in. The grass at our feet is absinthe green. It's like he's saying, "Look at these girls, this place, this moment. It's not what you think it is."

I'm sitting here staring at it right now, and after all this time, it holds up, sick in the best possible way. If anything, it's even more powerful because you know everything that's coming at these girls, all the blessings and beasts hidden in the oncoming traffic. It's just a fucking amazing piece of art.

We did a shoot at Zuma Beach, where I was laid out, spread eagle on the burning-hot sand with a halo of curly mermaid hair.

David scattered perfume bottles and cash on the sand like seaweed and beach treasures. Surfers stand around me, heads out of frame, holding their surfboards, like "phallic symbol much?" but I was laughing so hard at the time I didn't even notice. I had mascara running from the corner of my eye down to my ear. There was a lot going on—people buzzing around, adjusting props, hair, sand, lights, makeup—so I wasn't even aware that a stylist moved the silky top aside to expose one nipple. I'm glad I wasn't aware, because I might have gotten nervous, and the magic of the picture is in the blissful oblivion, the fully languid lack of attitude.

David became more intense and elated. I was caught up in the feeling that something incredibly cool was being created. It was thrilling. Energizing. The opposite of exhausting even though I was working my ass off. A lot of photo shoots are syncopated by this endless robotic mantra—*yes yes beautiful beautiful gorgeous gorgeous yes yes*—but David never did that.

"Turn off everything," he said. "Friends, boyfriends, girlfriends, parents. Think about what you're giving, not what you want to get."

It was after midnight when he said, "We have to shoot at your grandparents' house."

"Let's go," I said. "We'll have to climb the fence."

My ADHD brain has no room for hesitation, and I'd gone up and over that fence more times than I could count. It wasn't a big deal. I opened the gate for David and his crew, and we crept into Papa and Nanu's living room, where everything was creamy and regal. Grand piano. Glass coffee table. China cabinets full of fragile treasures. Brocade chairs and spotless drapes. Immaculate ivory carpet. Grecian statuettes on the mantel. A dignified oil portrait on the wall. It was all very stately, very . . . Hiltonesque. Like the lobby of a luxury hotel.

The irony was so easy.

Papa and Nanu were upstairs sleeping, so we had to be quiet, and that made the energy all the more intense. David lit the shot and threw a few random objects—fluffy white bathrobe, detangling brush, telephone—on the floor between my feet. He wanted me to go full trash punk wild child. I leaned into an edgy Courtney Love persona, with a hot pink micromini and a fishnet tank with nothing underneath. The only accessories: sunglasses, silk gloves, and an unlit cigarette. The stylist messed my hair up, choppy and loose, and gave my lips a nice plummy gloss. Strappy black platform heels made me six feet tall.

Sliving.

I was back. Here. In this house where my family had celebrated two Christmases and countless birthdays without me. In this room where my cousins and siblings got to snuggle on the sofa with Nanu and tell her about their bad dreams. Maybe David felt my mood slipping; he teased and catcalled me. Finally, ready to wrap it up, he flipped me off and said, "Fuck you."

Feet apart, chin up, I raised my middle finger and said what I wanted to say to the whole fucking dynasty. David caught the exact moment the *F* took shape in my mouth.

Try it! Bite your lower lip and let that F-bomb drop.

It's not pretty, but it feels fantastic, especially when you've been holding it in, when you feel like you've been hidden away and dismembered. It felt like Jack Nicholson's hatchet through the bathroom door in *The Shining*. I was just in the moment then, but I look at this iconic photograph now and see my declaration of personal independence.

These portraits manifested everything I was feeling inside: a celebration of freedom and fresh sexual energy with an undercurrent of bottled-up rage. They were so weird I didn't really expect them to go anywhere. I thought we were just having fun. He didn't even tell me he was showing them to *Vanity Fair*. When he called to tell me everyone there loved the photos and wanted to publish several of them, I was like, "*Whut . . .*"

I knew if my mom saw those pictures, she'd be pissed beyond belief. And my dad—holy shit. I tried to pitch it to them like, "Well, the good news is, I'm going to be in *Vanity Fair*!" but the nipples, the finger, Papa and Nanu's living room—they were literally like, *What. The. Fuck.*

My mom is incredibly savvy about business. She gets the intersectional chemistry of fashion, art, and celebrity and quickly recognized what this photo shoot might do for me, but this was not the image she wanted Nicky and me to present to the world. She'd been teaching Nicky and me since we were little girls taking high tea in Peacock Alley, teaching us the ways of polite society. These photographs did not fit that narrative.

My mom called David LaChapelle and ripped him a new one. She called the editor at *Vanity Fair* and demanded they pull the pictures, but they had model releases—signed, sealed, delivered—and David held his ground, defending the artistic integrity of his work. It was a fight for a while. Ultimately Mom and Dad had to go along with it. All they could do in terms of spin control was participate in the accompanying article that was being written by Nancy Jo Sales.

I'd like to lie and say I got no pleasure from their distress, but after so many years of lying as an automatic fallback position, I'd rather just own it: I did get a little thrill out of the whole thing.

Nancy Jo observed Nicky and me at a Times Square nightclub called Saci. We arrived after midnight, because this was an after-party following the Council of Fashion Designers of America Awards. Nancy Jo described Nicky as a "tall, blonde, ghostly girl" and called her sparkly Union Jack miniskirt "an expensive costume for an Austin Powers movie."

When Nicky saw that, she was like, "What do you want from me? It was all Dolce!"

That part of the article is really all about Nicky, possibly because that night at the club, I was offsides, networking away. Ben Stiller was there doing research for a movie about male models, shooting test footage with a little handheld camera, and scouting out interesting people who might be cool for cameos.

I don't know whose idea it was to have Nancy Jo interview my family as a unit, and thank God there was no such thing as reality TV back then, because we'd have won an Emmy for Most Awkward Family Dinner.

Mom tried to coach us all in advance on what to say and not say. This was *Vanity Fair*, not Page Six or some disposable tabloid that comes and goes in a weekly rinse cycle. We were all freaked out and nervous—for different reasons. For me, this was a huge opportunity, but Mom was not into the idea of me being famous. She was there to protect our family and the Hilton name.

The Hiltons are not new to the gossip economy. We've been in the tabloids since the invention of the flashbulb. Conrad Hilton lived in an over-the-top Bel Air mansion called Casa Encantada. When he was fifty-five, he married twenty-five-year-old Zsa Zsa Gabor. My great-uncle Nicky was briefly married to Elizabeth Taylor. The gossip economy was just getting warmed up back then, but Papa learned quickly that it was better to avoid that kind of exposure. My dad is a very private person. He was intensely uncomfortable with the revealing pictures and the whole idea of an article about the outsized nightlife of his teenage daughters.

The plan was to have lunch on the patio at my parents' house in Southampton. Super casual. Just another day at Casa Encantada.

Dad was there as silent as a stone. Mom orchestrated everything with chatty energy. I felt intensely nervous and shy, just wanting it to be over. Nancy Jo asked a few general questions about my friends and who I was dating. The paparazzi had taken some pictures of me with Eddie Furlong, and she'd heard rumors about Leonardo Di-Caprio. I hate it when articles define women by who they're dating. Like that's their résumé. Ick.

I tried to steer the conversation toward the movies and music I was working on, but Nancy Jo seemed super interested in the Leonardo DiCaprio rumors.

"We, like . . . we hang out at parties," I said. "He's nice, but—"

"Did you see the story?" Mom cut in with the spin. "A full page in the *Enquirer*. They just make this stuff up."

There was an awkward silence. Mom said something about her friends calling her "Mrs. It" because I was the It Girl but that my nickname at home was Star. Nancy Jo looked at me like she was working out a math problem.

"Paris, your eyes are so blue," she said.

"They're contacts."

I almost said "thanks," but then I thought she might be trying to trap me so she could call me out for pretending. (Which reminds me of another rule for life I wish I'd figured out sooner rather than later: STOP FUCKING PRETENDING. It takes too much energy and makes you paranoid.)

"Mine are real," said Nicky.

Dolce and Sebastian pawed my ankles, begging for bits of grilled chicken.

"Are you close?" Nancy Jo asked me.

Nicky and I both said, "Very."

She asked what we liked to do together, even though she'd already seen us doing it at the club. I didn't know what else we were supposed to say—jump rope? Mom chimed in with shopping, golf, ice-skating, skiing. She said we liked Tahoe. Dad said we liked Vail.

The baby voice came out of my mouth and said, "I like going to pet stores with my dad. Sometimes we go in and buy a puppy."

"Will you be going to college?" Nancy Jo asked.

"I decided to take a year off," I said. I felt Mom's eyes drilling into the side of my head and added something about my parents wanting me to go to college. I had no smooth answers for questions about normal teen things—SATs, prom, graduation. I had stock answers to those questions, as did my parents, but it made me sad to be a liar when David's pictures were so full of truth.

"She knows she'll have to work and support herself," said Mom. "She's finally figuring that out."

Nicky waved a fly from her plate and scoffed, "This is so ironic."

(See? No pretending. It actually works!)

"People want to be heard," said Mom. "They want to talk and chat. And I see people at parties doing this, and I think to myself, 'What are you *doing*?'"

I didn't know who she was talking about, but I felt the need to defend myself. With Dolce on my lap for courage, I said, "I'm not just some party girl. Whatever people think. I have my own business. I do music. And I'm fundraising for breast cancer because my grandmother is sick. I want people to know about all that."

"Well, then," Mom said. "Speak up!"

"I'm trying to," I said tightly, "but you keep interrupting me."

We glared at each other across the table, tied to each other like we were in a three-legged race. Shame bound us together in an unspoken pact: *Don't tell anyone about the you-know-what.*

But for anyone who's willing to see it, those David LaChapelle photos said everything I couldn't articulate as a teenager: *I'm here! I'm free! I am young and angry and sensual, and I am me.*

Mom and Dad were nervous, waiting for the issue to drop.

"You can't control these things," Dad warned me. "You don't know how they're going to cast it."

Ultimately, the article casts him as an "angry Hemingway character." It says Mom was wearing a "kooky flowered hat" and a "cheek-high" Lilly Pulitzer skirt, which was unfair. I mean, I wasn't a fan of the hat, but my mom looked classy and beautiful, as always. I didn't love the description of my shoes—"Lucite sandals that look as if they would by worn by streetwalkers on the planet Zorg"—but she also said I looked like a "1930s movie siren" so I was happy.

The photo spread appeared in the September 2000 issue of *Vanity Fair*. Gwyneth Paltrow was on the cover with a steel-blue header: THE "IT" PARADE. On page 350, superimposed on the picture of Nicky and me on the sidewalk outside the Grand—visual pun obviously intended—the lede says:

> Hotel pioneer Conrad Hilton strutted a parade of showgirls on his arm, and Zsa Zsa Gabor as his second wife. His son, Nicky, notoriously wed and divorced Liz Taylor. Now a fourth Hilton generation—19-year-old Paris and her 16-year-old sister, Nicky, in her wake—is setting society on its ear. Planning a cosmetics line, starring in a documentary about herself, and denying tabloid tales of a romance with Leonardo DiCaprio, Paris is the very model of a hip-hop debutante.

For three generations, the Hilton men were the movers and shakers; the Hilton women were either show horses or "behind every man there's a good woman" women. They had their own ambitions and rich inner lives, but first and foremost, they were Mrs. Hilton. Nicky and I were supposed to marry good men and carry on the old traditions. My brothers were supposed to marry nice women and carry on the Hilton name.

And then there was me.

Before he died, Papa used to joke: "Most of my life I was known as Conrad Hilton's son. Now I'm Paris Hilton's grandfather."

Those David LaChapelle photos are the inflection point where all that history tipped into the future. They opened a floodgate of opportunity for me, lifting my name from tabloids to A-list fame above and beyond the gossip economy. I went from model to supermodel, walking in major New York Fashion Week shows. My side hustle, getting paid to party, turned into real money. Like, a *lot* of money. The more people saw me, the more money I made—not just for myself, but for everyone around me.

All this was happening in the middle of the dot-com renaissance. Perez Hilton says he began blogging in the early 2000s "because it seemed easy." And it was. The internet was a massive black hole, sucking up every bit of content it could find. Suddenly all these eyeballs were out there with no rules about what you could put in front of them. Celebrity gossip was the Chicken McNugget of the new information age: not especially good for you but delicious. And irresistible.

I was at the eye of that perfect storm.

"We've always had the celebrated ones," David said, but this was something different. People didn't start saying *influencer* until 2015, so I didn't know what to call it or what it might become when it started happening. I didn't know how to do anything other than live my life, for better or worse, so I just kept doing that as it all became larger than life.

You probably know what happened next.

Paris Hilton happened.

16

I ended up with a cameo in *Zoolander*, Ben Stiller's male-model movie, along with David Bowie, Cuba Gooding Jr., Natalie Portman, Fabio, Lenny Kravitz, Sting, Gwen Stefani, Winona Ryder, Lil' Kim, and Lance Bass. Oh, and Ben Stiller! It was a quick scene, but I was thrilled to be part of it. And I had dialogue with Ben himself!

> ME: Hey, Derek, you rule.
> BEN: Thanks, Paris. I appreciate that.

When they talked about all the fun *Zoolander* cameos in the press, they referred to me as "style icon Paris Hilton"—probably because they didn't know what else to call me—and I liked the sound of that.

In February 2001, I turned twenty, happy to leave the dumpster fire of my teens behind. Nicky graduated from Sacred Heart School, and we celebrated with a big party at the Bryant Park Hotel. Mom and Dad were so proud of the fabulous young woman she'd become. I was overjoyed that Nicky was free and available for adventure. Now she could come and go between New York and LA—and London and Paris and Tokyo—to walk runways, go to parties and premieres, and just hang out with me and my friends.

I started dating Jason Shaw, who was really the perfect boyfriend. If I could have been the perfect girlfriend, maybe we'd still be a thing. I first saw him on the curb in front of the Four Seasons in LA, waiting for valet parking, and recognized him from the towering Tommy Hilfiger billboard that featured him stretched out in his underwear like ten stories tall in Times Square. He was with Mark Vanderloo, and they looked like a couple of Greek gods out for a stroll.

Jason never intended to be an underwear model. He wasn't the *Zoolander* stereotype. Key to his unique look was a rare authenticity. He was a lovely, down-to-earth guy from Chicago. He had a degree in history. According to legend, a scout spotted him, signed him to a huge agency, and like ten seconds later, Tommy Hilfiger offered him the kind of crazy multiyear deal we all dreamed of. Whenever my schedule allowed, I went with him to shoots in Amsterdam, Milan, and anywhere else Hilfiger was sending him.

Jason bought a house on Kings Road where we could live together, but we were never home for long. During the aughts, I was in the air and on the road 150 to 200 days a year. (Between 2010 and 2020, that ramped up to 250 days a year.) In spring 2002, I celebrated my twenty-first birthday with that first epic skydive and global birthday rager. Jason gave me a silver Porsche—dream car, dream guy. I got to see all the people I loved and thousands of people who loved me. And I looked amazing.

Gram Cracker died a few weeks after my birthday. We knew for a long time that it was coming, but it still felt like a body slam. Mom, Kim, and Kyle were all with her at the end. Mom told me they were holding her hands and crying when she died. Suddenly they heard cupboard doors banging open and slamming shut. They ran to the kitchen, and there was no one there.

The hospice nurse said, "She was saying goodbye."

Hearing that comforted me. I liked the idea of Gram Cracker's spirit—and my own spirit someday—moving through the room like a windstorm on the way to Heaven. I believe in God, and I hope that Heaven means we'll all be the best versions of ourselves, but death scares me. It's my only real fear.

Mom took it so hard. I didn't know how to help her. She did all the things you're supposed to do when someone dies, all the business and details. My mom is incredibly strong on the outside, but she feels things deeply. The loss of her mom—and the loss of Nanu two years later—was brutal. My mom's defining character trait is joie de vivre. She's joyful—like, full of joy—so it scared me to see her so sad. I hate to admit it, but maybe this was the first time I was as sensitive to her feelings as I was to my own.

For me, it was strange to think of Gram Cracker as gone, because I felt closer to her than ever. She was with me. Hummingbirds came and went, just like she said they would. A general hum of energy and light carried me through acting classes and auditions, both of which I hate. I get so insecure, and I hate feeling judged. I just wanted to work.

Summer came, and so many good things were happening. Tinkerbell! What a gift when she came into my life. I did a horror flick called *Nine Lives* and an artsy short called *QIK2JDG*, had a fun bit part in *Wonderland*, which starred Val Kilmer, Lisa Kudrow, Carrie Fisher, and Christina Applegate, and did a cute cameo in a rave scene with Mike Myers in *The Cat in the Hat*.

I met with producers at Fox, who pitched me an idea for a show that crossed the streams between fiction and reality, a mash-up of the scripted, fish-out-of-water sitcom *Green Acres* (starring Papa's ex-step-aunt-in-law Eva Gabor) and a documentary-style reality series with the added twist of episodic challenges. There had never been a show like this before, and there hasn't been one since. *The Simple Life* was a reality TV groundbreaker that no one—including me—has ever been able to repeat.

I was instantly on board. Producers initially wanted it to be the Hilton sisters, and I begged Nicky to do it with me, but Mom and Dad were not in favor. Too many unknowns. Too many people. Too close to home.

"Don't be insane," Nicky said. "You'll embarrass yourself."

"Not if it's funny."

"I don't want to be funny," she said. "I want to be classy, and if their intention was for us to look classy, the show would be about us living our lives as runway models at New York Fashion Week. This is not that."

She had a point.

The theme song kinda says it all:

Let's take two girls, both filthy rich,
From the bright lights into the sticks.

There was no doubt about how it was supposed to play out:

They're both spoiled rotten.
Will they cry when they hit bottom?

Notice it says *when*—not *if*—they "hit bottom." People expected this to be about two unrelatable rich bitches who get put in their place by "real" people. There was huge potential for humiliation. I needed to partner with someone who had no fear of looking silly—no fear of *being* silly—a brazen prank caller who knew how to party and was willing to lean into the ridiculous. This show would not have been what it is with anyone other than Nicole Richie.

I didn't have to beg. She was there from hello, 10,000 percent.

The tight production schedule started in May 2003, and we worked sixteen-hour days through the oppressive heat of the Arkansas summer. We were given broad direction for building our characters—Nicole as the sassy troublemaker, me as the beautiful airhead—going for a Lucy and Ethel 2.0 dynamic. We had no clue how any of the crazy scenarios would play out; all we knew was that whatever happened, we were supposed to make it hilarious.

I think a lot of people assumed Nicole and I would look down on this rural family, act like bratty princesses, and then get put in our place. Again, I was the beautiful ditz; Nicole was the troublemaker. Tale as old as time. But we were living in a shiny new millennium, and that old storyline didn't work for us. We wanted to tell a story about girls who go out into the world full of *game on* and conquer every obstacle in a completely creative, gutsy way. We had to dance along a very fine line: irreverent but respectful, sexy but approachable, bold but not bitchy. We had to slay the daily challenges by flipping the script in some funny way and then make some good come out of all of it. We didn't overthink it at the time, but looking back, I hope the takeaway is this: *The future belongs to girls who refuse to do as they're told.* Girl power doesn't come from being rich or beautiful; it's a combination of courage, kindness, and laughter.

The first season was shot on location in Altus, a small town in Arkansas. The production budget was not huge by Hollywood standards, but it meant a lot to this community. They welcomed us with open arms and went along with all our shenanigans. The mischief was never mean-spirited or disrespectful. Everyone in town knew us and wanted to be part of it.

We loved the Leding family. They were the kind of family Conrad Hilton aspired to and never had—the family my parents tried to force into existence until it blew up in their faces. The Ledings remind me of Carter's salt-of-the-earth Midwestern family, which is the kind of family Carter and I hope to raise. Their multigenerational home was filled with functional love and support. I grew especially close to Curly, the grandmother, who was strong and fearless—like Gram Cracker—and to Braxton, the toddler who instantly fell in love with Tinkerbell. I don't think it's a coincidence that producers put us in a house with two teenage boys—Justin and Cayne. Our mission was to tease and torment them, but we adopted them as our little brothers instead.

The director had Nicole and me flirt and make out with a couple of local boys, Anthony and Chops, who we were supposedly dating. (Nicole and I were both in relationships IRL.) Randomly, I ran into Chops a few years ago at Netflix, where he's now a finance executive. Apparently, he took to show business better than we took to cattle insemination.

Bunking together slumber party style on the Leding's enclosed porch, Nicole and I lay there at night, cracking each other up and coordinating our outfits for the following day. Every morning, our thirteen-year-old selves came out to play. We had a crazy amount of fun and laughed until we cried, but I won't lie; by the end of the shooting schedule—eighteen weeks of eighteen-hour days—we were beyond exhausted. It was so unbearably hot in Altus. At some point during the dog days of August, I called my mom, crying, trying to cover the phone with my hand, and said, "I hate it here."

"Only three more days," said Mom. "You can do this, honey."

And then she sent a private jet loaded with food from Mr. Chow's, a vivid demonstration of both the love of privilege and the privilege of love.

The big movies that summer were *Finding Nemo* and *Matrix Reloaded*. Six months before the debut of *The Simple Life*, the biggest shows on TV were *CSI*, *Friends*, and *Joe Millionaire*. We didn't know yet who we'd be competing with or following. Obviously, a time slot following *Joe Millionaire* would be perfect, so we were praying for that.

While the first season of *The Simple Life* was in postproduction, Friendster and Myspace launched. Social media wasn't a huge thing, but it was starting to be a thing, and I was interested. Here was a space where you could connect with Rupert Murdoch (user name Dirty Digger) or a friend from first grade. You could launch your homemade music in the same space where Nine Inch Nails were launching their new album. You could reinvent yourself and amplify whatever you were up to, which was incredibly exciting for us as the *Simple Life* rollout took shape.

The show started getting tons of great press. Nicole and I were working it, showing up, doing interviews. I was out clubbing almost every night, posing for the paparazzi, talking to everyone about this crazy, wonderful show about to come out, promising everyone that they'd be blown away. I shuttled between New York and LA, working the red carpet at premieres and award shows, and wherever I went, the growing army of paparazzi followed. I was having a wild-child moment, and it was sort of glorious.

I loved Jason, and we talked about spending the rest of our lives together, but I knew I wasn't in the right place to make that kind of commitment. It had nothing to do with him. He was a good, good guy. I didn't understand it at the time, and I can't explain it now. I just wasn't capable of being honest or loyal or whole. I was damaged in ways I couldn't tell him about, and the fact that I never confided in him about my past—that says it all, doesn't it? Secrets are corrosive. Secrets destroy anything you try to layer over them. It's like using concealer to cover a black eye. You can hide it, but that's not the same as healing.

When I realized I was pregnant, it was like waking up on the ledge outside a fortieth-floor window. I was terrified and heartsick. The hormones sent my ADHD symptoms spiraling. I felt paralyzed by an anxiety that took root in my body and grew like poison ivy. Everything I knew about myself was at war with everything I'd been raised to believe about abortion. No one can ever know how hard it is to face this impossible choice unless she's faced it herself. It's an intensely private agony that's impossible to explain. The only reason I'm talking about it now is that so many women *are* facing it, and they feel so alone and judged and abandoned. I want them to know that they're not alone, and they don't owe anyone an explanation. When there is no right way—all that's left is what is. What you know you have to do. And you do it, even though it breaks your heart.

Over the years, I've looked back on all this with sorrow, even though I know I made the right choice. In my loneliest moments, I romanticized the entire time and tortured myself with melodrama—thoughts like *What if I killed my Paris? What if Jason was the one who got away?*—but the fact is, there was no happy little family at stake. That was not going to happen. Trying to continue that pregnancy with the physical and emotional issues I was dealing with at the time would have been a train wreck for everyone involved. At that moment in my life, I was in no way capable of being a mother. Denying that would have jeopardized the family I hoped to have in the future, at a time when I was healthy and healed.

Facing that reality forced me to face the truth about how wrong it would be to stay in this relationship. I hate it that I broke Jason's heart. I broke my own heart. But I know we did the right thing—which is almost never the easiest thing. I'll always love Jason, but we tried dating again for a short time in 2010, and it didn't work. I was traveling eight months out of the year, and he wasn't one of those losers who were eager to follow me around. It was weirdly comforting to know for sure we absolutely were not meant to be forever. Until I met Carter, I wasn't totally convinced that forever was a thing for me.

I spent a few days crying, and then I went back to work. I didn't know how else to get through it.

I signed with a manager (for real), Jason Moore. He didn't flinch when I told him what I wanted to accomplish: household name, high-end endorsements, solid movie roles, Marilyn Monroe cachet. I liked the way he talked about me and my career as a work of art. When a deal was in development, he'd say, "the painting isn't finished" or "it's just a sketch." When people started saying I was "famous for being famous," he told CNN, "When all the artists were doing what we now call Impressionism, critics couldn't name it at the time, so they just said 'squiggly painting' or 'crazy artist.' That's what 'famous for being famous' sounds like to me: people not being able to define what a movement is."

JM and I started out great but ended up at war after I found out that Facebook had come to him with an offer, wanting me to be the first celebrity on the open platform, and he *fucking turned it down*. He said, "Paris Hilton is so big, we're going to do our own Facebook." Stuff like that is why we need the face-palm emoji. There are no words.

I was in Australia when he called to tell me that a thirty-seven-second video clip of me having sex was circulating on the internet.

My first reaction was, "What? No! I never did anything like that."

I thought someone made a fake video or something. It took me a minute to make the connection to that private video. I had to close my eyes and breathe. I felt like I was going to throw up. It was inconceivable to me. There's no reason to think a random guy you meet in a bar could be that rotten. Or that smart.

Within hours, news of the tape was everywhere, along with rumors that there was a full-length porno pending release. Everything I'd been working so hard for—I felt it all crumbling to shit.

I called him and begged. "Please, please, please, don't do this."

He sounded distant and cool, saying it was too late, it was already out there. He said he had every right to sell something that belonged to him—something that had a lot of financial value.

More value than my privacy, obviously. My dignity. My future.

Shame, loss, and stark terror swept over me. I hung up the phone, trying to think what I should do next. I'd have to tell the producers of the show. Worse than that, I'd have to tell my parents. I couldn't even wrap my head around it. At first, all I could do was cry and cry—wrenching, raw, chest-deep sobs. I felt like my life was over, and in many ways, it was. Certainly, the career I had envisioned was no longer possible. Everything I wanted my brand to be, the trust and respect I was trying to rebuild with my parents, the sliver of self-worth I'd been able to recover—all that was instantly in ruins. With my work on *The Simple Life* and the success of my new business, I'd cultivated an inner core of security and strength. Suddenly, I couldn't feel it anymore. I felt that old weight returning to my posture.

I got on a flight back to the US, trying to hide behind my sunglasses, but the lady sitting next to me could tell I was crying.

"Are you okay?" she asked.

I shook my head.

Over the course of the fourteen-hour flight, she was incredibly kind, and eventually I opened up and told her what was happening. The next day there was a picture of me on the cover of *Us Weekly* with the headline "Paris Hilton Exclusive: My Side of the Story," or something like that.

Mom was livid. "Why would you do an interview before you have a chance to process this?"

"I didn't!" I kept insisting, and then I remembered the lady on the plane. She must have recorded the whole conversation. I don't know who placed her in that seat next to me, but I imagine their kid went to a very nice college at my expense.

The thirty-seven-second clip provided proof of concept, I guess: a teaser to show how big a deal this was going to be, how much buzz it would create, and how much people would pay to see it. I imagine someone would need that in order to set up financing for production and distribution. If that was the intention, it worked. It was a very big deal. That was immediately obvious. Buzz was off the chain because—*comedy gold*—it was too easy. The potential for blond jokes, the opportunity for self-righteousness, the degradation of someone living a posh life. It was like an X-rated version of *America's Funniest Home Videos*.

When the full version of the tape was released, the initial price point was around fifty bucks, which must have had a massive profit margin, because no one had to invest a dime in marketing. Late-night comedians, bloggers, and tabloid editors provided that for free. The tape was everywhere, and everyone was talking about it, shaking their heads, and saying I had no decency. Funny, no one mentioned the decency of people who watch creepy sex videos of teenage girls.

One morning I stopped into a neighborhood newsstand on

Sunset Boulevard, a place where I went for coffee and magazines on a regular basis, and there was a huge display: "YES! We have the Paris Hilton Sex Tape!" The owner seemed baffled when I ripped the poster down and threw it in his face. He couldn't understand why I was crying.

"What's wrong with you?" I screamed. "You're not a porn shop, you're a family newsstand! My little brothers come in here to get ice cream!"

The impact the tape had on my career is impossible to quantify, but the absolute worst aspect of this horror show was the impact on my family. My mom just crumpled into bed and stayed there. My dad, red faced and furious, worked the phones, calling lawyers, calling spin doctors, trying to help me marshal any hope of damage control. The knee-jerk reaction was to summon a pack of rabid lawyers, but the consensus was that lawsuits would only bring more attention. Mom's standard advice was "Don't give it oxygen," and that made sense to me. It often does, in a world where tearing down is so much easier than building up.

My parents were still living at the Waldorf, and a newspaper was left outside the door of every room first thing in the morning. Nicky got up early and ran down the hall, turning all the papers facedown, so Mom and Dad and the boys wouldn't have to see the headlines and feel like they were walking a gauntlet. Barron and Conrad were plenty old enough to understand what it all meant, and they were so weirded out, they could hardly look at me. During the previous three years, from the time I got out of Provo, I had been trying to rebuild relationships with my siblings and mend the shattered bond between me and my parents. Now we were back to zero. Left of zero. Worse than ever.

I didn't know at first if Fox would even go ahead with *The Simple Life*. All the positive energy and amazing buzz the team had worked so hard to build—everything about the show was dwarfed by the sex-tape scandal. I couldn't face the cameras. I stayed hidden for several weeks, turning down every opportunity—interviews, club appearances, runways, magazine covers—sacrificing all the income I would have normally brought in. If Nicole or anyone else went out to continue the launch effort, questions about the sex tape dominated the conversation.

On December 2, 2003, *The Simple Life* debuted on Fox with thirteen million viewers, an astounding 79 percent of the adult audience. Reviews were moon-shot awesome, and the team decided it was time for me to step out of the shadows and address the scandal in some way. There were a lot of options. Every show wanted me to come on and be interviewed, but the one that made the most sense to me was an offer to play myself in a segment with Jimmy Fallon on *Saturday Night Live*'s "Weekend Update." It was a risk, but the script was brilliant, Jimmy was pitch perfect, and the sketch lives on as one of the great moments in *SNL* history.

> **JIMMY:** As we agreed, we won't be discussing the scandal
> that's been in the paper the past few weeks.
>
> **ME:** Thank you, Jimmy. I appreciate that.
>
> **JIMMY:** So, your family—I don't know if people know—
> owns hotels all over the world, right?
>
> **ME:** Yes. They're in New York, London, Paris . . .
>
> **JIMMY:** Wait. So there actually is a Paris Hilton?
>
> **ME:** Yes, there is.
>
> **JIMMY:** Is it hard to get into the Paris Hilton?
>
> **ME:** Actually, it's a very exclusive hotel, no matter what
> you've heard.
>
> **JIMMY:** I've heard the Paris Hilton is very beautiful.
>
> **ME:** I'm glad that you've heard that.

JIMMY: Do they allow double occupancy at the Paris Hilton?

ME: No.

JIMMY: Is the Paris Hilton roomy?

ME: It might be for you, but most people find it very comfortable.

JIMMY: I'm a VIP. I might need to go in the back entrance.

ME: It doesn't matter who you are. Not gonna happen.

Like I said: comedy gold. And I made a lasting friend. Jimmy Fallon was so cool and so kind. This was another moment when I needed to be reminded that kindness exists, and he was there for it. When he calls me to come on his show, I'm there.

The second episode of *The Simple Life* surpassed the series debut with 13.3 million viewers. The show was a massive hit, sparked a whole new reality television marketplace, and stands as a comedy classic. I promise you, someone is streaming it right now, and I hope they laugh until their ribs ache.

I'm deeply grateful to the Leding family and incredibly proud of Nicole and me and the whole crew who worked so hard on that first, groundbreaking season. I know in my heart that the success we earned was despite the sex tape, not because of it, but some cynical people will always claim that we couldn't have done it organically. I wish we'd had the chance to find out.

It makes me want to vomit when people suggest that I was in on the release of that footage on the internet or involved in the video that was released later and—in a stunning fit of bad taste—dedicated to the memory of victims of 9/11. (WTF!) The release of that private footage devastated me, personally and professionally. It followed me into every audition and business meeting for years. Even now, in a corporate world dominated by men, I look around a conference table knowing that most of the people sitting there have seen me naked in the most degrading way imaginable. No matter what I do—despite everything I've accomplished in the past two decades—90 percent of the articles written about me see fit to mention it. It wouldn't matter if I solved climate change by inventing a Fanta-powered bullet train, the headline would be "Planet Saved by Paris Hilton, Who Did Sex Tape When She Was 19."

The release of that video cost me an insane amount of money, and more important, it devastated my family. And it will never go away. It's out there waiting for my children, who will be confronted with it someday. I think some people want to believe I was involved in the release of the tape—or that I benefited in some way—because it's unpleasant for them to think about the cruelty and complicity of their own response.

Please, hear me when I say I would never—NEVER—under any circumstances be involved in the production of an amateur teen porn video, and if I had been involved in this one:

- The lighting would have been better.
- I would have had proper hair, makeup, and wardrobe.
- The camera angles and editing would have been more flattering.
- I wouldn't have packaged it like a sleazy low-budget piece of garbage.
- I would not have had the poor taste to dedicate a porn flick to the victims of a terrorist attack. (Seriously. What the actual fuck does that even mean?)

Most important: If this was something I had *chosen* to do, *I would have owned it.* I would have stood tall in my Louboutins and said, "Yup, that was my choice, and anyone who wants to judge me can pound sand up their ass." I would have stood by it, capitalized on it, licensed the shit out of every frame, and then boogied on over to the bank without apologizing to anyone.

I'm not judging any woman who *does* choose to do all that.

I'm saying that choice was taken from me, and it hurt me.

It makes me so angry to think about how many girls are exploited because of flabby, toothless laws pertaining to revenge porn and other unauthorized use of private images. If I were to take a photo of a teenage boy, slap it on an inflatable hemorrhoid ring, and sell it for fifty bucks, you know what that would be?

Illegal.

How is it that the law allows me to trademark and protect the word *sliving* but refuses to protect a woman's right to control images of her own body?

Not long ago, I was in my hotel suite in Washington, DC, getting ready to do a press conference and meet with legislators about the federalization of laws guaranteeing oversight and regulation in the troubled-teen industry. I looked in the mirror, inspecting the sleek line of my black business suit, trying to decide if the modest scoop neck was better than an alternative look with a high neck and silk bow—not as comfortable, but it left no skin showing below my chin.

"Carter? Babe, what do you think?" I presented myself with the scoop neck and then held the second look in front of it. "This or this?"

He kissed me on the forehead because my lips were freshly glossed.

He said, "You look great, and we need to go."

"I'll take this with me." I stuffed the high-neck blouse in my bag. "Just in case someone screams 'whore.'"

Because this is something I've had to think about every day since that sex tape was released. People screaming "whore" at me—that's a thing. I have to anticipate and steel myself against it, and I resent every particle of energy this drains from my emotional life force. I can't even let myself think about what my life could have been if I hadn't participated in something I knew was a bad idea at a moment when I was so vulnerable, working so hard to put my life back together. It destroyed a huge sector of my business before I even had a chance to build it. No matter where I went or what I did after that, I carried a scar.

My family and friends celebrated the premiere of *The Simple Life* with a party at Bliss, a hip new restaurant on La Cienega. The paparazzi swarmed the street outside. When the limo pulled up, I sat in the back seat with my heart hammering, knowing what everyone was talking about, not knowing what to say.

I turned to my dad and asked, "How do I look?"

"Like one in a million," he said, gripping my hand.

Instead of the cute little dress designed for this big occasion, I opted to wear a sleek pink tuxedo, and that choice holds up to history. A lot went into that look. Check it out. It reads classy, sexy, proud, and strong: the pink satin manifestation of "sorry not sorry."

The door opened. Flashing lights and shouting poured in. There was nothing defensive about Dad's stance as he walked me into the restaurant. His posture was proud, and he was smiling ear to ear.

Remember that sound cameras used to make? The click of the shutter followed by the whirring advance of film through the little drum? That *click whirr click whirr click* in rapid succession, multiplied times ten times ten times ten—it was like music to me back then, and I kinda miss it now. Digital cameras capture images in sterile silence most of the time. That visceral *gotcha* noise is optional. Back then, it was ubiquitous. (Isn't that a great word? *Ubiquitous*: all over everything like Hollandaise sauce.) Sometimes when I'd lie in bed after a long night out, I could hear that sound along with the blood rushing in my head.

gotcha gotcha

My first step back onto a big red carpet was at the 2004 Grammys. "Paris! Paris! Look left! Paris, over here! What do you have to say about the sex tape? Wait! Paris, we just want to talk to you! Over here, Paris!"

gotcha gotcha gotcha gotcha gotcha gotcha gotcha gotcha gotcha

Janet Jackson was scheduled to perform with Luther Vandross that night, but a week earlier, the infamous Super Bowl halftime "wardrobe malfunction" happened, so CBS/Viacom told her she was blacklisted and no longer invited to be part of the show. To his credit, during the acceptance speech for one of his multiple Grammy awards, Justin Timberlake did apologize for exposing Janet's breast. So that's not ironic or anything.

Look, I'm not asking anyone to feel sorry for me. I take full responsibility for the public and private choices I've made, and I'm not apologizing for any of it. I'm just saying, there's plenty of shame to go around, and girls have traditionally dealt with more than our share. And we're over it. I know I am, and I think Brit, Lindsay, Shannen, and a whole lot of other women would probably agree. Girl-shaming as a sport and industry needs to be over.

People say I invented the selfie, but that's not true. The Grand Duchess Anastasia took pictures of herself a hundred years ago, and hundreds of years before cameras were a thing, artists were painting self-portraits. What I did as an influencer was strap a jet pack on the idea that I—the person in the photograph—deserve to benefit from that image more than people who create and sell images of me without my consent.

Since women like me and Kim made Instagram our bitch, the kind of paparazzi insanity that killed Princess Diana has all but disappeared. It'll never be that way again. There's still a market for candid pictures of celebs—especially if the celeb looks embarrassingly fat, skinny, ugly, drunk, or compromised in some way—so the paps are still out there, but it's nothing like it was in 2003, when the street outside a club sometimes devolved to hard-core hand-to-hand combat with people fighting each other to get photos that sold for seven figures.

Ultimately, it's about supply and demand. The demand is what it always was; you can trace it back to Helen of Troy. But now the supply is up to me.

The rise of selfie culture isn't about vanity; it's about women taking back control of our images—and our self-images. I don't think that's a bad thing.

Discuss amongst yourselves.

17

Facebook launched in February 2004, and I kept hearing about it, but it was for college students only.

"Don't take it personally," Nicky advised, and I didn't, but it was a strange reminder that there was once a little girl called Star who dreamed of becoming a veterinarian. But I didn't go to college. The people who were paid to educate me failed, so I've had to educate myself by doing, dreaming, and experimenting, by reading and listening, by screwing things up and fixing them again. I had to forage for my education on the all-you-can-learn buffet of life. My self-education is a collage of experiences glued together with towering role models.

Again: I was born to privilege. I'm not minimizing that. But I could have coasted, and I never did. I worked. And every time my life fell apart, I worked harder. One priceless bit of advice my great-grandfather gave my grandfather, and my grandfather gave me: "Success is never final. Failure is never fatal."

I've seen both up close.

Anyway. No college. So, no Facebook for me in 2004. Probably for the best. I'm sure there was a lot of garbage gossip about me. I didn't need that kind of negativity or distraction.

The Simple Life was a massive hit, and my business was booming. Working with Parlux Ltd., I started my lifestyle brand and released my first fragrance—Paris Hilton, female and male variations—which did so well, I decided to buy a big house. Wendy White helped me find a place on Kings Road above the Sunset Strip, and I remodeled it to include "Club Paris," the ultimate after-party venue, with an amazing sound system, full bar, and pole-dancing pole.

I loved curating music and collecting people who made these all-night events strange and magical: musicians, models, artists, actors, and just a lot of random people doing wildly interesting things with technology and media. So many fresh faces showed up at my door. Anna Faris recently reminded me about the night she arrived, starstruck and shy, new to a world that was moving so fast. I took her upstairs, and we sat in my closet, talking and laughing while I showed her how to do the smoky eye that was about to be retrending.

This may be the real beginning of my life as a DJ, because I never let the music stop. I steered every party like I was piloting a starship, never allowing anyone to be left behind. The 2004 soundtrack was defined by Outkast's double album *Speakerboxxx/The Love Below* and Snoop Dogg's "Drop It Like It's Hot."

There were so many great movies that year: *Mean Girls, Anchorman, The Notebook, 13 Going on 30, Napoleon Dynamite, Shaun of the Dead, Howl's Moving Castle, 50 First Dates.*

Nicole and I started filming season two, which had us driving all over the country on a road trip, working odd jobs to finance our journey. One of the situations was at a dude ranch, which I was excited for. I love horses. I felt confident about riding, even though I hadn't done it in a while. Everything started out fine, but I think my horse was jumpy because of all the unfamiliar camera equipment and people around. He lurched forward and picked up speed. I lost the natural rhythm and started bouncing high off the saddle, so when the horse bucked and kicked, I couldn't hold on.

I hit the ground hard. The wind was knocked out of me, so I lay there for a minute, struggling to breathe. By the time crew people got to me, I was sitting up, saying, "I'm okay, I'm okay." And then I felt this weird sensation like molten lava pouring down the side of my body. I'd fallen in a patch of stinging nettles, weeds that look soft and fuzzy but are actually covered with millions of tiny needles, each one as fine as an eyelash and filled with acid. It felt like a javelin went through my torso. I tried to stay in character and make this funny, but I was in agony. The big joke in the show was one of the cowboys offering to pee on me, which was supposed to take away the sting. No thanks.

(FYI, that's a myth, probably stemming from a situation where some cowboy peed himself because it hurts so bad.)

As the show got more and more popular, the bits Nicole and I came up with went everywhere. Walking down the street in New York, I'd hear girls giggling and singing, "Sanasa sanasaaa!" "That's hot!" caught on the same way it had back in sixth grade. After we wrapped season two, I trademarked the phrase. I wasn't sure what I wanted to do with it; I only knew I didn't want anyone else to get there first.

Nicky was nineteen and killing it. She debuted her high-end clothing line, Nicholai, at New York Fashion Week and unveiled a collection of dresses and rompers for her Chick ready-to-wear label. We did a collab with Samantha Thavasa, a Japanese company that made high-end handbags. Nicky was the designer and signed the bags, and we were both the faces, modeling for billboards, runways, and ad campaigns. Every time we went to Japan, fans went crazy. It was like the Beatles had landed. Promoters packed the schedule with a month's worth of work in seven days.

We loved working as the Hilton sisters. For a while we lived together at my place on Kings Road, and we did a lot of traveling, promoting our product lines all over the world, and having a lot of fun.

That summer I got into a weird moment that was not huge, compared to some of my other moments, but it was upsetting: the first of many break-ins at my house on Kings Road. Not the Bling Ring break-ins. And not the stalker with the knives. Somebody else. People broke into that house like it was a Cadbury crème egg.

The place had been ransacked and was a straight-up crime scene. I wanted to get inside to get away from the paparazzi, but the cops had it all taped off, so I popped across the street and climbed over the fence at a neighboring property, which happened to be the home of my former boyfriend Jason Shaw, and I got so tangled up on the gate that the alarms were set off. Cops came swarming, followed by the paps. It was beyond.

Nicky said, "I'm calling Elliot."

Back in the 1960s and '70s, Elliot Mintz hosted *Headshop*, a television talk show where he interviewed legends like Bob Dylan, Mick Jagger, Timothy Leary, and Salvador Dalí. He was a close friend of John Lennon and Yoko Ono and was by Yoko's side after John was murdered. To this day, Elliot is a regular at my parents' Thanksgiving table. He had a deep understanding of fame and media and a vast network of interesting friends who trusted him, which is a rare thing in Hollywood. People called him a "Hollywood fixer" or "spin wizard." If you ask Elliot Mintz what he does, he says, "I clean up what gets tainted and magnify what glows."

Nicky made the call, and Elliot was there within the hour.

As he fought his way through the crowd, I noticed he had no trouble making the paparazzi behave. Access is Elliot's superpower; they were in awe of it. When he rolled up, they parted like the Red Sea. He dealt with the cops, got me back into my house, and crafted a media statement that magically shifted focus away from my violated household and fence-climbing effort to my emerging brand and new fragrance.

When it was all said and done, Elliot ordered some food to be delivered, and we sat talking for a long time. I liked his Jiminy Cricket integrity and the deliberately thoughtful way he spoke. All these years later, this is still the one thing that most impresses me about Elliot: He never speaks without thinking. Every word is a precise footstep.

"What is your plan?" he asked. "Your wish? Your ambition? I ask this of all my clients: What do you want to achieve?"

I didn't lie. I said, "I want to be famous. I want people to know who I am—to be aware of me—and I want them to like me so I can sell them things. My product lines. Nicky's product lines. Designers, makers, anything I like. If I say something is beautiful, then they know it must be beautiful. If I go to this club or spa or resort, then everybody wants to go there. I want people to appreciate my opinion as a tastemaker. As an icon. And I want to monetize that, like *a lot*."

"Your immediate presence has been established," Elliot said. "You're past the embryonic stage of this career you're developing."

I nodded. "It's going pretty well."

"Like a runaway train," he said. "Do you worry about overexposure?"

"I don't believe in overexposure."

"There are parameters. There's a turnaround factor. You have to be aware when it becomes obnoxious."

I shrugged. Agree to disagree. For the moment. We talked for a long time about the changing landscape of media and what it means to be a celebrity.

Elliot said, "My specialty is how much can a person do where they're promoting their own work, where they become secondary in that dialogue and it's about that performance in the movie, that innovative sound they created in the music, what was revealed in the book that altered people's lives. That, to me, is the key to great media—*lasting* media. You can't simply be about the sale. Remember, there are such things as limited editions."

"Maybe," I said. Exclusivity. That was more my love language.

"If you reach a smaller number of people with real potency and power, they will stay with you forever," said Elliot.

I didn't fully understand it then, but he was describing my Little Hiltons, a rock-solid core group of fans who became my family in many ways.

"You have a career of forty years," he said. "You don't have to burn it all out in five. Artists aren't like athletes with a limited number of years they can be viable. There are countless examples of artists who continue to create and inspire two and three generations of fans after decades and decades of doing the good work."

Looking for some concrete strategy for how to apply all this theory, I showed him the flood of media requests and messages that poured into my phone every day.

"Your life," he said, "is a whirlwind. People seldom realize how much of your life you have to devote to keeping yourself famous. It's a round-the-clock, full-time experience. When you go into Ralph's at one in the morning, you're on. When you're sick, you're on. When you're tired, you're on."

"I know."

"When you climb a fence—"

"Elliot," I said, "I'm in on the joke."

He knew what I was talking about. And he knew why I needed him to know. That's what made Elliot an indispensable part of my working life for several years and an indispensable part of our family to this day. He curated requests and helped me practice a few talking points, but more than that, he helped me figure out a philosophy that grounded me in the middle of this firestorm I'd started. In terms of crisis management, Elliot gave me the same advice he gives all his clients: "Don't lie. Learn from Clinton and Nixon. You're better off if you just cop to it and move on."

Even when we were momentarily mad at each other or busy with other things, I knew I could call him if I needed him.

As it turns out, I needed him a lot. Nicky had the foresight to know that in advance.

Days and weeks rushed by in a continuous loop: work, party, travel, party, runway, party, repeat. Elliot crafted a tasteful announcement for every engagement and a sensitive statement for every breakup. Whenever my personal bullet train went off the rails, he provided the same kind of clarity and calming presence I could always depend on from Wendy White. Several nights a week, Elliot went out with me and my friends. As the designated driver, he sipped chardonnay and carted us around without judging. Brit and Nicole and I always called him Chardy. Nicky and I loved to torment him on the phone.

"Elliot, Nicky says she wants to tie you up."

"Elliot, Paris wants to make out with you."

'Cause we're sophisticated like that.

Elliot was consistently unfazed.

We usually headed out into the evening at about nine, had dinner, hit a few clubs, collecting our entourage along the way. Nicole, Brit, Kimberly Stewart, Bijou Phillips, and Casey Johnson were among the regulars, but we never knew who we might run into, and there was plenty of room in my Range Rover. By the time the clubs closed down, we'd have our after-hours raging options laid out.

Elliot spent a lot of those after-parties people-watching or looking at the host's art while we danced and drank until four in the morning. Then, with the skill of a lion tamer, he steered us through the maze of waiting paparazzi and drove us all home.

The *New York Times* did a story about Elliot in 2006, which he didn't like but commented on because they were going to do it with or without his participation. The piece speculated about why this guy who was a legend in the industry—a man Yoko Ono described as "a dear friend who went through storms with me for 25 years"—would be hanging out with a twenty-three-year-old party girl and her silly friends. The author of the article seemed to think he should be spending his time on better people—people who didn't need him because everyone loved them no matter what—which really misses the essential element of who Elliot is: the guy who can be trusted when you can't quite trust yourself.

YouTube launched in 2005, three days before my twenty-fourth birthday, taking the potential for self-promotion and self-embarrassment to a whole new level.

Within the first six weeks of the new year, I hosted *SNL* with musical guest Keane in February, announced and broke off my engagement, and wrapped a third season of *The Simple Life*. In May, I blew a lot of tiny minds, wearing a bikini and washing a car while eating a Carl's Jr. burger in a Super Bowl ad, which was later banned from TV for being too sexy. So, no one was terribly surprised to see me on the cover of *Playboy*.

Except me. I was surprised. And not in a good way.

Back when we lived at the Furley house in LA, Jen and Nicole went out with Hugh Hefner every Wednesday night in a Hummer stretch limo with a bunch of other girls. I started going along with them, clubbing on Wednesdays, and to parties at the Playboy Mansion on Halloween and Midsummer's Night, and other special occasions. This was back in the day when those parties were so dope. I lived for events like that.

Hef kept wanting me to be a Playmate, and I thought that would be awesome, but when I told Mom about it, she said, "Are you insane? No! You're not being a Playmate. That is so trashy." (Fun fact: Hef had asked my mom to be a Playmate when she was a teenager, and Gram Cracker shut it down for the same reason.)

Years later, as I got more famous, Hef really wanted me to do a *Playboy* cover. He kept offering me more and more money, saying I wouldn't have to be totally naked, just topless. And then saying, I didn't have to be topless, just sheer. And then saying I could wear whatever lingerie I wanted. Even when he offered seven figures, I turned it down, because I knew my mom would lose her mind, and because I had already been branded as a slut after the sex tape. I felt like a *Playboy* pictorial would just cement that in people's minds.

One morning a friend called me and said, "I love your *Playboy* cover."

I was like, "*Whut?*"

Hef had "honored" me with the Sex Star of the Year Award, which means they can claim it's "news" and not a pictorial. He got a picture from an old test shoot with a woman photographer who was really great. It's kind of an old-school pinup-girl vibe: red bustier and heels, black fishnets, very little actual skin—nothing as sexy as the Carl's Jr. shoot. I imagine it sold well because people expected to see me naked inside the magazine.

Surprise, suckers. They got nothing. Same as me.

My parents were pissed, and I cried, but none of us confronted him, because you just didn't do that.

That summer, I starred in *House of Wax*. The poster featured my face and the tagline: "Watch Paris die!" I didn't mind that marketing approach, and I wasn't naïve about why they chose it. And I like that movie. It stands as a campy classic. I starred in National Lampoon's *Pledge This*, and I got to play Barbara Eden doing her iconic *I Dream of Jeannie* character in *American Dreams*.

I made huge money during those years, and I did waste a lot of cash, but only the percentage you should waste as you move through your twenties, which should be an exploratory decade no matter how many zeroes show up on your paycheck.

"You're young," Papa told me. "You can tolerate high-risk investment."

He was talking about mutual funds and real estate, but I believe you can apply that advice across the board, financially, emotionally, professionally, and fashion-wise.

I screwed up sometimes. I said some things I wouldn't say now. I hurt people's feelings, and I'm sorry. I drank a lot and had some unfortunate moments. Some I can laugh about, others not so much. I'm not going to wallow in any of that here. I'm not offering explanations or asking anyone to explain themselves to me. So, no walk of shame here. Sorry, not sorry. The only people who don't screw up are people who never do anything.

I wasn't fully prepared for the tidal wave—love and hate—that came my way, so I focused on the love and recognized the hate for what it was: Pigface.

Hollywood's Pigface is not a person; it's a mentality. A power trip that comes from a deep well of helplessness. When Provo Pigface put you "on bans," no one was allowed to talk to you. Hollywood Pigface is great at shunning, shaming, and canceling people who don't play the tribal games.

Provo Pigface mocked and bullied kids and got them to rat each other out. She had only one goal—to control us—and her power came from turning us against each other. As soon as I figured that out, I was no longer afraid. I took delight in messing with her. This got me slapped around and thrown into solitary. But I survived it. There was nothing Hollywood Pigface could do to me that was worse than what had already been done.

I was twenty-three years old, working on the third season of *The Simple Life*, when *South Park* did an episode about me. This was so trippy! *South Park* was my favorite cartoon. I'd met cocreators Trey Parker and Matt Stone at a party and found them cool and interesting. If anyone could stand up to Pigface, I would have thought they could.

Womp womp.

The episode—directed by Trey and written by Trey, Matt, and Brian Graden—is called "Stupid Spoiled Whore Video Playset." I'm the title character, but they also apply that epithet to Britney Spears, Christina Aguilera, Tara Reid, and all the little girls who were fans, which upset me more than anything ugly they could say about me. It also upset me that the episode graphically portrays Tinkerbell being shot and killed. The thought of that made me sick. I've been involved in some pretty edgy media, but I don't even know where something like that comes from.

When someone on a red carpet asked how I felt about the "Stupid Spoiled Whore" episode, I said, "Oh, I didn't see it," and then I mumbled something about imitation being the sincerest form of flattery. What was I supposed to say? Frankly, I didn't want to draw more attention to it. I always heard Mom's advice in the back of my head: "Don't give it oxygen."

When a journalist told Matt about my muted red-carpet response, he said, "That shows how fucked up she is."

Prior to #MeToo, we were taught to be cool, rise above, and accept stuff like that. My not wanting to watch his cartoon about my dog being shot and me coughing up ejaculate—that's evidence of how fucked up I am. And what's really fucked up is that I did accept it. I kept quiet about it. For decades. I debated even bringing it up here, because *ick* and because I hate hate *hate* conflict. They're obviously better at bashing me than I could ever be at bashing them. Stuff like this was what Rap was all about. The only way I got through it was to stay quiet and stare at the floor.

I just can't do that anymore. Advocacy work has taught me that "silence means assent"; if you don't speak up when something is wrong, it's the same as agreeing with it.

I'm so sad that Matt and Trey went that route. Sexualized bashing of young women is worse than politically incorrect; it's dangerous. And it's boring. It's a failure of imagination. I keep wondering why they fall back on it, stretching for any remaining shock value. There's another *South Park* episode in which Cartman is granted one wish by school faculty, and his wish is to have Selena Gomez beaten while he watches.

Process that script with me for a sec: A teenage girl is brought in to be beaten for the gratification of the protagonist. Someone beats her and then says, "All right, get her the fuck out of here." As if the girl they've just assaulted is a piece of garbage to be disposed of. That's the bar now.

Selena Gomez is one of the sweetest people you'll ever meet in your life, and at the time that show was aired, she was dealing with a terrifying stalker in real life. But this isn't about who she is; it's about who we all are. How is something like that accepted—by all of us—as *funny*? How do we not see that the treatment of It Girls translates to the treatment of *all girls* in our culture?

I'll say again: I love *South Park*.

I'm not saying *South Park* is a terrible show or that they should be canceled. But I do hope that someday Trey and Matt will consult their better angels about the need to keep streaming "Stupid Spoiled Whore Video Playset." And the Selena Gomez ep. Or the thing about Britney Spears and Miley Cyrus being murdered while people take pictures of—

Look, I've done and said some things I'm not proud of. I used to wear those horrific Von Dutch caps. I once went to a Playboy Mansion Halloween party dressed as Sexy Pocahontas. At eighteen, I got drunk and performed a totally inappropriate version of Snoop Dogg's "Gin and Juice" at a party, and yes, I knew *aaaallll* the lyrics. When I was put on the spot in an interview, I pretended I voted for Donald Trump because he was an old family friend and owned the first modeling agency I signed with—and when I left to go to another agency, he was furious and intimidated the shit out of me on the phone. The truth is even worse: I didn't vote at all.

Am I standing by these choices? Would I make the same choices again, knowing what I know now? Of course not! None of that reflects the person I am now.

People evolve. We have the capacity to learn. And we all make mistakes when we're young. We have to let go of the CEDU "dirt list" mentality and find a way to do accountability and grace at the same time.

They don't match, but they go together.

You wake up one morning and say, "Wow, that was not a good look." You make it right if you can. You apologize—in private where it counts, in public if it helps. And then you move on. I'm not pretending to be, like, the Dalai Lama in Louboutins here. I'm just saying, grace is available to all of us if we make it available to each other.

The Simple Life ran for five seasons. Lots of laughter. Lots of drama. During that time, boyfriends came and went: a Backstreet Boy, a couple of Greek heirs, a lot of hungry tigers, and what Demi Lovato calls "clout chasers."

My book *Confessions of an Heiress* debuted at number 7 on the *New York Times* bestseller list, and I toured all over the place, connecting with hundreds of thousands of fans, loving my Little Hiltons. I did modeling, movies, and television, released several more fragrances, and collaborated on eyewear, skin care, shoes, bags—everything from phone cases to pillow shams. Eventually my brand expanded to encompass retail spaces, spas, and specialty hotels.

During all this—and everything else that was going on from summer 2007 to spring 2008—director-cinematographer Adria Petty followed me around with a handheld camcorder, shooting a crazy amount of footage for a doc called *Paris, Not France*. It started out as a behind-the-scenes thing for the album I was recording, but she so beautifully captured the frenetic pace and edgy vibe of my life at the time that we looked at this amazing footage and agreed: "This isn't some DVD extra, this is a fucking film." Adria put it all together with brilliant music, smash-cut editing, and commentary from Camille Paglia that elevated the film to a discussion of what celebrity had become.

Adria got the film into festivals all over the world—Cannes, Toronto, everywhere—and that scared me, because there was some stuff in it about the sex tape. And if that wasn't enough, one day while we were filming, Elliot called to tell me that someone had "acquired" the contents of an old storage unit filled with my personal belongings, including family photos, private journals, and medical records. They wanted me to pay a huge sum of money to buy back my stuff, and if I didn't, all these intensely private documents would be published on a subscription-based website, much like the sex video had been.

Before I had a chance to respond, the website went up and got 1.2 million hits in the first forty hours. My private medical history—including bills and statements pertaining to the pregnancy years earlier—was available for people to judge and gossip about. I guess this was the scene where I was supposed to explain a miscarriage or justify an abortion, and I was like, *Fuck that.* No woman, famous or not, should be forced to discuss her reproductive health with strangers. Robbing a woman of her right to privacy is a physical and psychological assault. People who do this kind of thing don't want to think of themselves as rapists, but that's what they are. Rape isn't about sex; it's about power. Sexualizing an assault is the most effective way to make a woman feel like rest of the world is judging and condemning her—which is usually the case.

I've survived it over and over again in different forms: the man who roofied me, the orderlies who molested me, the ex who released the sex tape, and every person who watched it. And this. Those people overpowered me and chained me down with shame and humiliation that rightfully belonged to them. It took me a long time to figure it out, and I'm still working on it, but when I place the shame where it belongs—on the people who hurt me—they lose their power, and I'm free.

Elliot rode in on his metaphorical white horse and chased the bastard down. He spared me most of the details, but my understanding is that it was like the situation that played out with Pamela Anderson and Tommy Lee and their infamous sex tape back in the day: someone got hold of my private stuff and tried to sell it, and because he was a buffoon, other people stole it from him and made money off it.

The situation went on and on for a couple of years until late one night, Elliot had a long come-to-Jesus conversation with this guy who'd made his living marketing sleaze and blackmailing celebrities, including me, Tom Cruise, and several others. Elliot felt he'd made some headway and arranged to meet with the guy, who seemed exhausted by his creepy life's work and genuinely interested in finding some form of redemption. Before the meeting could take place, the scandalmonger hanged himself in the shower.

Karma's a bitch.

18

Maybe I should have organized this book as the story of my life in telephones, starting with the private line in my bedroom when I was a kid. I thought it was cutting edge because there was no curly cord; you could roam all over the house and out to the backyard without dropping the call. As a nonstop working model, I carried a beeper in the 1990s and upgraded to a flip phone in 2001, which I loved because it was easy to BeDazzle. I perfected the art of pretending to be on a call to dodge unwelcome conversations.

In 2002, I had a cute little clamshell. Most people used a dorky phone holster; I clipped mine like a barrette on the low waist of my pink velour track pants, a nice little pop of shine against a bare midriff below a Von Dutch crop top. In 2003, I rocked a rhinestone-encrusted Nokia with the tallest hair of my life. My 2004 Formula

One flag girl look: flip phone with a high tech (at the time) LCD screen, pigtails, and tennis skirt. So cute.

The T-Mobile Sidekick II launch event in 2004 was like the It Girl Armageddon. I went with Nicky (this was her flawlessly sultry brunette phase) and partied with Nicole, Fergie, Bijou, Lindsay, Elisha Cuthbert, and others. That Sidekick was everything—phone, camera, messaging, email—and there was a hot pink Juicy Couture Limited Edition. This might be the flashpoint that began the smartphone era. Snoop Dogg and I became the faces of Sidekick, doing launches all over the world. Those events were epic, and we had so much fun shooting commercials.

Unfortunately, my Sidekick got hacked in 2005, and all my private contacts and pictures gushed out onto the internet. All these blah blah blah messages—that endless stream of thumb-typing in your phone—sites published them as if they were a new Gospel.

new yrs eve special big $
geoffrey coming in on 6th
hive movie Miramax
if u wanna leave ill pretend i hsve to pee u wait 3 mins come
  by urslf to back entrance
right on olive right on alameda 3 mi
party at rumi

It went on and on like this. I don't know why anyone thought that was newsworthy. I mean, maybe if you need an alternative to Ambien, then sure, try scrolling the random text messages of a person with ADHD, otherwise—no. The invasion of my privacy was annoying, but I was more upset for my friends whose numbers got leaked than I was for myself. Honestly, I was numb to it by that time.

The next few years saw a flurry of cutting-edge smartphones. I tried BlackBerry and Razr and kept a couple fresh flip phones in the repertoire. I did another big launch event for the Sidekick 3 in LA and yet another for the Razr rollout in Japan. This tech wave was all about sexy, all about color, all about functionality that took users seamlessly into a whole new mode of social and commercial interaction.

My ADHD was diagnosed sometime in my early twenties. I don't remember that much about it, because I didn't realize it was that big a deal. The doctor must have given me a brochure or something, but I don't remember him talking to me about it that much. He wrote me a prescription for Adderall, and I took it. It did help sometimes, but I hated it for a lot of reasons. (Dr. Hallowell put me on Vyvanse in 2022, and it was life changing.)

Over the years, as I learned more about how ADHD rewires the brain, it made perfect sense with my tech obsession. I was always *onto the next thing, onto the next thing, onto the next thing.* Finally, the rest of the world seemed to be catching up. It was thrilling to discover tools that kept pace with my personal rhythm—tools that instantly adapted to the hands they were in. Apps were developing. AI was learning. I couldn't wait to get my hands on the next new thing, and I had the money to get it. With my laptop and a high-speed internet connection, I was never alone in my bed at night. Somewhere in the world, someone was up, doing something interesting.

In 2006, Facebook opened up to the general public. (Thanks again to my first manager for screwing me over on that.) Twitter did a soft launch in 2006 and then went huge at SXSW the following year. Twitter was an ADHD wet dream—a steady stream of new ideas, images, directions, and possibilities.

At twenty-five, I was just having fun, shouting out little things that made me happy. But there was no denying the commercial power—the direct, bankable *influence*—of that happy little shout-out. If I tweeted about a bag or a shoe or a shirt I loved with a link to the designer or store, there was an instant surge of sales. It wasn't an advertisement—and most of the time I didn't get paid for it. I wasn't thinking about how I might control and monetize it, and I think that's why it worked. It had to be organic. The smartest thing I did was keep living my life, figuring it out as I went along.

Meanwhile, designers and marketing trend spotters noticed what I was doing and started sending me all kinds of gifts—clothes, accessories, sunglasses, dog toys, the newest gadgets, and even cars— hoping I'd post about them. Every day UPS pulled up and unloaded a ton of boxes. Every closet and spare room was overflowing. Faye Resnick was helping me renovate my house and suggested I ask Kim Kardashian to help me organize it all.

Kim had started a business where she went into the closets of famous people, took whatever they didn't love, and sold it on eBay. It was genius and generated tens of thousands of dollars for charity and fun money. She did an incredible job, and we had so much fun working together.

We balanced each other. I was a disorganized night owl; Kim was an efficient early riser. It felt good to have someone I knew I could trust and depend on. We went everywhere together—New York, Las Vegas, Miami, Australia, Germany, and Ibiza.

The song of the summer—at least my summer—was "Stars Are Blind." For me, it will always be the quintessential beach blanket song: a little vacation-destination reggae, a little boardwalk ska, all love and sunshine. Sheppard Solomon and Jimmy Iovine were working on an idea with Gwen Stefani in mind, but when Warner Bros. told them I'd been signed to do an album, Shep said, "I have something that might be perfect." Shep fleshed out the song, tailoring it to my voice and style, and I loved it. The song was produced by Shep and Fernando Garibay, who knows his beats. I trusted their instincts, and they trusted mine. That song felt right in every part of me.

It made me happy.

You can hear it in the music.

There's no tricks, no extra tech. That's *me* being the most me I'd ever been up to that point in my life. I stood in the booth, relaxed and joyful, and for a little while, all the sadness of my teen years fell away. The character I played on *The Simple Life*—a character who was taking over more and more of my life in the real world—is nowhere to be found in this song. Every line was produced with care and precision. Every time we punched in a moment, a breath, a word—every little nuance—it got better and better. I couldn't wait for the world to hear it.

"Stars Are Blind" dropped June 5, 2006, reached number 18 on Billboard's Hot 100, and then took on a life of its own. To this day people tell me how it defined that specific summer for them, along with the movies *Nacho Libre*, *Talladega Nights*, and *The Devil Wears Prada*. A few years ago, Charli XCX tweeted, "Stars Are Blind is a pop classic" and cited it as a major influence. In a red-carpet interview, Lady Gaga said, "'Stars Are Blind' is one of the greatest pop records ever. You laugh, but it would be interesting to get such an iconic blond woman in the studio with me."

I'm so proud of that song! I just want it to live forever. I recently remastered it, inspired by Taylor Swift taking control of her backlist.

In 2019, I got a letter from writer-director Emerald Fennell, asking for permission to use "Stars Are Blind," which she'd written into a pivotal scene in *Promising Young Woman*. The movie sounded funny but dark, and she had a genius idea for this song that was her "ultimate bop." She said, "I need a song that, if a boy you liked knew every word to it, you'd be incredibly impressed." If you've seen the movie, you know what she means. (If you haven't seen the movie, go now and watch it!) The scene takes place in a drugstore. Cassie (Carey Mulligan) dances with Ryan (Bo Burnham), an old acquaintance, and their passing friendship evolves before our very eyes. They fall in love in the sweet, happy space of this song. *Promising Young Woman* is a rape revenge story full of latent female rage, but that moment lets in the light and air that has to be there for us to know that Cassie's baseline innocence is still alive in her.

Promising Young Woman was released for streaming on Christmas Day, 2020. The world was deep in quarantine mode, so it never got the full theatrical premiere it deserved. It got Oscar noms for days—Best Picture, Best Director, Best Actress, Best Editing, Best Original Screenplay, and the screenplay won—but I would have loved showing up in full splendor for that premiere.

Instead, Carter and I watched it in bed. We were on a yacht somewhere on a Christmas vacation. In the sweet, happy space of that song, I let myself feel my own baseline innocence—a baseline joy—that no one could ever take from me. I loved this good, good man. And he loved me. I had it in me to love and be loved. What a relief it was to know that about myself after years of reasonable doubt.

In 2007, Tumblr launched, and Apple unveiled the iPhone. I felt something momentous beginning, but at the same time, an era was ending for me. *The Simple Life* was in its final season—the one where Nicole and I were camp counselors—and it seemed like there was a shift in the party vibe. The wide-open windows of social media made it easy to go viral one day and get swallowed whole the next. People popped up and disappeared so quickly, you never had a chance to know who they really were. My peers and I went hard, and not everyone lived to look back on it. I saw so many people pass through the meat grinder of fast fame.

I wanted everyone to love me—constantly on, constantly moving—making connections, finding ways to work with people I admired. I was out with boyfriends or girlfriends every night, and most of the time, Elliot went with us as our designated driver. But every once in a while, I just wanted to do my own thing. I love to drive, so I usually took my own car to and from work.

September 7, 2006, I got up around three in the morning and dozed in the chair while I got glam done for the second day of a music video shoot for my song "Nothing in This World." The storyline is about a kid who's getting bullied at school until I move into the house next door and go to school with him so he can be a big man on campus. It's sort of a callback to when I went to prom with the sweetest, nerdiest kid. His big sister asked Nicky to go with him, and she didn't want to because she had a boyfriend, but I was like, "Yaasss!" I was twenty-three and wasn't completely over the fact that I never got to go to prom. We did the whole thing—corsage, limo, mom taking pictures in the backyard—and when we showed up at the dance, everybody lost their minds. "Paris fucking Hilton is here? With *that* guy?" It was one of the greatest nights of my life.

So, this video is really sweet, but there were a lot of moving parts. We worked for about sixteen hours, and I never had a chance to eat anything, but when we wrapped at the end of the long day, I joined the crew in a toast with a margarita. I felt fine, but on my way home, I got stopped for speeding and blew a 0.08 on the Breathalyzer—the absolute minimum required for a DUI in California. I pulled up into In-N-Out drive-thru, waiting for a burger and fries, which probably would have solved it.

It's the least spectacular flameout in celebrity flameout history.

And the most expensive margarita in margarita history.

I went through the whole processing feeling stupid and angry—at myself more than anyone else. It was way after midnight. I couldn't decide if it was worse to call my parents and ruin their sleep or let them wake up to the news in the morning. I called Elliot, and he picked me up from the station house. I just wanted to go home, but I knew the paparazzi would be waiting. I suggested maybe I should go to a friend's house, but Elliot said, "You should go home. They need to see that you're stone cold sober."

When he pulled up to the gate, I sensed I wasn't in for the usual dance I'd always done with the paps. There was a different sort of energy. Even through the closed car window, I could hear one of them mocking me in a high voice—"*Hee hee hee hee, I'm here!*"—as I waited for Elliot to come around and open my door. I got out pretending to be on the phone.

"Paris! Paris, how ya feeling? Paris! Can you tell us what happened?"

"She's not going to make any comment this early," said Elliot. "I'll come out and see you in about ten minutes."

"Okay, bye. I love you," I said to the imaginary person on the phone. I punched the code into the alarm on the gate and flashed a smile for the cameras before I went in. The guys must have gotten paid well for staying up late; I saw that footage over and over again on the news the next day, followed by a brief Q&A with Elliot.

"You saw her moments ago," he said to the paparazzi outside my gate. "She clearly was not intoxicated. She was not drunk. But the officers did what they have to do in a situation like that. They took her to the station. She went through the same procedure that everybody else does. When it was determined that she's obviously not a flight risk and she's not inebriated, they released her on her own recognizance."

He emphasized that I'd had only one drink and received no special treatment during processing.

"Will Paris spend time in detox?" they asked. It seemed like that's what people wanted. A big addiction/redemption sob story, but I didn't have one, and I remembered Elliot's advice the day we met: "Don't lie. Just own it." I called Ryan Seacrest and gave a calm, candid interview on the radio the next morning, accepting responsibility, making no excuses. I went to court and got three years' probation, a fifteen-hundred-dollar fine, a four-month suspension of my license, and court-ordered alcohol education classes.

Fair enough. I accepted that. Even if they were stretching to charge me with DUI, there have been times when I probably was over the limit and didn't get caught.

Pause for an important message: DON'T DRINK AND DRIVE.

It's stupid and dangerous and will fuck you up. Even if you don't feel drunk, just don't go there. Also DON'T TEXT AND DRIVE. Same reason. DON'T DRIVE if you're distracted, upset, sleepy, or whatever. Even though I was only on the fringe of testing positive for tipsy, I was way too tired to be driving, and I've heard that's worse, even though it's not illegal. I deserved to take a knock for the stupid choice I made.

I didn't deserve what happened next.

I was told by my lawyer that I couldn't drive at all for thirty days and then for ninety days after that, I could drive only to and from work. The day the suspension was lifted (according to him), I was driving to work and got stopped for speeding. And I didn't have my lights on. The city street was brightly lit, but that's such a stupid mistake, it still hurts my head. What seriously screwed me is that my lawyer, who'd never handled a DUI, didn't have the drive-for-work waiver he thought he had. He told Elliot and Elliot told me that I could drive as of that day, but that's not what the paperwork said. My license was straight-up suspended.

The lawyer threw Elliot under the bus, and Elliot blamed himself, but I was a grown woman driving around in a five-hundred-thousand-dollar vehicle. It was my responsibility to handle myself. I should have read the fine print in the paperwork instead of depending on someone else to tell me what I could or couldn't do. And even in the brightly lit street, I should have had my lights on. I deserved a ticket for that, just like anyone else would get. The miscommunication about the suspension took it to another level. Now I was looking at going to jail, and that terrified me.

My parents were heartsick, but they were with me. My family closed ranks around me and loved me. All the grace I could have asked of Mom and Dad when I was a teenager—it was here for me in this moment. Mom could see how scared I was, and she let me cling to her like a little tree frog.

Elliot tried to step up and testify that he had told me it was okay for me to drive to and from work, but the judge wasn't having it. He was literally days from retirement and seemed to relish this last big moment, his fifteen minutes of fame. He sentenced me to forty-five days in jail and specified that I had to spend that time in county correctional—maximum security for violent offenders—not the "glamour slammer" for nonviolent offenders or on house arrest like most people would in a similar situation. I was to be the example for all the dangerous party girls out there. The tabloids ate that up. Elliot told me that when the judge arrived at church the following Sunday, the congregation gave him a standing ovation.

My lawyer appealed on the grounds that this sentence was far outside the norm. Elliot put out a public statement saying what he wasn't allowed to say in court, taking it on the chin when the tabloids made it sound like I'd fired him in a rage. The fact is I was really pissed off at him, the lawyer, the judge, the tabloids—I was mad at everyone in the whole goddamn world, starting with myself.

I called Elliot the next night, and we talked for a long time. If there was ever a moment when I needed him on my side, this was it. He put out another statement, saying he was my publicist again, and when a reporter commented on the revolving-door turnaround, he said the most Elliot thing I ever heard him say: "I don't choose to revisit that which is divisive. I'm only interested in that which is healing."

When I said I wanted to be the most famous person in the world, I knew what I was signing up for. I knew every mistake I made would be on full display. I never expected anyone to cut me any slack; I'd seen what happened when Martha Stewart went to jail a few years earlier. Comedy gold. I get it. I could handle that part of it. What killed me was how vividly everything came rushing back. Strip searches. Solitary confinement. Cement walls and metal doors. The sound of footsteps and screaming down the hall.

The nightmares had never left me. Now I was awake. It was real, and I couldn't tell anyone why this wasn't like Martha Stewart making the best of a bad situation. People weren't talking about being "triggered" back then. PTSD was something we associated with war zones. I had no words to express the gut-deep anxiety I felt.

There were endless conversations about how and when I should turn myself in. It occurred to me that the transporters had been right; if I'd known they were coming, I would have run. The urge to run now was overwhelming. I felt it like an acid in my leg muscles. But where could I go? I'd gotten my wish. I would be recognized anywhere in the world.

My team theorized that, because paparazzi would be expecting me to turn myself in at the last possible moment on June 5, I should go to the MTV Awards on June 3 and then go to jail after. Every photographer in town would be focused on the after-parties, and they'd expect me to be there. This was my best opportunity to do what I had to do without the paparazzi crawling all over it.

I got dressed up. Hair. Makeup. The whole thing. I did the red carpet, smiling for cameras, signing autographs, putting on my breathy baby voice for one interview after another.

Make a mad face.

Make a happy face.

Make a face with no emotion.

In her opening monologue that night, Sarah Silverman made some jokes about me that she herself later described as "hard core," and the material landed just like any comedian would hope.

"Paris Hilton is going to jail," she said, and a chorus of cheering and hooting went up. So many of these people regularly partied at my house. Now they were laughing and celebrating my humiliation. I felt the Rap closing in around me. I sat there, trying to maintain my mannequin face—the protective shell Pigface could never crack—but I was dying inside as the bit went on with an oblique reference to the sex tape. I'm not going to repeat the whole thing here.

I don't choose to revisit that which is divisive.

I'm only interested in that which is healing.

When I was younger, I thought "rise above it" meant swallowing negative feelings, pretending nothing was happening. That was the way my parents operated, but now I see how buried pain and anger can damage your soul; the only way to resolve it is exposing it to air and sunlight.

In 2021, fourteen years after that MTV Awards show, Nicky was on my *This Is Paris* podcast, and we got on the topic of the *New York Times* documentary *Framing Britney*, which sparked a long-overdue conversation about the demeaning way Brit and I and other young female celebrities were treated by the media back in the aughts.

This led to an unpleasant memory of David Letterman drilling down on the jail thing after promising not to talk about it. I'd been on the show many times, and he'd always had fun at my expense, but he'd never been actively cruel like that. Nicky remembered waiting in the wings as I came off the set crying and shaking.

"To have a young girl up there, asking her questions designed to humiliate her," Nicky said on the pod, "it's cruel. And I don't think that would happen today."

"It's such a different world now," I agreed. "There's a lot that wouldn't happen today."

"You know what would not happen today?" said Nicky. "Sarah Silverman going onstage at the MTV Awards . . ." and she went off like only a little sister can, outraged all over again. I cringed at first, thinking, *Oh, God! Don't bring that up! Don't give it oxygen!* But then it struck me how present and real that hurt was, undiminished by time, in my sister's voice. All these things I tried to rise above—they didn't just hurt me. They hurt my little sister, my nieces, and the daughter I hope to have someday. For the first time, I saw that Letterman interview and the MTV monologue in the context of an entire culture that reveled in the degradation of young women, and there was just no way to bury it anymore. I understand the "don't give it oxygen" thing, but there's a point where you end up cutting off your own oxygen as well. I finally let go of that idea and spoke for the first time about that incredibly painful moment.

The beautiful plot twist is that Sarah was on my side. The next day, she said on her podcast, "Paris Hilton on her latest podcast calls me out for jokes I did about her when I hosted the 2007 MTV Awards. Here we go."

I held my breath, bracing myself for the scathing comeback.

"You know," said Sarah, "she said herself on the podcast, that would never happen today. And she's right. I would never do those jokes today. I've actually dedicated the past several years trying to do comedy that attempts to marry hard-hitting jokes with actual heart. Back then, the consensus seemed to be that was not possible. And I fully accepted that. I came up in a time when talk-show hosts and comedians were hired to make fun of pop culture. We were roasting the biggest celebrities and pop culture icons at the time, and nobody was bigger than Paris Hilton. So here we are in an awakened world, and I am totally into it. It's how we grow. It's how we change. I'm super down with reflecting on the past and my part in perpetuating real ugly shit. And yes, we can continue to litigate the past. But I do believe that maybe that should be coupled with taking into account any growth that has come with those passing years. . . . Comedy is not evergreen. We can't change the past, so what's crucial is that we change with the times."

She said she didn't know I'd be in the audience at the MTV Awards, that her heart sank when she saw the look on my face, and that she'd written me a letter to apologize. She chose "that which is healing." A brave choice. An honest choice. Oxygen. In a good way. It brought tears to my eyes. I wish I'd received her letter back then. It would have meant a lot. All these years later, she could have blown it off like, "Hey, I tried to apologize. Bitch ice-burned me." I love that Sarah put herself out there instead and offered this template for moving forward.

I'm not always successful, but I am trying to follow her lead and allow for growth in people who've hurt me, and I'm hoping the people I've hurt will allow for continuing growth in me. I think about what might have happened during CEDU Raps if all the kids had said, "No. We're not doing that." It never crossed our minds—the idea that we could band together instead of tearing each other apart. We were so terrified. We thought we had no power over the people who turned us against each other. We didn't know that kindness was our only hope.

Revisiting the aughts from a post-#MeToo/#TimesUp perspective is wrenching. I had fun—*tons* of fun—and I refuse to remember it any other way. Other than a few occasions that left me curled up in a ball, I didn't let haters get to me. Because, honestly, we took it for granted, didn't we? Girls like me assumed we would be judged and belittled. We *expected* girls to be sexualized and then condemned for their sexuality, punished for both silence and speaking out, told we should accept responsibility for our choices and then called crazy or stupid or slutty if we didn't live by the rules other people chose for us. I'm happy to see a new generation of girls—and guys—rejecting that tired way of being.

I think we can be better. I believe kindness and decency will win eventually because it's good business. The market for assholes is simply not sustainable. It should come as a great comfort to all my fellow fuck-ups: redemption is a thing. Sometimes it's hard to find. Other times it comes out of nowhere and makes you cry.

The night of the MTV thing, I turned myself in at the LA County jail and went through the whole process: mug shot, cavity search, orange. On the way to my cell, people were yelling at me—*rich bitch, cunt, I'm gonna fuck you*—and I felt my stomach turning. I couldn't breathe. It was like a big fist reached into my chest and closed around my heart. I seriously thought I was dying. A doctor came. Or a nurse. She examined me and held a paper bag in front of my face. Night ground into day and into another night. I couldn't stop crying. I lay in my cell, doubled over with dry heaves that made my ribs feel broken. I was having severe panic attacks and PTSD.

My attorney provided evidence of medical necessity and received permission from another judge for me to spend the rest of my sentence on house arrest, but that crusty old man who was supposed to have retired stepped in and insisted that I be rearrested, brought back in handcuffs, strip-searched again, and processed back into county lockup. I don't know why it meant so much to him. These extraordinary measures were not about me being treated the same as other people; they were about me being treated worse.

The warden felt it would be too disruptive and dangerous to put me in general population, so he put me in solitary. My cell had a narrow cot, a toilet with a tiny sink above it, and a wall-mounted desk with a little round stool built in. I was alone there twenty-three hours every day. For one hour, I was taken to the shower and allowed to use the pay phone. I could speak to my parents through a Plexiglas window once a week.

Media outlets offered up to a million dollars for photos of me in the orange jumpsuit. All the talk shows wanted to get me on the phone. A male guard kept coming into my cell, rubbing my head, and offering to bring me a Sprite. I woke up in the middle of the night to find him standing over me with a camera. I pulled my blanket over my head and screamed bloody murder until another guard dragged him out and took me to the warden, who was annoyed to see me but was actually on my side.

"This is ridiculous. We don't have beds for the people who pose a genuine threat to society. This is a joke. What a waste of resources," and on and on like that as he paced back and forth in his office.

I didn't know what I was supposed to say. Somewhere down the hall, a TV was blasting CNN. *Heiress Paris Hilton blah blah blah.* My lawyer promised to keep fighting it, but a weird, exhausted calm settled on me. I told him, "No. Just leave me alone." I huddled on the small cot, hugging my knees to my chest, and made myself go to that place I used to go to during those long hours in Obs.

My beautiful world.

I was not surprised to check in and find that, overwhelmingly, the life I was living was very much the life I had visualized. What didn't make sense to me was how I could be having so much fun and feel so little satisfaction. I had everything I wanted. But it wasn't enough. Maybe there was no such thing as enough, and my only salvation was to just keep grinding. Do more projects. Date more guys. Partner with this person or that manufacturer. More fragrances, properties, movies, music. More parties. More people. More money, more money, more money.

I read *The Secret*, a book that had always given me faith in myself and the world. A compassionate guard played the audiobook on the speaker system so everyone could hear Rhonda Byrne's reassuring words. *Energy... trust... love... abundance... education... peace.* I believed in these things. I wanted to receive and give them. I thought a lot about how much I had changed—and had not changed—over the past ten years. For a minute it seemed like I had my arms around it all, but now it was impossible to know what my world would be like after I was released, impossible to say how this would impact my brand—the brand I'd built and should have been protecting. It was all I had. In many ways, the brand was me; if I failed to protect it, I was failing to protect myself, and then what would I do?

It was about how I wanted to feel. Not what I wanted to get.

I would not forget that again. I would not be vulnerable.

The character I played—part Lucy, part Marilyn—was my steel-plated armor. As a teenager, I created her: the dumb blonde with a sweet but sassy edge. I used her to get into clubs, portrayed her on TV and in movies, and let her out to play with the paparazzi. People loved her. Or they loved to hate her, which was just as marketable. I leaned into that character, my ticket to financial freedom and a safe place to hide. I made sure I never had a quiet moment to figure out who I was without her. I was afraid of that moment because I didn't know what I'd find.

The answer came the week before I was released. They opened my cell door and brought in several plastic bins full of letters from Little Hiltons all over the world. *I'm with you. Stay strong. You inspire me. You can do this.* Among these thousands of letters, there was not one that expressed anger or judgment—it was all love. It was all kindness. I spent the last several days of my sentence writing back, answering as many letters as I could. Little Hiltons, I don't have words to tell you all what you mean to me. You've given me life a million times over. I'm so grateful and so proud of the beautiful people you are inside and out.

I also started writing a song that pretty much sums up the whole experience:

CNN and MTV, all cameras focused on me
Helicopters up above, oh what a travesty
There's a crazy world at war
Right outside of my front door
They're wasting time on me
I'm just a jailhouse baby
Oh, I'm singing so sweetly
Oh, jailhouse baby
Oh, no window to the world
I'm a little, I'm a little jailbird

Cold nights and freezing water, fluorescents always on
Stuck here behind this glass, my parents see their daughter
Judge, you're no celebrity
You're a desperate wannabe
Seems like you'd rather leave
Real criminals on the streets

All those lonely nights of terror
I thank you for your letters
Words from around the world
For the lonely little jailbird

In the state of California, you get one day off your sentence for each day of "good time" served, so I was there for twenty-three days. The evening I was released from jail, helicopters filled the air while paparazzi and mainstream media pressed against the chain-link fences that created a long alley I had to walk down to get to the car where Mom and Dad were waiting for me. The air was full of flashing lights, chopper blades, and shouted questions.

The press line was bigger than any red carpet or film festival I'd ever seen. I was wearing jeans, a stubby ponytail, and no makeup, but I walked out of there like a fucking supermodel. I just walked—and then ran, unicorn trotting in my Louboutins—into my mother's arms. In all that madness, I felt a calm core of pure happiness. I had stepped out of hell for a second time.

In the months that followed, the paps were relentless. I eventually had to sell my home and move to a gated community up off Mulholland. I loved my new house, but it was hard to leave the happy party house on Kings Road.

It felt like the end of an era.

PART 4

*Sometimes good things fall apart
so better things can fall together.*

MARILYN MONROE

19

Coachella and I have a history. We both entered the grown-up world in 1999, struggled for a few years, found our footing, and spent the next two decades raging in all our neon glory.

Coachella is held every spring at the Empire Polo Club, a seventy-eight-acre field about twenty minutes from Palm Springs. During the year I lived in Rancho Mirage with my grandmother, we spent many Saturday afternoons at Empire Polo Club, wandering the grounds and watching the games. I loved looking at the horses. She loved looking at the men. It was very much the same vibe as the polo scene in *Pretty Woman*, which was shot at the Los Angeles Equestrian Center in Burbank but is pretty much a copy and paste of a typical Saturday afternoon in Coachella Valley. Gram Cracker and I were always dolled up and sophisticated in summer dresses and ballerina flats. You couldn't wear heels; that would make for a brutal afternoon walking around on the turf.

In the early aughts, Coachella—officially the Coachella Valley Music and Arts Festival—was called the "anti-Woodstock" because they provided plenty of restrooms, food, and water for a crowd of beautiful people, who were generally nice and well behaved. This new generation of festivalgoers had zero interest in wallowing in the mud. If you're in the mood for mud, I'll see you at Glastonbury.

In 2009, Brent Bolthouse created the Neon Carnival, an A-list, invitation-only after-party. (Remember Brent? He's still killing it, and we've been together since that sweet-sixteen birthday party at Pop in 1997.) From the first year, I was obsessed. Someone asked me last week, "Will you be at the Neon Carnival?" and I said, "Honey, I *am* the Neon Carnival."

I'm writing this in 2022. Festival season is finally alive again after being murdered by COVID two years in a row. I'm a little stressed out about my wardrobe. I'm usually a control freak about wardrobe for Coachella and Burning Man, dissecting every detail months in advance, but I've been insanely busy working on a mirror event—a Neon Carnival in the metaverse—so at the last minute, I called my friend Shoddy Lynn, who owns Dolls Kill, this sick raver store that sells glitzy, Goth, artistic, crazy, sexy clothes and accessories. I love supporting this woman-owned small business.

I also had Michael Costello make me a few daytime dresses—flowing boho chic—that I can wear with ballerina flats from Nicky's French Sole collab. I'll be a beautiful, lacy angel in the afternoon and a sexy raver princess at night. Every look involves glam and a photo shoot, so it has to be planned in advance or it eats up too much fun time, which is already limited because I can only be there for one weekend. Normally, I'd never miss the second weekend of Coachella, but Carter has a business function I need to attend along with all the other supportive spouses.

I'm weirdly thrilled by domestic "wifey for lifey" duties like that.

Carter and I know how to work a room together—a power-couple dynamic we both learned from our parents. I don't know how to explain it, but it's a thing—this graceful, sweeping ease, a form of unspoken communication that can't be learned or faked. It only happens if you genuinely respect, trust, and support each other. Maybe the best word for it is *alliance*. We're in this together. What's important to Carter is important to me. What's important to me is important to Carter.

Even so, I'm afraid the FOMO will be real when I see everyone else posting pictures from Coachella Weekend 2.

A lot has changed for me since the last time I was at Coachella. I've changed—for the better, I think—but the biggest difference is having Carter with me. The first couple years of our relationship coincided with quarantine. This is our first festival season together. Right now, Carter is standing in the foyer, in shock when he sees the quantity of luggage I need for a three-day weekend: two dozen suitcases and garment bags, multiple bins containing bags, crowns, sunglasses, several cases of glam and tech equipment, and a life-size cardboard cutout of Fisher, founder of Fizz hard seltzer. It all makes sense. Trust me.

I don't think about it on a conscious level, but Coachella is a good example of how my ADHD perception of time translates to trend spotting: In the eye of the Spirograph, I walk the polo field with Gram Cracker and the Neon Carnival with Carter. I feel the earth beneath my sturdy boots and pretty ballerina flats. If the right influencer says the best of both worlds is a pretty platform boot, then someone—preferably a small, woman-owned business—is going to sell a ton of those.

We load out and leave before sunrise, fly to Palm Springs in a private jet, and relocate to our home-base hotel suite, where my team helps me reorganize everything in a walk-in closet. Friday morning, we pull up behind the main stage at Coachella in an RV the size of a Greyhound bus. In the next seventy-two hours, I get maybe ten hours of actual sleep. I'd get even less if I didn't sleep while people do my hair and makeup.

Marilyn Monroe used to do that, too—lie there sleeping while the glam squad did their work as if they were putting makeup on a corpse. It's not good-quality sleep. More like a power nap. I'm okay with it for the weekend. It's kind of fun to wake up with iridescent lips and Sailor Moon space buns, and I have to make the most of my only weekend at Coachella.

First and foremost is the music. In between mainstage acts—Megan Thee Stallion, Harry Styles, Billie Eilish, Swedish House Mafia with The Weeknd, Doja Cat—there's a constant rotation of amazing performers on eight stages. I have to map out a schedule and literally run from one stage to another in my platform boots, making sure I have time for all my favorite DJ sets and—my favorite thing—the Neon Carnival.

The Neon Carnival is the last echo of the LA party vibe we loved at the turn of the century.

"New York had Studio 54," Brent said to me not long ago, "but we had the nineties and 2000s. You could go to a club in LA on a Monday night, and it felt like an Emmy party."

I'm not the only one who still wants to party like it's 1999.

The Neon Carnival is a curated experience that makes me think of those wildly fun, colorful turn-of-the-century parties. In the beginning, it was staged inside a giant airplane hangar, but after ten years, they moved it to the HITS (Horse Shows in the Sun) Equestrian Center. The guest list is limited. There are no tickets or tables for sale. It doesn't matter if you have money or a massive Instagram following.

There are celebrities like me and venture capitalists like Carter, but fame and money aren't the be-all-end-all. You're just as likely to bump into a skater poet from Venice, a race-car driver from Australia, models from Japan, advertising moguls from Kenya, people from different cultures, people with different abilities, loud people, quiet people, straight people, gay people, drag queens, drama queens, introverted extroverts and extroverted introverts. The only thing we all have in common is that we're alive and lit up with milky neon magic.

For Neon Carnival, avant-garde fashion is the rule, not the exception, so the clothes, hair, and makeup are out of control, but not as expensive and hard to move around in as the avant-garde looks you see at the VMAs and the Met Gala. I love seeing everyone breaking away from the expected, expressing their personal freakiness, whatever that is. I think I'll wear a little black dress with neon green beads that come alive in black light, plus sunglasses from my new Quay collab, a fleecy neon rainbow bomber jacket from Dolls Kill, and a little hologram backpack for my phones, ketchup packets (Heinz and fries, always), extra tiaras (designed by Melissa Loschy of Loschy Crowns, who makes these glorious bespoke headpieces and sells them on Etsy) so I can gift them as the spirit moves me, a couple of fragrances (sometimes I wear a men's scent), a makeup kit, and a little battery-operated fan. Because it's hot. Temperature-wise.

In the wake of the 2008 economic collapse came the Web 2.0 democratization of the internet. We started talking about the "long tail" concept of creator content that breathed outside the box. No more product-launch windows. No more gatekeepers. Now you could create and direct your own marketing from the palm of your hand. I was on the bleeding edge of it all, with all the name recognition—for better or worse—powering my platform, which got me some great opportunities in movies, television, and traditional media.

Some people were saying the old world and the new were separate and incompatible, but for me, it was a healthy symbiotic mix. There was no established path for me to follow, no role models for me to learn from. I just spread my wings and the updraft took me.

During the 2008 presidential election, the McCain campaign

inexplicably chose to use images of me in their ads as the example of the worst thing they could think of: a "Hollywood celebrity." I guess their intention was to equate Barack Obama with me and Brit—vacuous celebs with nothing to contribute to the dialogue. A relatively new website called Funny or Die came to me with a brilliant idea, and I did a series of "Paris for President" faux campaign ads, which include some of my favorite dialogue ever.

> ME *(sitting on a chaise in a cute swimsuit)*: Okay, so here's my energy policy: Barack wants to focus on new technology to cut foreign oil dependence. McCain wants offshore drilling. Why don't we do a hybrid of both candidates' ideas? We can do limited offshore drilling with strict environmental oversight while creating tax incentives to get Detroit making hybrid and electric cars. That way the offshore drilling carries over until the new technologies kick in, which will create new jobs and energy independence. Energy crisis solved! I'll see you at the debates, bitches.

I studied the scripts so there wouldn't be a teleprompter and it would be clear that I knew what I was talking about. No baby voice. Just me. The crew came to the Hamptons to film, so I got to hang out with my family at the same time.

"You'll be back for Thanksgiving, won't you?" Mom said.

I probably made some vague promise that I would, and I didn't purposely avoid those holiday weekends. I didn't make a point of not going, but I didn't make a point of going, either. I was in a good place with my parents.

In 2010, Instagram and Pinterest launched. The big movies were *Inception* and *The Social Network*. The party vibe was noticeably shifting now with the knowledge that whatever you did, wherever you went, someone there had a camera, and anything you said or did could be out there for the world to see within seconds. Casey Johnson died just a few days into the new year. She'd been best friends with Nicky and me since we were little girls, and she looked so happy in the last photos I saw on Instagram. Rocking a sparkling gold mini with snakeskin pumps and a Chanel bag. I clicked that little heart. It was beyond imagination—the idea that Nicky and I would never see her again.

In 2011, I turned thirty. It was a new era for social media as an art form. Twitter bubbled up, followed by Instagram, and I was in the first wave of users. I saw it as an opportunity to expand my global brand. Along with the potential to build my own interests, I looked for opportunities to lift up people and causes I believed in.

I tried on a new reality series with Mom—*The World According to Paris*—some of which was shot during my community-service hours from a minor possession bust. No big story there, just a small amount of weed, which is legal now and should have been legal then—especially for people with PTSD—but it wasn't legal then, so it was a fair shake. I put in my 200 hours of service, and then we were having so much fun I put in another 350 hours. I was happy that we were able to direct some attention to deserving organizations serving the homeless in LA.

The show was fun, and Mom was great. Traveling so dominated my life, I decided to do a Passport Collection of fragrances—Paris, South Beach, Tokyo, St. Moritz—and rolled around the world promoting them. I sponsored a motorcycle team in Madrid and walked at Brazil Fashion Week with Lady Gaga's "Born This Way" booming in the background. I had lots of fun posting about my travels on Twitter until I discovered that when you post about all the exciting places you're going, people know you're not home, and they rob you.

I was stunned to find out that a group of high school students later known as the "Bling Ring" had entered my home on several occasions while I was gone, taking jewelry, shoes, clothes, cash, and whatever else they wanted. I know, I know—it's hard to feel sorry for someone whose closet is so overflowing, they don't immediately notice a million dollars' worth of missing stuff, but when I was finally home long enough to realize what had happened, I felt violated and angry.

I'd worked so hard for my space. I was so exhausted when I came home. This was supposed to be my sanctuary. It took me a long time to feel safe there again, but I couldn't contemplate the thought of moving. I was done running away. And anyway, this house was so special. When Sofia Coppola was shooting *The Bling Ring*, she asked me if she could shoot here.

"There's no way to re-create it," she said. "It has to be the real thing."

It was healing, in a way, to turn what had happened into a great piece of art. I love Emma Watson and the entire cast. The crew was respectful of the fact that this was a real home where a real person lived her life.

My life, my business, and my brand were all about loving your look "hot," living in gorgeous houses with pretty things and adorable pets, and hanging with girls who know how to have fun. I came of age during the most turbulent pop culture period since Cleopatra. While it was happening, it all felt like fast-forward. Runways, parties, appearances, skiing, skydiving, cuddly pets, beautiful people, iconic photo shoots, sisterhood, business, fragrances, family, fans, nightclubs, lashes, bags, redefining femininity, creating music, placing beauty in the eye of the beholder, making art an experience and experiencing art as a way of life—it's a lot. I know. I'm okay with extra.

We transformed what it means to be famous, the Little Hiltons and me. More important, we transformed what it means to be yourself.

20

Amnesia is where I go to forget. Whatever you're trying to leave behind, trust me, it's no match for the indescribable energy of this arena-sized club that sits at the center of Ibiza, an island in the Mediterranean Sea somewhere between Spain and North Africa.

I first heard of this place when I was fifteen, living with my family at the Waldorf. I begged my dad to let me go there, but he talked to the concierge, and the concierge said, "No, no, no. Not Ibiza. This is a notorious party island. This is not a place for good girls to go."

So, no Ibiza for me until I was old enough and had made enough money to get there on my own.

In 2006 I organized an epic girl trip for myself, Caroline D'Amore, and Kim Kardashian. We all stayed in a teepee behind my friend Jade Jagger's house. It was very bohemian and cool. Kim was not much of a clubber in general, and neither of us had ever experienced anything like Amnesia. The super clubs don't open until bars around the island perimeter are ready to close, so the party doesn't even get started until 3:00 a.m. Most people are there to dance and enjoy the music, not drink. Kim and I were smart and looked out for each other. Reliable backup is an essential element of the girlfriend trip. The nonstop music is too loud to hear someone calling out, so you collect a nice crew of trusted party pals and keep eyes on each other.

Production values at Amnesia were off the chain. Insane sound systems. Epic laser light shows beaming across the crowd. Music pulsing a particular kind of house style—the Balearic beat, a unique sound that was born in those islands. We were up in a VIP area with an amazing view of the booth where the DJ was operating an elaborate array of decks and mixers. This was the first time I really paid attention to what the DJ was doing and saw how powerful it was. Killing it like a rock star, he conducted the whole room, thousands of people in the palm of his hand.

And then they fired up the foam cannons.

There's a dress code—shorts, T-shirts, and flip-flops were not allowed—but most people had swimsuits under their clothes. I pulled my cocktail dress off, tied it around my waist, and kept dancing in my bikini.

"Paris! *Ven aqui!*" The foam girls waved me over to the railing.

I took control of the cannon and blasted lemon-scented suds all over the crowd below. People went crazy, bobbing around like rubber duckies in a bubble bath. Kim and I couldn't stop laughing. Our faces lit up with the kind of joy you see when little kids come down a waterslide. That electrifying happiness—that's what I wanted people to feel when they came to the Foam and Diamonds party I hosted for five years at Amnesia. I wanted them to leave like we did, exhausted and elated, squinting in the early-morning sun.

I wanted to go back to the hotel and sleep, but Kim wanted to experience the day life in Ibiza, so we made our way to the beach and lay on the white sand.

Kim shaded her eyes with her arm and laughed. "That was lit."

"That DJ's hot," I said. "One day I'm going to be up there."

"A girl can dream."

"It says in *The Secret*, 'Life is not happening to you. You are creating it.' I'm going to create that."

"You and *The Secret*," said Kim. "You're obsessed."

"For real, though."

"I believe in you." She was half asleep but sounded like she meant it.

I said, "I believe in you too, babe."

The water was cool and intensely blue. Caroline and I linked arms, floating on inflatable rafts, so tired from dancing all night that we fell asleep and woke up half a mile offshore.

It was years before I actually started DJing, but this is definitely when it clicked. I was still in my teens when I discovered I could get paid to show up at a party, and I learned a lot, going to the best parties and the best clubs all over the world. People would show up to see celebrities, but only a great DJ could create the electrifying experience we saw in Ibiza that night. I knew if I applied myself to learning the technology, I could do both.

The first thing I learned was that it's a lot harder than it looks, but still—I'm smart enough to ask questions instead of pretending to know everything. A brilliant guy named Mike Henderson, aka DJ Endo, taught me the basics of the hardware and software. Over the next few years, between a million other things I was doing, I spent hundreds of hours learning everything there was to know about DJing, teaching myself all the tricks I could find on YouTube, and inventing a few new tricks of my own. I went to every big festival—Burning Man, Coachella, Ultra, Tomorrowland—observing, absorbing, feeling the energy, learning how to keep people jumping and raging.

Like any woman in an overwhelmingly male-dominated business, I met with some knee-jerk resistance. When I started playing gigs, some people didn't want to believe it was really me. I couldn't make space in my head for that. I worked harder, proved myself, and made my way up. I was booking major music festivals and megaclubs in the US, China, Europe, and the Middle East. And then, I finally made it back to Ibiza.

During my five-year residency at Amnesia, family, friends, and thousands of fans—so many of my Little Hiltons—so many fun, beautiful people came from all over the world, and it was everything I envisioned. It wasn't easy for me to carve out several weeks every summer, so I knew the closing party in 2017 would be my last visit to Ibiza for a while. I loved being there, but business was booming.

My fragrances had brought in almost three billion dollars, and I was working nineteen other lifestyle brands including skin care, shoes, clothes, bags, lipstick, lighting, home décor, pet fashions, and anything else I could bounce off a mood board. My real estate holdings included spas and nightclubs, and I even followed in my great-grandfather's footsteps, opening hotels of my own. I was writing and recording music, and I was always up to shoot a movie or make an appearance in the right place for the right price.

For twenty years, while every inch of my skin was laid bare to the world, I kept certain things hidden. The effort left me lean and detached, strong enough to survive head-spinning success, soul-crushing betrayals, and staggering amounts of my own bullshit.

But sooner or later, everyone leaves Ibiza.

Amnesia never lasted long enough for me. No matter how hard I worked, no matter how hard I played, eventually I had to sleep, and in my nightmares, I remembered. It was as if the time I spent in jail opened a basement door that I'd kept locked a long time. The nightmares had never left me, but going to jail for twenty-three days took them to a new level. It was real again. Immediate. Physical. Dangerous. I didn't just wake up screaming; I woke up struggling for air as if I were trapped on the bottom of a muddy river.

Sometimes I got up and pulled my laptop into bed with me. It was not a healthy habit. The first time I googled "Provo Canyon School," I was stunned to see that it still existed. After all these years. No one had done a damn thing about it. Including me. The guilt was like the sting of a wasp. Because this is what pedophiles and abusers and rapists do: They make you complicit in their wrongdoing by giving you the one thing that threatens them: Now you know. You could stop them. If you do nothing, the next one's on you. Of course, this is absolute bullshit, unfair and untrue, but I know I'm not the only one who carried that burden. So many survivors have shared their stories and cried with me, both of us heavy with regret for every child who suffered while we tried to leave that place behind. Our sanity—sometimes our very survival—hinged on forgetting that place and creating a life in which we'd never have to think about it again.

With the dawn of Reddit and other forums, survivors of Provo and CEDU began to piece together a terrible history of abandonment and abuse. The extent of the wreckage was heartbreaking: addiction, PTSD, suicide, shattered sleep, ruined families. And the mass of the money—*so much money* it took my breath away. Billions flowed into these facilities via private and public funding. It was so fucking wrong the way they continually changed corporate entities to dodge lawsuits and accusations. CEDU Education had been sold to Brown Schools in 1998. They declared bankruptcy in 2005 and were taken over by United Health Service, Inc. They disappeared and reappeared like Whac-A-Mole. Some efforts had been made to hold them accountable, but no one was able to pin anything on them.

I had to look away. I had to tell myself, *This isn't my fault. There's nothing I can do.* I couldn't be part of this. What if someone on one of these forums remembered me? Hated me from back then? All that Rap stuff. The kangaroo kick. The stabbing plot that got blamed on me—all of it. My brand was more than my business; it was my identity, my strength, my self-respect, my independence, my whole life. I had to protect my brand. Anything off brand—*no*. Circle with a slash. Can't have that.

I retreated to my safe ground: work.

Facebook acquired Instagram in 2012, and Twitter acquired Vine. I launched a line of eyewear in Shanghai and toured with my fifteenth fragrance, Dazzle, which is still one of my favorites and gave me a break from the Spanish model I was dating. I'd gone into a franchise deal that involved forty Paris Hilton retail locations, mostly in Europe and Asia, selling handbags, skin care, sunglasses, and other branded merchandise.

In 2013 and 2014, when I wasn't doing DJ residencies in Atlantic City and Ibiza or playing shows in Spain, France, Portugal, South Korea, and the US, I was in the studio working on music of my own. I built new singles, "High Off My Love" and "Come Alive," into my set along with my classic theme music. More than ever, I felt Ultra Naté's "Free."

I couldn't shake the thought of the children being held at Provo Canyon School, but I felt exactly the way the school had trained me to feel: powerless.

I wanted to help, but I didn't know who to go to. Anything I did meant risking my carefully constructed narrative. It meant potentially hurting or embarrassing my family.

I felt protective of Papa. He was healthy for his age, but some of the spark went out of him when we lost Nanu in 2004. He was never a super sentimental guy, but as I grew into my life as a businesswoman, we shared a lot of common ground. That relationship was important to me. In 2014, I leaned into my real estate interests, opening Paris Beach Club in the Philippines, and he was all about it. Whenever I took him out to dinner, I'd ask him if he wanted to go out the back way to avoid the paparazzi, but he was proud and happy to take my arm and go out the front.

It meant a lot to me to see my mom and dad so proud of everything I'd accomplished. I won Best Female DJ at the NRJ DJ Awards, and *Time* magazine reported that I was the highest-paid female DJ in the business, making up to a million dollars per gig. I'm still working toward the day when we can drop the "female" part of that conversation. There are so many killer women DJs out there now, the term feels dated and out of touch. Opportunities are plentiful; the boys have nothing to be afraid of. If you're good, you'll get work. Competition is healthy, right?

Nicky was killing it, too. Her book *365 Style* was published, and she was engaged to James Rothschild, who was (a) wonderful and (b) a Rothschild.

All of which is to say, I didn't want to rock the family boat by bringing up unpleasantness from the past.

In 2015 "High Off My Love" reached #3 on the *Billboard* club list, I played to a crowd of fifty thousand at Summerfest in Milwaukee, and Nicky married James at Kensington Palace. The low point was losing Tinkerbell, my sweet companion through so many highs and lows. She died of old age at fourteen.

TikTok launched in 2016, an instant sensation. Donald Trump became president. And I became an aunt when Nicky and James had a gorgeous daughter, Lily-Grace Victoria. Her little sister, Theodora Marilyn, was born in 2017.

Being Aunt Paris brought out a new level of fierce in me. As I watched these amazing little creatures grow, memories of my own early childhood bubbled up from the back of my mind. I was once that joyful, a free-spirited little mermaid of a kid. And then . . . things happened.

TikTok and Instagram made it easy for me to pretend my life was a perfect fairy tale, but in fact, my fairy tale life is the one that didn't happen: elite prep school, Ivy League college, graduate studies abroad, a career in animal science, a nice husband and children. All that disappeared before I had a chance to even imagine it. Now I was trapped inside that *Simple Life* caricature, this me-but-not-really person who was out in the world living my life.

Social media became the new reality.

Selves became selfies.

Privacy was commodified.

Our collective attention span became ad space.

An entire generation of children grew up numbed by Ritalin and somehow managed to reinvent the art of connection.

I was carried by a tide of empowerment. It rose up under me as women of all ages grew weary of the way we'd been dismissed. Now I was working hard to shed my skin and leave behind the character with the baby voice. I wanted to be the woman Marilyn never had a chance to evolve into: It Girl gone Influencer.

Everything I do is tied up in swiftly advancing technology: music, social media, DJing, visual arts, product development and design, NFTs, and whatever comes next. Carter and I talk a lot about how we'll raise children in the thick of it.

(We talk a lot about kids in general because we're so excited to have kids one day.)

"I can't imagine what it means to be a thirteen-year-old girl in this day and age," I said. "We'll have to be strict about screen time."

"Our parents faced the same challenge," said Carter, "except they had to be strict about computer time and video games. And their parents had to be strict about this new thing called television."

It's mind blowing, isn't it? It's all happening so fast.

But I had this brick wall built up around me. I worked hard at keeping it there. Made some poor choices. Allowed some toxic influences. I wasted so much time on hungry hangers-on and beautiful bullies who always seemed to need money, constant attention, or both. If I accidentally connected with a man who was man enough, I always found a way to torpedo things.

"I don't feel that bad for you," Nicky said after I broke up with someone I hardly remember. "If you wanted kids and wanted a husband, you would find a way to make it happen. Maybe you don't want it. You think society expects that of you, but it's a huge responsibility. If you don't genuinely want it, you shouldn't do it."

I did want it. Genuinely! But some part of me just wasn't open to the kind of partnership I saw in Papa and Nanu, Mom and Dad, and now Nicky and James. I accepted that it was something I wasn't capable of. I didn't see myself ever unlearning that old lesson: *I'm better off on my own.*

I traveled 250 days a year. My time was consumed with creating and cultivating. Making things happen. That was my lifeblood. And all this activity insulated me from memory. Every gig, flight, and photo shoot, every cameo role and disposable boyfriend, was a brick in the wall I built around myself. No one knows me better than Nicky. The fact that I never told her what actually happened during the time I was supposedly "away at boarding school in London" is proof of how deeply I buried it.

I turned thirty-six in 2017: the same age Marilyn Monroe and Princess Diana were when they died. Whatever path they blazed for me ended here. A strange *something needs to happen* feeling settled on me.

Reality TV offers were a constant thing in my life, and I usually turned them down without taking the meeting. I didn't want to go backward. But I kept hearing from Aaron Saidman, who was executive producer on the documentary *Leah Remini: Scientology and the Aftermath*. I was won over by the level of homework he did and the substance he was going for.

At our first meeting, Aaron told me, "I went down kind of a rabbit hole, reading a lot of press. A lot of it was, honestly, unflattering. Critical. I started thinking about the audience consuming all those articles. We spent twenty years obsessing about Paris Hilton, gossiping about the Hilton sisters, but you weren't talking about yourselves. We were all having that conversation, but every time a scandal broke, the family did this circling of the wagons. They sent the PR guy out to take the flack."

I had to smile, thinking about Elliot sipping his chardonnay.

I clean up what gets tainted and magnify what glows.

"As a nonfiction storyteller," said Aaron, "I became more curious about what you might say if you really had a chance to speak in the first person."

I was curious, too. I'd recently produced and starred in *The American Meme*, a documentary about social media influencers, and I wanted this film to be equally cinematic, scary, funny, entertaining, and poignant. (Also my vision for this book, and I hope I've succeeded.) I agreed to participate in a documentary about corporate-branding diva Paris Hilton jetting around the world, being a girl boss, greeting fans, playing major music festivals, and dating hot guys. I wanted to bring fans into my Beverly Hills home,

Slivington Manor, and show some of the day-to-day hammering away it takes to build a global corporate entity in the tradition of my great-grandfather's insane hotel empire.

I had no intention of disclosing the truth about my "boarding school" years. But then Demi Lovato rocked my world.

I'd known and loved Demi for a while, but I was as stunned as the rest of the world by how real, vulnerable, and courageous she was in the *Demi Lovato: Simply Complicated* documentary in 2017. Not long after my last show in Ibiza, I was the DJ in the house party scene at Demi's, the setting for her "Sorry Not Sorry" music video shoot. In the doc, Demi shared a painful reckoning with a difficult past; in person, I saw her in the midst of an intense journey of self-acceptance and discovery.

I envied that acceptance. I wanted that discovery for myself. But most of all I was inspired by Demi's courage. Seeing it in her sparked courage in me. Instead of worrying about what it would mean to my brand, I started thinking about what it would do to the troubled-teen industry if I stepped out of the shadows and told my truth.

I was elated when Alexandra Dean came on board to direct *This Is Paris*. (Her documentary *Bombshell: The Hedy Lamarr Story* explores the hidden life of the movie goddess who was also a brilliant scientist.) Alexandra and her crew started following me, keeping up with my intense schedule, one continent after another, shooting events and interviews, showcasing the fans who show up for me no matter where I go, geographically or stylistically. This was the only relationship that ever seemed to work out: me and all these people I don't know. It felt like love until I was alone at the end of every day. I had to leave the well-lit world and try to sleep, knowing the nightmares would always be there, waiting patiently between the wallpaper and sterile hotel art.

After several months of shooting footage of airports, gigs, stores, and my closet, we landed in Seoul, South Korea. I was exhausted, and Alexandra wanted to capture that authentic moment. I let her bring a handheld camera to my hotel room. She filmed me peeling off my lashes for the night and then sat quietly while I tangled myself in blankets, searched for my phone, rummaged my bags, and complained of the cold. She didn't throw questions at me the way most people do when they've got an interview to deliver. She just stayed with me, hour after sleepless hour, and her silence was like a magnet.

I downed a shot of Dream Water. The label said, "Wake refreshed!"

"In my dreams," I said. "I never wake refreshed. I'm so fucking tired. I'm just—literally my mind is going through what the upcoming months are, and it's nonstop. Travel all around the world, and I see nothing except hotel room, club, stores. I don't even know who I am sometimes. I'm always putting on this façade—like a happy, perfect life. I had this plan. I created this brand and this persona and this character, and I've been stuck with it ever since. And I didn't used to be that way."

It was that skydiving moment. Telling the truth gave me that horribly wonderful, wonderfully horrible feeling of free fall into empty sky.

"Something happened to me. In my childhood."

Alexandra sat cross-legged on the bed, holding the camera in her steady hands as it all poured out of me.

"They took away all of my control, and I wasn't allowed to be any, like, have, just like—basically, they take away all of your human rights, and you just like, have *nothing*. And you just, you literally can't control—you can't even like walk or talk or go to the bathroom or cough—everything a normal human being would do, but you have to ask permission. And be locked up. And controlled. And given fifty million rules that like—it made no sense whatsoever. It was just like, literally, create this impossible—I don't know, it's like psychological torture. Crazy! It doesn't even seem real. Like when I talk about it, I'm like, *I don't even know how this is real.* But all these other survivors online—I get now that other people like me are out there, and they understand, but they are not being heard. They are not being *believed* that children are in these places that are worse than prison."

In scattered bits and pieces, I told her the story I've told you in the pages of this book. By the time it was all out, the sky was showing a glow of early dawn. Outside the window, Seoul was a deep blue sea dotted with traffic signals and high-rise offices. Alexandra and I lay on the hotel bed, physically and emotionally drained. We were both crying. Her arms were trembling with fatigue from holding the camera still for hours. I'm in tears now, thinking about her stamina and patience and the generosity it takes to just *listen*.

"I wish I could bring a camera into my dreams and show you what it's like," I said. "It's terrifying. And I think the only way to have these nightmares stop is to do something about it."

Throughout the filming and editing of *This Is Paris*, Alexandra coaxed me far beyond my standard comfort zone, and there were some intense moments when we clashed. I was beyond nervous when she reconnected me with the few girls I knew at Provo, and the final moments of the film follow us to Provo Canyon School, where I stood with fellow survivors on a mission to break the "code of silence" and close down that particular hellhole.

The scariest moment of the whole process was sitting down with my mom and talking to her about what really happened. Studying the expression on her face, I saw disbelief at first and then shock and then deep sadness. All the times I cried for her—so many terrifying nights and miserable days when my heart kept sobbing *mom, mom, mom*—it's as if she heard it all at once. Overwhelmed, she covered her face with her hands, pressing her fingers against her forehead, silent for a long moment. When she looked up again, her face was composed and pretty. A mask of grace under pressure. She had to process it in her own way.

At first, I thought she might still be the queen of sweeping things under the rug, but a few days later, I got a text from her with a link to an article about Provo Canyon survivors, as if she wanted me to know she was ready to follow me down the rabbit hole. From there we began a slow, careful conversation about the past, respectful of each other's feelings, neither one of us wanting to pile on any more pain.

As my advocacy work expands, I'm focused on urgently needed legislation that protects children still in custody, but I'm agonizingly aware of the families torn apart by the troubled-teen industry—families who start out in crisis and end up utterly dismembered with crippling debt and deep, deep emotional scars. They need help, too. They need healing.

Having my mom beside me on legislative action trips gives me hope for those families. Privately, we haven't sorted through it all. I don't know if we ever will. Publicly, her willingness to talk about it shows astonishing courage. Her presence sends a simple, powerful message: *Mom's here.*

21

Carter likes to say he cured me of my *clubitis*, which, I guess, is another word for FOMO. And my FOMO was next level. I compulsively kept going, year after year, feeling like I had to make up for lost time.

The carousel ride went around and around, following the same global path year after year: Cannes Film Festival. Let's go. After Cannes, it's the Monaco Grand Prix. From there we all fly to Ibiza, then Saint-Tropez, Tomorrowland, Coachella, Burning Man, Ultra Music Festival, Art Basel, Miami, EDC. There was a full calendar of events that could not be missed, and in between the regular stops were red carpets, film premieres, and epic after-parties. I remodeled my new house with acres of closet space, a recording studio, and an updated, grown-up version of Club Paris where I gathered my friends whenever I was home.

Carter and I crossed paths many times during those years. He was at a lot of the same festivals and events, and he tells me he and his brother, Courtney, and cousin Jay crashed several parties at my house. I didn't invite them—didn't even know them—but we knew so many people in common, they had no trouble fitting in. Apparently, Jay spent an evening with Snoop Dogg and Suge Knight smoking weed in an upstairs room. He went home to Michigan and told everyone about it, and it became one of the favorite family legends: "That Time Jay Got Stoned with Snoop and Suge."

Carter's family always gathers for the holidays. He grew up in a small town outside Chicago. He's a Midwesterner, and I love that about him. After college, he worked for Goldman Sachs until he and Courtney moved to LA to start VEEV, a high-end alcohol brand—one of the fastest-growing private companies in the US—and founded their venture capital firm, M13 Investments, in 2016.

He likes to think we knew each other because we were in the same place at the same time on so many occasions, but the truth is, I didn't notice him. I was too busy being Queen of the Night. In August 2019, while *This Is Paris* was in postproduction, I was at Burning Man. A friend came over to say hello and get a quick photo, and Carter was there. I looked right through him.

It's weird. Like maybe we were meant for each other, but God didn't let me see him until I was ready.

In the fall, holiday plans began to evolve, and Mom wanted me to come to the Hamptons for Thanksgiving with family and friends. This was something I hadn't done for fifteen years. I always worked. Always had a reason to be in London or India or anywhere other than the dinner table with my parents. That was a hard *no* for me, especially when I heard Nicky and James were going to Abu Dhabi.

"I'm not sitting there alone with Mom and Dad," I said. "That would be incredibly lame."

"Paris," Nicky said in her bossy-little-sister voice, "go see your family. Don't be an orphan. The girls will be there! You haven't seen Lily Grace and Teddy for a while, and they're growing so fast."

I told her I'd think about it, and looking around LA, I was surprised to realize that I was tired of being detached and wandering, sick of parties where I had to play some scripted part.

I felt ready to go home.

Thanksgiving week was busy with cooking, eating, and social calls. Mom was invited to dinner at her friend's house, and she invited me to go with her. She expected me to make some excuse about needing to sleep or go shopping, but I said, "Sure."

I expected to be bored out of my mind, but I got there and saw this cute guy—tall and athletic with an amazing smile and kind eyes—and I thought, *Okay, this might be interesting.* Carter's sister, Halle, is married to the son of my mom's friend. Carter's dad had passed away suddenly two years earlier, so Carter was there with his mom, Sherry, a small steel-magnolia kind of lady. The way Carter looked after her was so sweet: attentive but not hovering, compassionate but strong. He always had her in the corner of his eye.

When Carter saw me, his face lit up. Carter says when he saw me sit by the fire with a cup of hot chocolate, he told his brother to run interference so he could talk to me alone for a while. We covered the *hi how are you* basics, and I realized this guy thought I knew who he was. He mentioned the Burning Man thing, and trying to be nice, I was like, "Oh, yeaaaaah. Of course." He asked me about my upcoming plans, and I said, "I'm supposed to go on this trip with the Dalai Lama and a bunch of other people."

He said, "Oh, I know some people going on that trip. Let me get your number so I can introduce you." He didn't actually know anyone on the trip. It was just a workaround so he could get my real phone number without seeming overly aggressive.

When people started mobilizing for dinner, I made a powder-room run to freshen up my makeup, and Carter headed for the table, situating his mom on his left, bogarting the chair on his right to keep it open for me. When I sat next to him, he didn't even try to be cool about it. He was just elated to be sitting there with me. As the evening went on, we talked about our families, art, life, business, and our mutually favorite thing: work. And then Carter kept on talking about work while I sat there thinking about how to get him outside so I could kiss him.

One of the servers leaned in and quietly said, "Miss Hilton, I notice you're not eating. Is there something else we can get you?"

"No," I said. "I don't like to eat in front of cute boys."

After dinner, I asked him if he wanted to go for a walk outside and basically jumped him. I pushed him up against the fence in the tennis court and kissed him, and then we made out like teenagers for ten or fifteen minutes.

Carter said, "Well. I was not expecting that."

"I get what I want," said the Queen of the Night.

"I should get going," said Carter. "We're heading back into the city tonight. I'm staying at the Plaza with my mom and my brother."

I was like *wait now—what?* That's it? And then they left.

Google emergency. I spent the rest of the night researching this guy, checking out his company, watching him on YouTube doing interviews and business commentary on CBS and Fox and *Hatched*, a show about entrepreneurs.

He was so damn cute. I was obsessed. I had to see him again.

"Don't go to the city," Mom said. "You'll look desperate."

And I *felt* kind of desperate. I stayed one more night in the Hamptons, got up, and packed my bags. I told Mom, "I have to see him."

I went back to my apartment in New York. Carter came over. We ordered Mr. Chow's and drank a bottle of wine and talked for hours and hours. I told him about the doc that was about to come out—the shocking secret that would be revealed to the world. He listened to my story with tears in his eyes.

For the first time in my life, I began a relationship on a foundation of full disclosure. I made a connection that didn't include separate corners for carefully kept secrets. We were honest with each other. Crazy concept, right? First you own it. Then you can share it.

Quietly, completely, my walls came crashing down.

For the next few months, Carter and I saw a lot of each other. I made room for that, made it a priority, turning down every invitation to go clubbing or jet-setting. My friends kept asking me if I was okay, and I told them, "I'm fine. I just don't want to blow it with this nice guy."

A few months later, in March 2020, the COVID pandemic shut everything down, and my noisy world became quiet. I couldn't remember the last time I was home for so many days in a row. This was something I always thought would make me crazy. But I liked it. Carter and I retreated into a world of our own. We cooked and cleaned and took care of each other. He was gentle with my newly opened heart. This was a new thing for me: a truly grown-up relationship with a man who is my equal. He returned me to the joy I knew as a child and made me feel ready for children of my own.

We knew this was forever. We knew we were a family. We started IVF with big dreams of our cutesy crew and life we'd build around them.

For Carter and me, quarantine was an oasis, but it was terrifying to see the death toll rise. So many of my fans endured loss and tragedy. So many of the people we love were especially vulnerable.

I felt guilty to be so blessed and lucky in the middle of such suffering.

I was heartbroken for Alexandra when the premiere of *This Is Paris* was swept off the table, but for me, it felt like mercy. I was grateful that it came in that extraordinary moment of mandatory shelter. I didn't know how it would be received by the public or—more important—by my family. There was no way to predict how it would affect every facet of my business and personal life.

This Is Paris was released on YouTube on September 14, 2020, and was viewed more than sixteen million times in the first thirty days. The immediate impact was beyond anything I could have imagined, but it was painful for my family to finally confront the truth about what happened. The healing is an ongoing process, which is probably the case in every family.

Since the release of *This Is Paris*, I've made multiple trips to Washington, DC, to meet with legislators and White House staff about the desperately needed changes in laws pertaining to regulation and oversight in the troubled-teen industry. With Carter's full support, I brought the impact producer Rebecca Mellinger into my staff. Her job is translating outrage into action: organizing protests and press conferences, managing position papers, and hosting our podcast *Trapped in Treatment* with Caroline Cole, who's also a survivor of the troubled-teen industry. Rebecca and I went through a legislative-action training course that opened my eyes to how much power we—as in We the People—truly have. My goal is to shut down every facility with a track record of abuse and to make sure that every child has access to proper care.

We want kids trapped in treatment to know: *We're here for you.*

And we want institutional abusers to know: *We're coming for you.*

The bills we've helped pass and the laws we've helped codify are the greatest achievement of my career, the thing I'm most proud of. I wish Papa and Nanu and Gram Cracker were here to see it. I kinda wish Conrad Hilton was here to see it! And I get evil delight from knowing that the people who harmed me and so many other children are seeing it. I hope they're scared shitless.

I finally showed up—for myself and for someone else—and it feels so powerful. I sleep at night, knowing that I'm doing everything I can to help kids caught in that spiderweb of lies, abuse, and silence.

Carter has been incredibly supportive of my efforts to raise awareness and bring meaningful change to the troubled-teen industry. He loves that I'm a warrior woman and an activist and a creator tycoon who lies next to him in bed working out a mood board or going over P&Ls while he works on a product pipeline or acquisitions paperwork. I can honestly say that exactly zero men ever have loved me the way Carter does, for all the reasons he does. I didn't even know a relationship could make you feel protected and empowered at the same time.

In February 2021, I testified before a Senate subcommittee urging them to pass Senate Bill 127, which was later passed by the House of Representatives, compelling regulation and oversight of youth facilities by the Department of Health and Human Services. Two weeks later, on my fortieth birthday, Carter asked me to marry him, and I said yes.

Our fairytale 11/11 wedding was documented (obviously) in the Peacock series, *Paris in Love*, so I won't go into all the details here. The show covers all the craziness that went into planning the wedding plus the incredible progress we made with advocacy, and a few baby steps forward in my relationship with my mom during that time. The wedding itself was three days of unmitigated bliss. The guest list was limited by the lingering effects of the pandemic, but Carter and I were surrounded by love and submerged in joy.

After three years together, we're a comfortable married couple. We love our Saturday mornings when we go to the farmers' market for fresh eggs, fruit, and veggies, which we haul home so I can cook an elaborate brunch, and then we sit there and eat and eat and talk about exquisitely nerdy things like cross-collateralization and negative pickup. We laugh a lot and take time to wonder and be grateful. We love our work, our homes, our jobs, and we adore our dogs.

The Hilton pets have their own social media platform and have been cast in a number of commercials. Diamond Baby stole the show in a series of Hilton commercials. Carter and I joke about Slivington refusing to lift his leg for less than a quarter mil. In addition to being their stage mom, I'm juggling product lines, developing my media conglomerate and metaverse world, and managing a full calendar of events. The opportunities that come my way on a daily basis are so extraordinary, I have a hard time saying no, but I'm learning. Carter and I are both keenly aware that money is a lot of fun, but the most precious natural resource we have is time.

I love that Carter is still an incurable romantic. Not long ago, on our monthiversary, he set up the patio with couches, pillows, presents, hors d'oeuvres, and a big movie screen for an outdoor showing of the Marilyn Monroe classic *Gentlemen Prefer Blondes*—the 1953 musical in which Marilyn plays Lorelei Lee, the iconic material girl who sings "Diamonds Are a Girl's Best Friend."

"If a girl spends all of her time worrying about the money she doesn't have, how is she going to have any time for being in love?" Marilyn says in her famous baby voice. "I want you to find happiness and stop having fun."

I laughed, feeling more alive, wider awake, and deeper in love than I've ever been in my life. That night I slept without dreaming and woke up feeling like a skydiver, ready to step into the open air, a future full of possibility.

That's what IVF is all about. Possibility. Hope. It's hard, but you're willing to go through anything to find your heart's desire.

I've always wanted twins: a boy and a girl.

"It's possible," our doctor said. "In a perfect world . . ."

If only my world were as perfect as it looks.

Month after month of injections, several egg-harvesting procedures, more IVF injections, new ADHD meds, my natural state of chaos—it's a lot. This is good love, a strong foundation for a family. Please, God, I kept praying, bargaining, and begging.

After Carter and I went through almost two years of IVF, there were babies on the way!

Nicky and my sister-in-law Tessa were both pregnant.

I was not.

It was a bittersweet moment. I was thrilled for them, but I always thought it would be so fun if Nicky and I were pregnant at the same time. Now she and Tessa were both gorgeous and happy and glowing, and I was jabbing another needle into my stomach, feeling left out and envious. I was sad about missing out on the whole pregnancy experience—gender reveal party, amazing maternity looks, Beyoncé-belly-among-the-roses photo shoot—but all that matters in the big picture is a happy, healthy baby. Whatever it takes.

For so many people, having babies is like plug and play, right? That's how it seems, anyway. And when you want a baby, it seems like everyone around you is popping them out like gerbils. It sucks, but I'm not alone. There are so many young women at the fertility doctor's office, so many families waiting to happen. My doctor says all the junk people eat and even the air we breathe has far-reaching effects we can't begin to understand.

I think the takeaway is that young women need to control their reproductive destiny. We need to know ourselves, know what's right for us—and when—and stay in the driver's seat. I know it's expensive, but if it means a lot to you, here's some big-sister advice: Don't put it off. Don't wait for Mr. Right to show up. Understand your options and take charge of your future. Harvest those eggs when they're young and feisty.

Carter and I kept trying for more girls. More injections. Another harvest. It's a lot on my body and mind, but it's always been a dream of mine to have two daughters and a son. The shots are painful. I felt like I couldn't take it anymore. I had to confront the fact that my mind and body had never fully healed—and probably never will fully heal—from the trauma I went through as a teenager.

As an adolescent, I was starved and beaten, pushed to the emotional breaking point. As a young adult, I put on a lot of miles, drank a lot of alcohol, and ate a lot of junk food. For decades, I was wild and driven. I lived those years to the limit, and I regret nothing, because I love where I am now, and all those choices brought me here. But I want to continue living for another eighty years at least, and that takes self-care—which is not the same as self-indulgence.

Carter takes care of himself because he wants to bring his best to the people he loves. Wellness as an act of love was a new concept for me. I'll never take it for granted again.

In spring 2022, I went through another round of IVF. More eggs were harvested. We had lots of potential boys, but only one potential girl. Enough for a football team, but only one cheerleader. We moved into a new house and started planning our new life: a shared nursery at first—then separate rooms, a pool where we'll teach them to swim, a terraced garden for flowers and vegetables, a green space where Mom and I would throw epic birthday parties.

We planned to name our girl London, because I've always had this vision of myself with a daughter named London. Not just a whim, like, "Oh, how cute would that be?" This was more than that. It was a key part of my vision of my perfect life. My daughter London. She would look like me. I would love her to the moon and back. She would be . . . everything.

In mid-September, I went to a doctor's appointment. When I came home, Diamond Baby was gone. We were in the process of relocating to our happy family home. The movers propped the door open, and she must have slipped through the wrought-iron fence. Maybe just adventuring.

I came unglued. Frantic.

At first, I was afraid she'd been taken by the coyotes that roam these hills, but then a pet psychic contacted Mom and told her Diamond Baby was alive and being cared for. We offered a reward, and in the avalanche of bullshit that naturally followed, someone sent a message saying that a neighbor's child had found Diamond Baby and was instantly in love with her. They said the kid's mom couldn't bear to part with Diamond Baby. No reward was worth breaking her daughter's heart. (This guy ended up being a scammer.) We thought about raising the reward, but we were afraid that, if we did, it would only make our pets more attractive to kidnappers.

Days and weeks went by. I couldn't stop crying. Losing Diamond Baby on top of the agonizing baby situation—it was too much. It was like losing my daughter, sister, and best friend all at once. DB was my everything. My arms and my heart and everything inside me ached with loss.

I had to suck it up and go to Milan Fashion Week. I was supposed to close the Versace show and DJ a party after. Donatella Versace is a dear friend. I couldn't leave her hanging at the last minute.

"I'll be okay," I told Carter. "I can work."

I can always work. I can always walk. Sometimes it's the only thing I know how to do: put one foot in front of the other. So, I went to Milan. Nicky went with me, and I was grateful to have her there. She knew how much I loved Diamond Baby and assumed that's why I was having such a hard time. I kept my magic sunglasses on during the fitting: a pink metallic mini with a shimmery bridal veil. This dress was a celebration of love in a show that was all about the bright future. Wearing my runway shoes, I went to rehearsal and followed the director around a runway that seemed to go on for eight miles. He never stopped talking, so it was okay that I didn't say anything.

"Good turn, okay? You want to mark it. The beat is pretty hot. Straight into the camera." He pointed to his eyes and then forward to where the camera would be. "Walking here. Staying center. Shoulders back, chin down, okay?"

I nodded and said, "Okay."

Emily Ratajkowski came and kissed me on both cheeks.

"Hello, gorgeous," I said.

"This is so exciting," said Emily. "I'm so happy to see you."

"You, too," I said. "The baby is beautiful."

"Thank you. He's here!" She lit up—literally lit up—at the mention of him. I was glad for my sunglasses.

I'd been giving it a lot of thought. Having my baby with me at work, on the road, backstage at Fashion Week. That's the world we live in now, and it's a potentially beautiful world if you can step over the intrusive thoughts. If you can hope. And keep walking.

If all goes well, by the time you read this, Carter and I will have a baby boy. We plan to name him Phoenix, a name that I decided on years ago when I was searching cities, countries, and states on a map, looking for something to go with Paris and London. Phoenix has a few good pop culture reference points, but more important, it's the bird that flames out and then rises from the ashes to fly again. I want my son to grow up knowing that disaster and triumph go around and come around throughout our lives and that this should give us great hope for the future, even when the past is painful and the present seems to have fallen to shit. It's weird how two ideas that are so different—so completely opposite—can coexist like that, but they do.

Freedom and suffering.

Joy and sorrow.

Love and loss.

Shoulders back, chin down, staying center, I waited in the darkness until it was my turn to step into the light.

That director didn't lie. The beat was pretty hot.

AFTERWORD

I wrote this book in an effort to understand my place in a watershed moment: the technology renaissance, the age of influencers. There wasn't room in this book for all the stories I wanted to tell, so I focused on key aspects of my life that led to my advocacy work: how my power was taken away from me and how I took it back.

I set out to create the truest possible representation of the life I've lived and the motivating factors that steered my course. The best and hardest thing for any of us to do is be honest, and I've tried to do that here. I hope you'll accept me as I am, but if you can't, I understand. Ultimately, I hope my story made you laugh and think and prompted you to love yourself a little more than you did at the start.

In telling my story, I've tried to be careful not to tell my version of the stories that don't belong to me. Not everyone who's important to me shows up as a character in this book. In addition to being Conrad Hilton's great-grandsons, Conrad and Barron grew up being Paris Hilton's brothers, but they both have their own stories. Fame is famous for inflicting collateral damage, and my little brothers were in that blast radius from the time they were small children.

Nicky has lived an extraordinary life in which I'm just a supporting player. I hope she and Mom will write their own memoirs someday, because intelligent, funny, hardworking, compassionate women rock this world, and sometimes their true stories get lost in the fog of toxic Real Housewives melodrama. My dad isn't the memoir type, but he could totally do a *Be My Guest*-type business book.

Conrad Hilton ended *Be My Guest* with a bulleted list of long-winded advice for entrepreneurs. Maybe someday I'll write another book on that subject, but for now, I'll just say:

- Follow your curiosity. It's calling you toward your true purpose.
- Don't waste energy living a life someone else designed for you. Life is one per customer. Let them do theirs. You do yours.
- Accept the necessity of endless reinvention. Staying the same is (a) boring and (b) impossible.
- There's no substitute for hard work. Keep killing it and something will happen. Probably not what you expected, but something.
- Know the star you are. And see yourself as part of a galaxy.
- Celebrate the positives, recognize value in the negatives, and be grateful for both because it all makes you who you are.

"You're a woman who lived eight lives at once," Elliot said recently. "You breathed Marilyn Monroe oxygen."

I was born to great privilege, and I'm living an extraordinary life. The sheer quantity of media surrounding my life story is staggering. I had to hire someone to help me make sense of it all. Sifting through thousands of pages for more than a year, we barely made a dent. I had to let all that go. This book is my way of walking through that looking glass.

With each passing year, it matters less and less to me how other people love, hate, adore, or dismiss me. Weirdly, that makes me feel closer to understanding people in general. I'm not trying to say I'm just like you. I'm trying to say I see you, and I think it's possible that we know each other better than one might think. I have secrets like every other woman in the world. Like every other woman in the world, I've had terrible things happen to me, and I've come out on the other side.

I know we're supposed to spin terrible things to make it sound like they were actually good, but that's bullshit. That heart attack did not save your life. Cancer is not a gift. Your abuser did not give you strength. Terrible things are terrible. Let's just acknowledge it. If you found strength, wisdom, or a new way of thinking, that's awesome, but notice that the strength, wisdom, and new worldview came out of you, which means it was all there inside you to begin with.

Advocacy saved my life. Carter is a gift. Good things are good, and I'm grateful. Terrible things can go fuck themselves, but I like to think that everything happens for a reason.

Every life story is a web of cause and effect. I was born at precisely the right time to exactly the right people. This cosmic alchemy made me who I am and placed me in a position where I could help someone in desperate need. And in the Spirograph of it all, advocacy work blessed me with the silver bullet that transforms my ADHD from disability to superpower: *purpose.*

For years I told myself I was incapable of focusing on anything; now I know that I can be a laser beam when I focus on something that truly matters.

When Mom and I went to Washington, DC, in 2022, Rebecca set up a replica of the Obs isolation cell so people could go inside and get an idea what it was like. Me going in there was an obvious photo op.

"Don't shut the door," I whispered to Rebecca. She hugged me tight, and I stepped in, trying not to cry.

Not because I was scared. I cried because I wasn't scared.

I cried because all day I'd been hearing stories: Someone saw my doc and decided not to send their kid to Provo. Someone's aunt heard our podcast and swooped in to get her nephew out. A girl who was at Provo when my fellow survivors and I marched on that place told me that staff had scrambled to cover the windows and force people into their rooms, but word spread like wildfire through the hallways among the staff and patients.

"What the hell—*Paris Hilton* is out there?"

The cops came, and media followed, shining their unforgiving light on an evil industry that can no longer hide in the shadows.

gotcha gotcha gotcha gotcha gotcha

That day, I wanted everyone inside those walls to know the same thing I want you to know right now: The people who hurt you don't get the last word. You get to tell the story of you, and your story has more power than you can imagine.

BONUS UPDATE

One year later...

Just before midnight on New Year's Eve, Miley Cyrus set the tone for 2023 when she took my hand and said, "This is gonna be slicker than shit."

She wasn't joking. Miami was hot and humid, and when the night air cooled down, a slippery film of condensation formed on the stage floor.

But this was also a good way to describe the new year we were about to slide into: Scary. Fabulous. Dangerous. Hopes and dreams condensing to make everything shiny and terrifying and wonderful. Plus, that electrifying awareness that you may be about to fall on your ass.

I was wearing six-inch platform heels and a rose-gold version of my twenty-first birthday dress. Only this version wasn't as well constructed as the original, and it was literally coming apart at the seams. People were frantically sewing me into it five minutes before I went on.

Miami wasn't the plan. I got offers from all over the world. Carter and I could have gone anywhere for the holidays, but I said, "Let's just go to Maui." We knew Phoenix would be coming at the end of January. We wanted to savor that last moment of being just the two of us before we started being Mom and Dad. So, I turned down every invitation, every DJ gig, every epic New Year's Eve party—everything—and I was thinking, *Hey, good for me. I'm getting good at saying no.* A good Mom quality.

But then Miley Cyrus called and asked me to sing "Stars at Blind" with her and Sia on her New Year's Eve special on NBC.

She said, "You have to come and sing it with us. Like, we start, and then—surprise! Out walks Paris Hilton, and everybody's going, *whaaaat?!* Paris, you have to come. This song is so iconic. Your voice is vital."

Nobody's that good at saying no. I was like, "Sorry, Carter. I'm definitely canceling Hawaii. This is too iconic."

"A hundred percent," he said. Because he gets me.

I texted Miley to tell her I was in, and she texted back:

Miammmmmmmmmi! This is gonna be so iconic! Me and Dolly hosting the show! Now with you and Sia! The internet is broken!

She asked me if I wanted to do the walk on and chill or spend some time in the DJ booth and introduce her and Dolly I was down for any and all the things.

*Just let me know whatever you need for me to prepare and I'll be
ready to rock it!*

I'm leaving out a lot of exclamation points and emojis, but you get
the idea. I texted back that this would be iconic AF, and we should
coordinate our looks. She sent me some dressing room pics of her
pink Versace cocktail dress and said, *I've got you the entire time. If
you need anything or feel scared I Got U. Lean on me fully!*

A few weeks later, with the clock ticking down to midnight, I was
in Miami in my falling-apart dress and platform heels engineered to
break my ankle. The horn section started a cool Cuban version of
the song, and you know this song always feels like an old friend for
me. When I hear that song, I feel happy, even if my heart is gyrating
like a hummingbird in my chest.

Before Miley went to her mark, she said, "Be. Careful. It's so
slippery."

"I'm freaking out," I said. "I'm so nervous."

She laughed. "I got you, girl. And just so you know, we do this
all the time, and we're as nervous as you are."

Sia confirmed that this was true. Even if they were saying it to be
sweet, it made me feel less alone, and I was grateful.

Miley went out first and started the verse:

I don't mind spending some time just hanging here with you . . .

Sia came out to sing harmony on the chorus:

*Even though the gods are crazy, even though the stars are
    blind . . .*

She was wearing an over-the-top floral kimono with a huge red bow on top of her signature over-the-top wig—and sensible shoes, unlike me and Miley. Sia is no fool.

While Sia sang the second verse, and they did another chorus, I waited behind a sliding set piece. I tried to tell people working backstage "I can't hear anything in these earbuds," but they couldn't hear me over the crowd noise, and then it was too late to do anything about it.

I heard Sia say, "Ready for *this*?"

The sliding doors opened. My earbuds came to life. (Apparently, they turn them on at the last second.) I started walking, singing the bridge.

Excuse me for feeling this moment is critical . . .

There was a collective *"WHAAAAT?!"*—just like Miley envisioned—and then the whole crowd lost their minds, cheering, laughing, singing the chorus with us, everyone jumping under the night sky. You know that energy when you plan a huge surprise, and it goes off without a glitch. Perfection.

Miley met me on the glassy catwalk. She kept her hand on my back, and then we linked arms, literally holding each other up. I was still incredibly nervous about singing with these two legends, but the thrill of the moment carried me. We got to the chorus, and Miley said, "Sing, Paris." And I sang. It felt so good. We ended the song holding hands, all three of us—Holy Trinity 2.0—celebrating with thousands of happy people.

Best New Year's Eve of my life. And that says a lot.

Seriously, I've been to some sick NYE ragers, and nothing compared to this feeling.

I didn't think it could get any better, but after the show, Sia texted me: *That was AMAZING. We have room on the private plane. Do you and Carter want to fly back with us?*

We were supposed to be going to Hawaii. For real this time.

I texted back: *Hell yeah!!*

The next day, on the charter flight back to LA, Sia and I talked about dogs, work, music, and Miley's amazing smile, but mostly, we talked about music.

"You were born to be a pop star," Sia said. "Why aren't you making music anymore?"

"I never really stopped," I said, but I could see how it looked that way. I did the occasional collab, and a home studio was an important thing in our new house, but for the past two years, my main focus was on creating a family, building my new company, and writing this book. Carter and I had kept everything about our baby completely private, so I didn't say anything about Phoenix being on his way, but we talked about my book and about my trauma and insomnia.

"The book was a huge project," I said, "but it means a lot to me. I think it could make a big difference in the troubled-teen space."

The truth is, I was really scared about putting this book out into the world. My main worry was how my family would feel. They didn't know about some of the hard parts—the traumatic experiences I'd endured—and I didn't know how to prepare them. We just don't talk about certain things in my family, so opening up about all of this has been terrifying for me and upsetting to the people who love me.

For me, that process started with the doc. This book was another huge step. I worked with a top-tier collaborator—this sweet boho grandmother who's so kind and has worked with lots of other people on memoirs that deal with trauma and recovery. We spent more than a hundred hours on Zoom and FaceTime. I talked. She listened. She reshaped what I said into chapters that made sense, and then I went over the pages, making changes.

We messaged back and forth on WhatsApp and text, sharing research material and discoveries. All the deep-dive stuff, uncovering the horrifying history of the troubled-teen industry. When it was too hard for me, I had to step away for a week or two. In 2021 I set it aside for four months so I could concentrate on my wedding and the first season of *Paris in Love*, then we worked on it for another year. It was a lot, but I was so proud of what we did together.

Flying back to LA on New Year's Day, I told Sia, "The book drops in March. This year I'm focusing on business. My empire. My brands."

There was the cookware that blew up on social media before Christmas, a jewelry collab, fragrances, and season two of *Paris in Love*. I had twenty people working for me. Depending on me.

"But the music," she said. "It was amazing last night, wasn't it? That song was perfect for you back when you first recorded it. You need to find the perfect songs for the artist you are now. Do you think about doing another album?"

"Always," I said. "But I don't have time."

"What if I was executive producer?" she asked.

Just like that, it turned into the kind of conversation that only happens thirty thousand feet above the ground. It took a month for the shock to wear off but less than a second for me to say, "*Hell yes!*"

I went to the studio that night and every day the following week. Sia sent me dozens of songs—all these amazing options from the most incredible songwriters. She was contacting all these people, saying, "Hey, I'm executive producing this album for Paris Hilton. What have you got?" So, every day I'm getting the sickest tracks you can imagine from people like Miley Cyrus, Meghan Trainor, Jesse

Shatkin, David Guetta, and so many others. More than I could do in a lifetime. And I'm listening to them all, trying to decide. Sia was so brilliant at this part, figuring out the difference between a track that was perfect and a track that was perfect *for me*.

I dove into all this thinking I had four weeks before Phoenix, and I had this whole idea of how it would all work out as far as timing. Carter and I had a plan for getting everyone out of the house, gathering all the supplies we would need, doing all the things you want to do in advance.

Phoenix had other plans.

Two weeks before his due date, we got a call telling us the surrogate was in labor, and we just exploded into a ball of joyful, nervous energy. It was like, *THUNDERCATS ARE GO!*, and we had to make everything happen in a matter of hours instead of weeks.

We were still keeping all this completely private. We put a lot of effort into protecting that time for ourselves and our baby. We made sure that season two of *Paris in Love* was filmed more in the single-camera style of the doc. Carter and I shot most of the personal stuff ourselves, just using our iPhones, allowing no cameras at the hospital or at home. We decided that, if we shared this at all, we wanted it to be like we were sharing the sweetest little home movies with our friends.

If you watched these scenes on *Paris in Love*, you know how over the moon in love we were from the moment we laid eyes on our precious boy. What you don't see is a lot of what came before that.

The hard part of the story.

In the last chapter of this book, I said I went to the saddest fucking doctor's appointment of my life and that I wasn't trying to be sketchy, I just wasn't ready to talk about it.

I think I am ready now.

I mean, I'm trying to be ready. And I think this is as close to ready as I'll ever get, because after this book dropped, I saw how profound the impact was, how it's a gift when we share our stories—especially the hard parts.

* * *

Rewind for a sec. Go back to spring 2022.

Like I told you before: I went through another round of IVF. Eggs were harvested. Enough for a football team, but only one cheerleader, remember? What I didn't tell you is that we had made the difficult decision to have a surrogate carry our babies.

A lot of people are ready with the side-eye when famous women become moms with the help of a surrogate. No one says a word about the men who are part of this process, but it seems like people jump in there to judge women no matter what we do. Everyone has an opinion, trying to shame us, questioning why we make the choices we make instead of trusting that we know what's best for ourselves.

Some people are so insensitive. They'll ask me to my face at a party or even in public—I'm talking red-carpet interviews—and the subtext is like "What's wrong with you?" I'm so shy about it, I never have a good answer. It is a long, painful, difficult process that involves so many tears and tough decisions. I can't sum that up in a twelve-second sound bite for their convenience, and I shouldn't have to.

No matter what I say, half these people will go ahead and print stuff that doesn't even make sense: "Paris Hilton used a surrogate because she wanted to keep her stomach flat." Oh, you mean, my stomach that I've been jabbing needles into for three years? Plus, have you seen Nicky's stomach? She's had three babies, and her stomach is as flat as your iPad. It has nothing to do with that.

For all the red-carpet curiosity mongers out there: You wanna know why we chose surrogacy? *NONE OF YOUR FUCKING BUSI-NESS*! No one other than me and Carter and our fertility team is entitled to an opinion about our reproductive healthcare choices. What our surrogates did for us was huge. I'll be grateful to them every day of my life, but I'm not going to talk about it because they deserve to be happy with their families and not have their lives blown up by paparazzi. Thank you for respecting our privacy, their privacy, and the privacy of all women in the future.

Byeeee!

Okay, back to the happiness.

Oh, my gosh. Happiness doesn't even begin to express it.

The dream was to have a girl and a boy, born separately but at the same time, so they'd grow up as twins. (Miscarriages are more common with multiples, so we chose not to implant one surrogate with twins.) Everything was going according to plan: Our embryos were implanted, and it worked! Our angel surrogates were pregnant, one with a boy, one with a girl. This real-life miracle was happening right in front of us, and I can't even explain how thrilled and happy and thankful we were. This was everything we hoped for. All those months of injections and the crazy-making hormones—it was all worth it. We would have the perfect family we had both been dreaming of: Mama, Dada, London, and Phoenix.

We told no one.

Our obstetrician said, "A lot of people choose not to say anything during the first trimester. First trimester miscarriage is not uncommon."

"Nothing's going to go wrong," Carter said, and I loved him for sounding so absolutely sure of it.

I was afraid to breathe. It was like keeping your eye on two little baby birds in a nest—so fragile, so precious, and completely out of our hands. When I'm scared, my instinct is always to do something—

anything—and Carter is the same. The more nervous he is about a situation, the more he wants to micromanage every detail. In this case, there was nothing we could do but wait. I just focused on working on this book and the show and all the busywork of business.

The weird thing is, I felt kinda pregnant—and not just because of the hormones. I felt so full of joy and possibilities and new life. I wanted to know what it felt like to be pregnant, so I bought a prosthetic stomach and wore it around the house for a day. I know that sounds crazy, but I wanted it to feel real—even in just this small way. Feeling that weight on the front of me, running my hands over it, envisioning a whole life ahead of us. It crossed my mind that if I went out like that it would trigger the typical *PARIS BABY BUMP* headlines. It might have been fun to punk the paparazzi, but I didn't want to make a joke of something so close to my soul.

This was a good mind game to play. By the end of the day, I was like, *This is so silly.* I didn't need to pretend. I was about to be a mom for real. I can't speak for other women who've had babies via surrogacy, but for me, the baby bump was something inside me—emotional, psychological—and I imagine that's probably what it feels like for men expecting a baby, too. It didn't matter that no one else could see that I was expecting. My emotional baby bump was real, it was precious, and I was so completely happy to know it was exactly where it needed to be, growing warmer and bigger every day. The only thing that mattered was getting the babies past that scary first trimester.

Spring turned to summer. June. July.

"Second trimester," the doctor said. "This is where most people feel comfortable sharing the news."

Carter and I were committed to keeping our secret, but we looked at each other like, Holy shit, this is happening!

Riding another wave of pure joy, we bought a house high in the hills and started planning our new life as a family. We decided to do a shared nursery at first, and then do an adjoining boy/girl room later on so that as they got older, they would have their privacy but always be close. We didn't do any babyproofing or decorating in advance because so many people were coming and going all the time, but when we were alone, Carter and I talked about nothing else.

We were constantly researching and pre-shopping online. How will we enclose the pool so it's safe for the babies when they learn to walk? When can they eat peanut butter? What kind of nontoxic plants should we grow in the garden? What kind of music makes a kid better at math? For years, we were so focused on the pregnancy part of it. Now we were thinking about a whole lifetime.

Of course, a huge question was how and when to tell our families. We weren't eager to share the big news. Having this moment just between us was kind of beautiful. Intimate. I felt more in love with Carter than I could have imagined. We held each other so close during that summer. I felt like we were living in a perfect bubble of bliss.

Three months. Four months. Summer ended, as always, with Burning Man. And then it was September. We were almost five months along. And that's when it happened. The saddest fucking doctor's appointment of my life.

Carter and I sat next to each other. Silent. Cold. Like we were made of hard plastic. And all this *"words words blah blah"*—giant blob of horrible words—was coming out of the doctor's face but I didn't hear anything after the word *miscarriage*.

Our baby girl was gone.

It was quiet for a few seconds, and then Carter made a sharp, terrible sound like someone punched him in the throat. I fell apart crying. I didn't want to accept it. I couldn't let go of this dream that had sustained me through the darkest parts of my life. *My London*. My perfect girl. The perfect life I'd promised myself. She was so close

I could feel her in my arms. Grief took hold of me like gravity, like falling down a flight of stairs.

"But . . . to be clear," Carter said. "You're saying the male fetus is still viable?"

The doctor told us we were now in a high-risk pregnancy, but yes, the second surrogate was still carrying our baby boy.

Lying in bed that night, we just held on to each other, shaking, crying, trying to sort out how we were even supposed to feel. We were devastated, but also—I don't know—were we supposed to feel lucky? Grateful? Because how are you supposed to feel two totally opposite emotions—heartsick and thankful—at the same time without being torn in two?

I was terrified for Phoenix, who seemed so fragile now. I ached for him, thinking about the nursery they were supposed to share. Now he'd be alone in the dark without his sister.

"Do you think he knows?" I asked Carter, and he shook his head.

"We have to focus on Phoenix," Carter said. "He'll get through this. He has angels with him. I know he does."

He was talking about his father, I think. And Gram Cracker. All our grandparents. So many people who loved us. All Carter and I could do was hold on to each other and pray for a healthy baby. And I tried to do that, but I was so scared of what might happen. It all felt fragile and sad and hopeless. And trust me, there are no resources out there for someone in this totally abnormal situation. We felt like we were going through something no one else could possibly understand.

You already read in that last chapter what happened next. Diamond Baby went missing. Heartbreak on heartbreak. More than I could stand.

I didn't sleep or eat for days. We searched the property, calling and calling and calling, "*Diamond! Diamond Baby!*" I paced back and forth in the house. I locked myself in the bathroom, sobbing and hyperventilating. When I finally did sleep, it felt like I was disappearing down a hole—like I would never wake up. That's when we decided to post online about Diamond Baby, and there was such an outpouring of love and empathy. Family, friends, Little Hiltons on social media—so many people were so kind. It helped me pick myself up again.

Over the next two weeks, Carter and I stayed close to home, but he mostly sat at his desk, looking grim, tapping on the computer keyboard, researching, gathering data, applying statistics, looking for options. This is his coping mechanism of choice, and it's weirdly comforting. He doesn't come unglued about stuff, but he's never afraid to be seen with tears in his eyes, and something about that is so endearing. So manly and upright and good. He just keeps going. Strong. Quiet. Determined. It makes me feel like I can keep going, too.

One night he came to me and said, "I need to tell you something. You know, Diamond Baby was getting up there, and you never know what might happen, so as an insurance policy, for lack of a better word, I took a tissue sample a while back."

"*Tissue sample?*" I couldn't imagine this going in a good direction.

"If you want to," Carter said, "we could try to have Diamond Baby cloned."

My immediate response was "No. You can't just replace her. She was special."

"I get that," he said. "We're talking about a different dog. But it would be a dog with all the characteristics that predisposed Diamond Baby to be Diamond Baby. Check this out."

He showed me a website: VIAGEN PETS & EQUINE: The worldwide leader in cloning the animals we love.

Of course, I know cloning is a thing. I understand the science of it, but the emotional part is complicated.

I said, "I'll have to think about it."

Carter and I had to face a much bigger decision: Should we do another round of IVF or give up? The thought of more injections and drugs made me want to shrivel up in a corner. I can't overstate the anxiety I feel about going into clinical environments—all those doctor's offices where I sat there sweating, my heart pounding, my hands shaking. But what if London was still out there? She was so real to me. She always was. I had to try.

I started IVF again before I went to Milan Fashion Week. Nicky was there, and she could tell I was having a hard time, but she figured it was because of Diamond Baby. In a big way, it was, because if there was ever a time when I needed Diamond Baby, this was it. I just told myself to suck it up and take my ass to Milan and get back to work because that's what I do.

When I got home, I saw that the book collaborator was on my calendar the following week. *Ugh.* I had totally forgotten. Boho Grandmother was coming to my house to help me finish the memoir, and there was no putting it off because the publisher had already been beyond patient, giving me more and more time, dealing with the extra layer of confidentiality I needed. The last step in the process was a table read, and I felt we needed to do it in person.

I wanted to have my hand on every page and paragraph in this book, so she came to my house with two copies of the manuscript printed out in binders, and we read the whole thing together. She read each chapter out loud while I made notes in the margins, flagged things with Post-its, and highlighted paragraphs I wanted to revisit. Sometimes we backtracked so I could read something out loud to see if I liked the way it would sound in the audiobook.

We spent five days in my upstairs studio space, going over every word in the book. We laughed a lot. And we cried a lot. Carter came and went, bringing me water and meds. One afternoon, he took a picture of me curled up on the sofa, surrounded by this blizzard of pages and pens and sticky notes, and he said, "I've never seen you so focused for so many hours at a time."

I was proud of myself. Proud of this book. Proud of my story. It was a powerful experience seeing it all on paper, especially now when I was feeling so raw emotionally. On our last day together, we got to that last part about "your story has more power than you can imagine," and I started crying.

"Are you okay?" she asked.

I said, "I think so. This has been the best kind of therapy for me. Work. But it's been even harder than the doc."

"The memoir journey takes a lot out of a person," she said. "You've been incredibly courageous. But I see you struggling with a lot of emotion today. Is it about the book or IVF or . . . something else?"

"The IVF has been hard," I said, trying to focus on the pages in my lap.

"I hear that," she said. "I sucked at fertility. We tried for years. Had two miscarriages. Then I got pregnant with twins, and we lost one at nine weeks, so we thought we were having another miscarriage, but then we were still pregnant, so that was a mind-fuck."

My stomach did a little somersault. "You lost a twin?"

"But our baby boy was born healthy and beautiful," she said. "And we had our fabulous girl two years later. And now that my kids are grown, I see pregnancy as such a small part of being a mom. Motherhood happens in the brain and the heart and the soul, not the uterus. I don't even have a uterus anymore, and I've leveled up to grandmother."

Now I was really crying, and it was kind of like that night with

Alexandra. I didn't plan to tell her everything; it just came out. She listened for a long time without saying anything, without trying to advise or fix me. She just said, "Oh, sweetie. That's huge." She asked if I wanted to be hugged, and I said I did.

We sat on the sofa for a long time and talked about motherhood and God and the idea of science and technology messing with Mother Nature.

"Mother Nature keeps trying to kill me," she said. "I'm team science."

I told her about Diamond Baby and asked her if she believed dogs have souls.

"I do," she said, "and I'll say this about Diamond Baby, wherever she is. It seems to me that what she did for you in this moment was force you to let people in—let them come close enough to comfort you—even though you couldn't tell anyone why you were in so much pain."

This was a weird way to look at it, but it's true. If Diamond Baby had been there in that overwhelmingly sad moment, I would have cried to her, sitting in my closet, and no one except Carter would have ever known how wrecked I was. I didn't know how to process the loss we'd experienced, so I would have kept all that loss inside me forever, even though I know how unhealthy that is.

Diamond Baby gave me the opportunity to grieve and an opportunity for other people to comfort me. When she disappeared, she left an open door for my family, friends, coworkers, and all my Little Hiltons all over the world to form a circle of love and care around me. Everyone knew how much Diamond Baby meant to me, so no one questioned me when I sat there sobbing, "*She's gone, she's gone, she's gone.*" They just held me, loved me, and brought me Taco Bell.

Who knew people could be such good emotional support animals? Turns out that humans—if you give them a chance—can love you almost as much as dogs do. That was the last gift of love I received from Diamond Baby, a darling little creature who gave me so much love for so many years. Part of me wishes I knew what happened to her, but not knowing lets me imagine she's out there somewhere, alive and well loved, so in my heart, she always will be.

The following week, we handed off the manuscript to the publisher. I chose not to include this story at the time because I didn't know what the outcome would be. I'm telling you now because I know everyone goes through something like this at some point in life. Maybe it's not a miscarriage—or not what we typically think of as a miscarriage. Maybe it's the loss of something else people can't see—some hidden part of yourself—and you have to honor that loss, even if no one else can see it, because it's huge.

It's a safe bet that someone close to you is hurting right now. Maybe they can't tell you because of whatever reason. A million reasons. That doesn't mean they don't need your kindness. So be kind, just in case.

And if you are going through a miscarriage, please be kind to yourself. The loss of a pregnancy is so confusing and hard, no matter what the rest of the situation is. There's no right or wrong way to feel about it. It's different for everyone, and it's not just the physical pregnancy itself. Sometimes it's the loss of a family you envisioned or a self you thought you'd be. It can feel like the undoing of a dream, leaving you with the hard work of learning to dream again.

As Boho Grandmother was leaving, I noticed white block letters on the back of her black T-shirt:

NOTHING ELSE MATTERS

"I like your shirt," I said.

She told me she got it in Germany when her daughter took her to see Metallica at Hockenheim, and I thought, *That'll be me and my daughter someday. Me and London.* She was meant to be. I was sure of it.

Fourteen months later, on November 11, 2023, London arrived: healthy, beautiful, bright-eyed, fascinated by everything around her. Now that she's here, it's easy for me to say that I always knew it would happen, but seriously, I knew. I've always known. There were moments when it crushed me how long it took and how hard it was, but now I hold her and Phoenix in my arms, and you know what?

Nothing else matters.

* * *

The first edition of this book dropped in March 2023, when Phoenix was about eight weeks old. It was so hard to leave him. I did a global book tour, but I was like a bullet train. I made sure my PR team packed events into every hour of every day—a whole week crammed into three days. I didn't want to be away from home too long. Everywhere I went, fans lined up for blocks, camping outside the bookstores to make sure they'd be among the first hundred people in the door. I was usually slated to be there for two hours, but I stayed until I had personally thanked every person who came out. Sometimes I was signing books and taking selfies with fans until two or three in the morning, long after the bookstore and everything else on the street was closed for the night. There was no way I could walk away and leave fans standing out on the sidewalk.

The book was an instant smash and spent eight weeks on the *New York Times* bestseller list. A starred review from *Kirkus* said it's "a master class in owning your story." I was on the cover of *Harper's Bazaar* Legacy issue with the headline "The Redemption of Paris Hilton" and on covers for other magazines from *Vogue* Arabia to

Glamour UK and Spain, including *US* magazine's biggest selling issue of the year.

That's the kind of thing that makes a publisher very happy, and I was happy that they were happy, but what meant the most to me was the flood of affirmation from readers all over the world.

I've gotten thousands of messages on every platform from people saying "This book changes my life" and "I knew Paris was badass, but this is insane!" People shared stories of kids being taken out of troubled-teen facilities, survivors being able to talk about their experiences for the first time, families being healed by new understanding. So many readers said they felt seen and heard for so many different reasons. If there were haters, I didn't notice. Or maybe I just didn't care.

My hope that this book would help one person was fulfilled and amplified times a billion when we made a deal with A24 to do a series adaptation of the book with Dakota and Elle Fanning executive producing. (A24 is the hottest production on the planet, the brilliant minds behind *Everything, Everywhere, All at Once.*)

Some of the revelations in this book were upsetting for my family. I can only imagine how hard it was for them. I've had two decades to work through everything you read about here. It hit them all at once. It meant a lot to me to have Nicky and Mom by my side when I introduced the Stop Institutional Child Abuse Act (SICAA) in front of the Capitol Building in Washington, DC, on April 27, 2023. Led by Rebecca Mellinger, my team and I had been developing the language alongside bill sponsors for two years. It was a huge moment when we introduced the bill with bipartisan sponsors and supporters.

Ever since that day, I've been calling, texting, and sending video messages, working to get additional support. So far, we have more than seventy-five bipartisan cosponsors in the House and twenty-two in the Senate. We're really close to passing legislation that'll make a major impact.

I'm also hearing from readers that this book and season two of *Paris in Love* have generated a lot of conversation about how to react when someone you love reveals that they've been sexually assaulted, recently or in the past.

Three helpful things you can say:

- "I'm so sorry that happened to you."
- "Are you okay, or do you need help connecting to resources?"
- "I'm listening."

Three super not helpful things you might avoid saying:

- "You should have *blah blah blah*."
- "Why didn't you *blah blah blah*?"
- "That's what happens when you *blah blah blah*."

If you've been sexually assaulted, please know you're not alone.

Help is available at www.rainn.org. You can chat with someone online or call (800) 656-HOPE.

With the book and the baby and a lot of other issues, season two of *Paris in Love* was even more intense and emotional than the first season. I hope you'll watch it. (Streaming now on Peacock!) There's so much in it about the arrival of Phoenix, my ongoing legislative action in DC, my evolving relationship with my family, and my first live concert performance at Fonda Theatre, which literally sold out in three minutes and paved the way for more music to come.

Off camera, Carter and I were fully immersed in parenting, music, tech, massive media deals, pink strawberry waffles, and diapers.

So. Many. Diapers.

I'm getting into the "Mommy and Me" space, developing fashion and product lines for kids. There's now a massive pink Paris aisle in every Walmart, and my new Roblox world Slivingland gets millions of visitors every day. I'm looking into AI, figuring out ways it might help us spend more time at home. For now, Carter and I take turns saying no. There was never any expectation on his part that my career would be put on the shelf during these years. There was a mutual expectation that we'd both make compromises in order to prioritize kids and family time, and so far, it feels like we've found the right balance for an equal partnership.

Carter and I have the babies with us whenever we can. They spend a lot of time hanging out in his office, and Phoenix loves to sit on my lap while I'm getting hair and makeup done. He stares up at me and pays close attention to everything that happens. People can hardly get their work done, because everyone's so mesmerized with him. He's an old soul, I think. There's just something about him that makes people feel calm and happy. Holding, loving, and caring for him have been healing in a way that took me totally by surprise. When he looks into my eyes and talks that secret language babies talk, it's like he's speaking to the little child in me—that little girl who was so hurt in so many ways—and for that moment, all I feel is love.

I have to clap back at people now and then, because I get a lot of "How are you working all the time? You're a mom now!" or "How can you do that sexy lingerie campaign? You're a mom now!" People who post these comments don't notice or appreciate the sexy, hardworking moms all around them, I guess. Which is kinda sad.

They're missing out. Meanwhile, no one questions Carter about how much he's working or what he's wearing.

Bottom line: I have to do motherhood my own way. Tons of love. No apologies. That's what it means to be a sliving mom.

I eventually decided to be on team science, and we sent the Diamond Baby skin cells to ViaGen to see if they could clone her. The embryo split, and in August, we brought two perfect little puppies—Diamond and Baby—home to meet the family. Phoenix loves all dogs, but he was beside himself to have these two tiny friends who are equally mad about him. Diamond and Baby love to entertain and snuggle and kiss him. We zoom around in circles in the foyer—me on my Airwheel slivcase, Phoenix in his walker—and they chase us as fast as their skinny legs can carry them.

Through all this, Sia and I have been working on my album, and I'm just going to own it here: It is fucking fire. You don't even know. Or maybe by the time you read this, you'll be listening to it and you will know. That would be perfect because, in so many ways, it's a natural soundtrack for this book. It's like a trajectory—the doc, this book, then the album—taking me farther and farther into this realm of emotion and authenticity I never felt free to express. It's about taking back my voice and providing a soundtrack for anyone fighting to reclaim their narrative.

What Sia did for me—or with me, or to me—on this album is insane. She took my voice to a totally different place and helped me connect with the music in a new way. I'm proud of all the music and musical collabs I've done in the past, but this is the me who lives and creates in the here and now, and I love it.

Beyond the music, Sia's friendship means the world to me. She's truly one of the kindest people I've met in this industry. She has such a big heart. I'll always be grateful to her for believing in me, opening my mind to what I'm capable of, and making my pop star dreams come true. She's also a dog person and was there for me when Harajuku Bitch passed away at age twenty-three (which is 161 in human years!). The end of an era.

One afternoon, Sia texted me:

Holy shit I just wrote you a super smash with Jesse
ADHD

"It felt personal," she said. She was listening to the audio edition of this book and thinking about our long conversation, and this is what came out.

Back on the road, up in the air, I'm so tired
Word in a book, so much to share, I'm on fire . . .

I've heard this song ten thousand times, and it still makes me cry. It so perfectly captures this aspect of my life.

I was so down, thought I'd never be free
My superpower was right inside, see?
It was ADHD
It's the anthem I needed when I was ten.

I also did a tribute to Ultra Naté's "Free," the anthem that lifted me up and carried me after I got out of Provo. What's crazy about this arrangement is how the subtle shift of the beat and the smallest change in the chord progression takes it from a rebellion to celebration. My version of "Free" is a love song to the eighteen-year-old me. I know she's out there somewhere, under the strobe lights, feeling that song in her bones.

There's nothing in the world that could bring me down
There's no one in the room who could take my crown . . .

The first time Phoenix heard this song, his face lit up and he squealed like a wombat. Every time I play it, he goes bananas in his little jumping swing or zipping around in his walker. His first word was *"Yaaaaaasssss!"* He already gets me. My little buddy. He's grow-ing so fast! By the time London arrived in November, Phoenix was standing up, clinging to my leg, almost ready to walk on his own.

I dance with him, holding London to my chest, supporting her sweet little head under my chin.

I'm free
To do what I wanna do
It's my life
I'll do what I wanna do

We slow it down for "Fame Won't Love You," another beautiful ballad Sia wrote after listening to this book.

Little dreams come crashing
Let them wave in passing
Cos fame won't love you like a mother, like a father should

Carter comes to sway with us, one arm around me and our baby girl, one arm extended so he can hold our son's hand. My goal for 2023 was getting to this moment, this dance, and I'll never take it for granted.

Life is beautiful at Slivington Manor. I wanted to share the joy with you here because you helped make it happen. And I wanted to share some of the sadness because I know a lot of people are going through sadness of their own. I hope this makes them feel less alone.

Carter and I celebrated Christmas with family and friends, but we made time to be at home, just the four of us.

The four of us.

I love to say it out loud.

My New Year's resolution for 2024 is to be real, authentic, and vulnerable. I'm finally strong enough to be all that, and I owe my children the best version of myself. I don't want my daughter—or anyone else's daughter—to go through what Britney and I and so many other girls went through. I want to help create a future where people think differently about girls—a future where girls think differently about themselves. Part of that is raising my son to be a man who treats women with love and respect. He'll be learning from the best—his amazing dada—and I hope London will be his best friend.

We flew into a tiny airport in Montana on New Year's Eve, stopped off for groceries, and drove to our house in the snowy mountains, where I made my famous Sliving Lasagna for dinner. We got the babies changed and fed and tucked in, and then we sat in front of the fire, full of love and gratitude and the most delicious lasagna that ever existed.

Best New Year's Eve of my life. And that says a lot.

ACKNOWLEDGMENTS

The opinions I've expressed in this book do not necessarily reflect the opinions of the Hilton family, 11:11 Media, or any organization with whom I do business. This is my story, to the best of my imperfect memory. If others remember things differently, I respect their right to tell their own stories from their perspective. I've tried to process it all with love and compassion, and I hope others do the same.

So many THANK YOUs need to be said! There's not enough room in this book or a whole library to say how grateful I am for the support, good humor, and love of my family and friends. Mom and Dad: You gave me the world and taught me how to live in it. I am forever your girl. Nicky: You can always read my mind, so you know how important you are to me. You are my best friend, and I can't imagine my life without you. Conrad, Tessa, and Barron: You make me happy just by being yourselves. To my cousins Brooke, Whitney, and Farrah: So many fun memories around the world together. To all my other cousins, aunts, and uncles: You rock. My found family—Nicole, Jen, Allison, Holly, Cade, Brit, Kim—and too many others to mention: You've been there for me with laughter, love, common sense, and insane amounts of fun when I needed it most. Little Hiltons: I hope you see yourselves in all the happiest parts of my story. I want every single one of you to feel my love and gratitude.

My life was forever changed by the documentary team who refused to settle for less than my real story. Huge gratitude to Alexandra Dean, Aaron Saidman, and all the talented people who worked on *This Is Paris*. My advocacy and legislative work wouldn't be possible without my impact director, Rebecca Mellinger, and supporting staff. With you on my side, I know we can change the world. Bruce Gersh, the president of my media company, does the impossible every day and keeps this whole crazy carousel spinning, assisted by everyone on my incredible team at 11:11 Media. Special thanks and love to everyone who works with me on my fragrances, product lines, podcasts, social media, metaverse—all of it—you make it work. And you make it fun.

My dream book team traveled with me through the looking glass and back. Albert Lee, my literary agent at UTA, found us the perfect publishing home. Editor Carrie Thornton and her staff at Dey Street moved mountains and created a gorgeous design. Joni Rodgers helped me find my voice and held my hand through the chaos, supported by her agent, Cindi Davis-Andress, and researcher, Patty Lewis Lott. None of that would matter without the people who read this book, so thank you for your time and thoughtful energy. I look forward to hearing from you on social media and seeing you out in the world. A huge thank-you to all my little Hiltons around the world.

To Carter: Conrad Hilton said good luck means being with the right people in the right place at the right time. Babe, you are my person, place, and time. Our family and our future—that's my everything. Thank you for making me feel like I'm a princess living a fairy tale every single day. You are my world, and just like I said at our wedding, I'm going to make you feel like the luckiest guy in the world for the rest of your life. Love you.

Paris Hilton
Spring 2023